McGraw-Hill Series in Speech
CLARENCE T. SIMON, *Consulting Editor*

TRAINING THE VOICE FOR SPEECH

McGraw-Hill Series in Speech

CLARENCE T. SIMON, *Consulting Editor*

Baird—ARGUMENTATION, DISCUSSION, AND DEBATE

Baird—DISCUSSION: PRINCIPLES AND TYPES

Baird and Knower—ESSENTIALS OF GENERAL SPEECH

Baird and Knower—GENERAL SPEECH

Brigance—A HISTORY AND CRITICISM OF AMERICAN PUBLIC ADDRESS

Callahan—RADIO WORKSHOP FOR CHILDREN

Hahn, Lomas, Hargis, and Vandraegen—BASIC VOICE TRAINING FOR SPEECH

Powers—FUNDAMENTALS OF SPEECH

Van Dusen—TRAINING THE VOICE FOR SPEECH

Training the Voice for Speech

A GUIDE TO VOICE AND ARTICULATION IMPROVEMENT

C. RAYMOND VAN DUSEN, D.Sc.
Chairman of the Speech Department
Director of the Speech and Hearing Clinic
University of Miami

SECOND EDITION

NEW YORK TORONTO LONDON
McGRAW-HILL BOOK COMPANY, INC. 1953

TRAINING THE VOICE FOR SPEECH

Library of Congress Catalog Card Number: 52-6007

THE MAPLE PRESS COMPANY, YORK, PA.

To Mother and Dad

O what is it in me that makes me tremble so at voices?
Surely whoever speaks to me in the right voice, him or her
I shall follow,
As the water follows the moon, silently, with fluid steps,
anywhere around the globe.

—Walt Whitman, "Vocalism," *Leaves of Grass*

PREFACE

We tend to follow traditional practices in educational fields and to repeat conventional techniques through habit. Although we make a real effort to discover new principles of learning and to find improved teaching procedures, we continue habituated practices regardless of new information. Thus we fail to adjust our practices to our findings, and our teaching methods remain static.[1]

This is no place for a treatise on pedagogy; however, it will be noted that in the revised edition—which has been long overdue—increased emphasis is placed upon ear training. Experience and research have shown that this phase of speech training deserves greater consideration than we have given it in the past. Unless the student is able to hear errors in articulation and defects in phonation, he will be unable to do anything to correct them. It is only when he hears his errors objectively and admits to their presence that he is willing and able to make the desired changes.

Use of the original edition in the author's classes gave ample opportunity to evaluate its effectiveness as a teaching medium. He saw its weaknesses and its strengths and had the opportunity to reconsider its contents. In rewriting the book, he hopes that he has made a more useful text for voice and articulation training.

Originally designed as a "guide to action" in voice improvement, this objective has been furthered by including additional approaches and exercises in the revised edition. At the same time, other features of the book have been strengthened. Materials which simplify and clarify the anatomical, physiological, and psychological aspects of voice and articulation have been included.

The book has been expanded to include training in articulation so that it may be used in courses encompassing both voice and articulation.

[1] Dr. Clarence T. Simon, Northwestern University.

Chapter 15, entitled "Articulation the Vowels and Consonants," was prepared by Jack Probst of the University of Miami. Chapter 16, "Pronouncing the Words," was prepared by Dr. Thomas Lewis of Florida State University.

Practice selections for the original edition were chosen under the hurried conditions of war, and many of them were found to be unsatisfactory. It is the author's hope that this feature of the present volume is greatly improved as a result of the revision.

A chapter has been added entitled "Suggestions to Teachers," which the author believes will serve the objective of making this text a better guide to action in speech training.

For her kind assistance with the part of the copy dealing with relaxation, the author is grateful to Mrs. Ellen C. Henderson. The author owes his appreciation to Dr. Robert E. Card and Miss Laurine E. Endelman for contributing some of the exercises included. For helpful suggestions regarding the revision the author is grateful to Professors Paul L. Bogen of the University of Nebraska and Richard M. Mall of the Ohio State University. He wishes also to acknowledge his indebtedness to those authors and publishers whose works are quoted and who are mentioned specifically in the book. Finally, to his wife whose inspiration and assistance have made this work a reality, he owes much more than printed symbols can express.

C. Raymond Van Dusen

Coral Gables, Florida
August, 1952

CONTENTS

PART ONE

INTRODUCTION

1

THE TRAINING PROGRAM

"His voice was terribly monotonous, I almost went to sleep listening to it." "Her voice was harsh and high-pitched. I could hardly stand to stay in the room with her." "He sounded as though he had mush in his mouth when he spoke. I had difficulty understanding him." These are just a few of the criticisms people make about voices.

Sometimes, a person will make similar comments about another's voice when his own speech is far from perfect.

A Detroit society matron criticized the voice of a lecturer she had just heard. She said, "He had such a flat, uninteresting voice, I could hardly sit through his speech." As she made the comment, her own voice was so muffled and weak that the listener had to ask her to repeat what she had said. Had someone pointed out the lady's problem to her, probably she would have been surprised and embarrassed. She would not have taken offense, however, for she was the sort of person who would want to do something to correct the difficulty.

Often, poor voice and articulation create a bad impression without the listeners or the speakers realizing what is happening. People with sensitive ears react negatively to a voice that is unpleasant in quality just as they do to the screech of brakes or the squeak of an unoiled hinge. The difference is only a matter of degree; the dissonance in either case is unpleasant, and many try to avoid it.

Individuals have as little chance to eliminate the unpleasantness in other persons' voices as they do the noise of automobile brakes. Yet there is something they can do; they can improve their own ability to produce pleasant vocal tones. If everyone would set out to do this, much noise and unpleasantness would be avoided.

On very rare occasions, a friend will make an adverse criticism about the harsh quality, the monotonous pitch, or the weakness of another person's vocal tones. The person who possesses the defective voice may become nettled at first, but the comment will start him thinking. "Perhaps, my friend is right! At least it won't hurt to check his statement." He does this by having a transcription of his voice made and playing it back. He listens intently and then utters dejectedly, "Is that me?"

Yes, unfortunately, it is. He decides that his critic was right and that he had better do something to improve. But then come the questions, "Where?" and "How?"

WHERE TO GET VOICE IMPROVEMENT

The college student can usually receive help from the speech department in his school. Others will have to discover different methods. Some of the possibilities are (1) the speech therapist in private practice, (2) a competent vocal teacher, or (3) self-instruction.

Most of the qualified practitioners are in universities and colleges, and a few are directly available to people not enrolled in educational institutions. However, some schools offer help to people other than their own students, and those who need speech rehabilitation would be wise to investigate the offerings of their state schools.

Singing teachers could assist if they were willing to deal with the speaking voice. Although they cannot handle severe vocal disorders (these, by all means, should be treated only by the physician and the speech therapist), they should be able to improve a generally poor speaking voice, since many of the principles that they employ daily are as useful to the speaker as they are to the singer.

HOW TO GET VOICE IMPROVEMENT

The word "improvement" implies *change.* The student who desires voice improvement must make tangible changes in his approach to vocalization—he must train his ear to listen for differences in sounds and develop his ability to discriminate quality, pitch, and loudness. At the same time, he must learn to use his speech equipment differently from in the past and alter his voice and articulation in accordance with his particular needs. For example, if the quality is hoarse or throaty, the pitch too high, the intensity weak, or the articulation infantile, he must improve his ability to hear the deviation and, concurrently, change the manner in which he produces the sounds.

The student who has made changes in his approach to vocalization may have difficulty retaining his newly acquired vocal habits. He may return to old (wrong) habits because they are more firmly fixed than the newer ones. His ear is accustomed to hearing the wrong sounds, and his tongue, lips, jaw, and other parts are accustomed to making them. Often, they seem correct to him while the improved sounds seem wrong. He must be on the alert against slipping back once he has recognized his problem and has started to correct it. Every time he repeats the use of his new habit, he fixes it more firmly in his habit patterns. Any returns to wrong habits make acquisition of the new ones all the more difficult.

The student must want to improve his speech and be willing to work hard to get results. He has little difficulty in making achievements if he (1) approaches the program with an earnest desire to improve, (2) practices the exercises sufficiently and properly, (3) applies his new techniques every time he speaks, (4) develops a well-trained ear to guide him as he practices, and (5) uses his newly acquired patterns.

Building new habits. Frequently, a person entering the speech clinic for the first time will inquire, "What will you have me do—read?"

It is necessary to explain that that will be the last step in the corrective program. Then it is pointed out, as Professor J. M. O'Neill did once, that "Practice makes permanent, not perfect" and that, since the speech is not right, some basic changes must be made first. The cause of the trouble should be located, ear training must be started, and then new and correct procedures learned and put into practice. Later, if the work is successful, old habits will be replaced by new ones which work efficiently, and the whole program will be a matter of achieving something new in speech, not conquering a handicap.

The approach in any case should be according to rules of good vocal hygiene. The exercises used should put no strain on the vocal mechanism. All attempts to improve the voice should be toward obtaining effortless vocalization.

Working for improvement. Merely to learn about new procedures in an abstract way would accomplish little or nothing in voice improvement. It is necessary to "dig in" and work in order to bring about progress. Every one who desires to improve the voice must practice regularly. At the beginning, three or four periods of 10 minutes each are recommended for daily practice. As the course continues and additional assignments are made, more time will be required. Many students have found that they can work vocal training into odd moments during the day—while they are walking to class, bathing, or waiting for the luncheon bell to sound.

The pupil not only will need to practice the exercises which are suggested for developing new habits; he will have to make use of them every time he speaks. He will have to apply the principles. At first, he will need to make a conscious effort to do this whenever he has anything to say. After a few weeks of practice and attentive application, new and correct patterns should appear automatically.

STEPS IN THE VOICE TRAINING PROGRAM

The author has found that the objectives of the voice training program are reached more quickly and effectively when the work proceeds in the order suggested below. Of course there will be some overlapping. For example, work on physical preparation will start shortly after the ear-training program begins. Although the major part of practice in vocalization and articulation is reserved for the latter part of the program, some of this work will be included from the very beginning. However, it is desirable to follow the general pattern as closely as possible.

The students who make the best improvement are those who have been willing to practice and to apply the principles consistently day after day—yes, minute after minute—without fail so that every speech situation, regardless of what it may be, calls into play the new speaking habits that have been developed.

In doing this work it is necessary to set up new patterns of muscular response, and this is no easy job. When we think of those habits which we already have and realize how long it took for them to become established, we soon realize that the work of making permanent a new set of habits cannot be accomplished without expending a great amount of effort during a long period of practice and application.

EAR TRAINING. One of the pupil's big jobs will be that of laying a foundation for voice improvement by attempting to improve the alertness of his ear to hear differences in voices. As a result he will be better able to compare his voice with other voices and measure objectively his own voice improvement.

A considerable part of the program should be devoted to this phase of the training program because of the close relation between hearing and speech. Students—like the Detroit society matron—do not hear their own voices as others hear them. They fail to hear differences because their ears are not attentive. They react favorably or unfavorably, but they are unable to tell why they like or dislike a voice. They need to listen carefully and analyze a large number of voices on the basis of differences in quality, pitch, and intensity in order to develop this requisite for speech improvement.

In many instances, the correction of vocal and articulation faults is merely a matter of training the student to hear his mistakes. Once he is able to do this, he can make adjustments that bring about rapid improvement. For this reason, this part of the program must not be neglected. It should start immediately and continue throughout the course. Several class periods and much outside practice time should be devoted to ear training.

PHYSICAL PREPARATION. The physical preparation for the relaxed movement of the muscles involved in the production of sounds is another important step in laying the foundation for good vocalization. The approach to this part of the procedure is through relaxation. The pupil starts with conscious control exercises which are designed to develop an awareness of the movement of the muscles and then learns, through active participation, what relaxation is and how it feels. First, he develops the ability to relax the larger muscles of the body—those of the arms, legs, trunk, and neck—and then proceeds to the smaller muscles of the larynx, throat, and jaw. After these controls have been developed, he is ready to begin working on the breathing.

Early in the program the student develops patterns of breathing which can be used to further the free, unrestrained activity of the small muscles used during vocalization. After suitable breathing procedures are established, he no longer needs to concentrate on this factor as he produces sounds.

VOCALIZATION. Objectives during this phase of the program should include (1) the elimination of individual problems and (2) the development of clear, resonant tones at a suitable pitch which vary in pitch and intensity and are heard easily by the listener.

Application of the physical controls becomes a vital matter during this period. Every time the student utters a sound in class, during practice periods, or in everyday speaking situations, he must make certain that he is using the new relaxation techniques and breathing patterns.

ARTICULATION. The final step in the program is work on specific speech sounds. Effort is made to produce clear, distinct, and properly enunciated sounds and words so that the person "out there" hears them easily and understands what is said. Here again, it is important that principles previously learned are put to use constantly every time the student speaks.

The successful student develops a clear, resonant, pleasant, lively voice which is easily heard, easily understood, and suitable to his age and sex.

THE CHECKUP

A checkup on the condition of the structures should be taken care of before any actual vocal exercises are started. A physician or properly trained speech teacher should be asked to examine the organs involved in vocalization (mainly, the larynx) to see if any abnormality exists which should receive treatment. This is an absolute requirement in cases of severe vocal disorder. If there is a structural abnormality, a physician should be consulted and treatment started immediately.

Students who are allowed to proceed with vocal exercises in spite of abnormalities of structure are apt to cause great harm to the voice. The pathetic story of the preacher who came to the author once for advice regarding his voice illustrates what can happen when precautions are not taken early. He had suffered from a bad case of laryngeal paresis (a partial motor paralysis of the larynx) which should have had the immediate attention of a physician. He continued in his calling (and it was truly a "calling"—in fact it might even have been termed a "yelling"—because he spoke before large out-of-door audiences without the use of sound-amplifying equipment) in spite of the disorder. His voice held out for a while, but the physical condition became worse, until finally he had to give up preaching and take a minor administrative position in the church. The new job did not pay a salary sufficient to support his family, and he was forced to seek the financial aid of relatives. He might have continued a useful and successful career for many years if he had seen a laryngologist during the early stages of his difficulty, carried out the physician's orders and pursued a sensible program of vocal rehabilitation. The specialist probably would have prescribed, among other things, general and vocal rest for this patient. He might have advised the man to take some time out from his work and to stop speaking for the time being. But never would he have suggested that the patient practice some [o] and [ah] sounds in his condition.

2

BASIC ELEMENTS OF SOUND

You produce and at the same time hear the basic elements of sounds (quality, pitch, and loudness) as you speak. Since these elements are part and parcel of both production and reception of speech sounds, it is advisable to study them at the outset of the program.

QUALITY

Speech sounds are either tones or noises. The vowels are, for the most part, tones, since they are the result of the periodic vibration of the vocal folds. One of the measurable characteristics of sound is *wave complexity*, which determines the individual quality of a voice. Other terms for this characteristic of sound are *quality*, *clang*, *tone color*, and *timbre*. This characteristic of tones makes it possible to distinguish persons by their voices only.

Voices are frequently as dissimilar as different musical instruments. The leader of a choir in which the author once attempted to sing used to say, "I want the tenors to sound like a section of trumpets, the basses like a section of bass horns, and the sopranos like flutes." He was seeking difference in quality in each section, and although it is improbable that anyone in the group could imitate exactly the instrument designated, the choir members knew what the leader wanted because they had heard the instruments played.

Voices differ in quality from individual to individual because of variations in the mechanisms that are involved in the production of voice, for example, the shape and size of the pharynx and mouth, the hardness or softness of tissue lining these cavities, and the size of the mouth opening.

The string of the violin when stroked vibrates over its entire length, but it vibrates in segments as well. The vibration of the string along its entire length results in the *fundamental*. While the string vibrates along its entire length, it also vibrates in segments—halves, thirds, fourths, etc. All these tones contribute to the complex that gives the sound individuality. The segmental vibrations are called *partials*. The first partial is the fundamental which vibrates at the lowest frequency. Segmental vibrations above (the halves, thirds, fourths, etc.) are called the *overtones*. The fundamental is the first partial. The fundamental and the overtones vibrating in varying degrees of intensity combine to determine the quality of the tone.

The quality of the note of a saxophone or a trumpet is determined by the relative intensities of the fundamental and the overtones. C# on the one instrument will be different in tonal quality from the same note on the other instrument. Similarly, an [ah] sound produced at exactly the same pitch by two voices will be different in quality because of differences in the intensities of the various partials.

Tones are usually a composite of the fundamental and the overtones. A pure tone results when the fundamental is sounded alone. The use of the word "pure" in this instance may be misleading. Such tones are not necessarily pleasant. In fact, they are generally lifeless and uninteresting. When, in a complex tone, the overtones are in exact multiples of the fundamental, they are called *harmonic partials*. If they are not exact multiples of the fundamental, they are known as *inharmonic partials*. The latter usually cause the tones to be less pleasing, while harmonic partials usually (but not always) add to the clarity and richness of the tone. The resonators select and intensify certain partials in the tone and thus play a vital part in determining quality.

Although the ear may not readily analyze and identify the overtones, they are present in the complex tones reproduced. The ear is very sensitive to over-all differences in quality once ability to discriminate differences in sounds has been developed.

PITCH

The term *pitch* is used in referring to a sound as it is heard by the ear and locates sounds on the continuous scale extending from the lower to the upper limits of tonal perception. The lower limit of audibility is usually set at approximately 20 double vibrations per second; the upper limit at 20,000 double vibrations per second. The hearing range differs from individual to individual. Younger persons usually hear better than older persons.

In general, pitch is determined by the rate of vibration of the tone-producing mechanism; *e.g.*, a violin string vibrates at a certain rate which determines the pitch of the tone produced. When the string is tightened, a higher pitched tone results. When the string is loosened, the pitch is lowered. The situation is somewhat similar as far as vocalization is concerned, except that other factors than tension play a part, these being length and thickness of the two vocal folds. In the adult male, the vocal folds are longer and thicker than they are in the female, and therefore the male voice is usually lower in pitch. When tension in the vocal folds increases, the pitch is raised. The same is true when the length or thickness is decreased. The amount of tension in the vocal folds is determined by the sum total of the tensions in the intrinsic and extrinsic muscles of the larynx. The pitch level of the human voice and variations in pitch result from the condition of the structures involved in vocalization, auditory alertness and discrimination, emotional tendencies and changes, and vocal habits.

LOUDNESS

The term *loudness* refers to the effect of a sound on the ear—its loudness or softness—as determined by the amplitude of the vibration and the degree of reinforcement by a resonating body. Loudness has upper and lower limits. It varies between the auditory stimulus which gives rise to a barely perceptible tone (the threshold of audibility) and stimuli so loud that they produce a sensation of feeling or pain (the threshold of feeling).

The ear distinguishes this basic characteristic of sound because it depends upon the strength of the sensation received at the ear. The capacity of the ear to register the differences in the degree of strength of the vibrations makes it possible for the listener to sense differences in meaning and thus interpret the speaker's intentions.

The voice would be extremely weak were it not for the resonators of the mouth, pharynx, larynx, and head. These structures and cavities add loudness to the speaking voice. The situation can be compared with the mouthpiece of a clarinet. When it is detached from the instrument, the sound is faint. When the mouthpiece is attached to the instrument and blown, the sound is greatly amplified and enriched. The reason for this change is reinforcement of the tone by resonance.

The two physiological factors that play the greatest part in amplifying the tone produced by the vocal folds are the force of the expiratory air stream and the efficient use of the resonators.

PART TWO

CULTIVATING A GUIDE

TRAINING THE EAR

Ear training plays a vital role in correct sound production. It is the method of working—the *modus operandi*—that everyone should use who desires to correct specific problems of vocalization or to achieve general voice improvement.

Until the student can hear his voice as others hear it and becomes consciously aware of its blemishes, he will be unable to eliminate his vocal faults. Some students will be able to improve the voice without using other corrective procedures once they have trained the ear. Others will need to take additional steps (such as finding their most suitable pitch range, relaxing the throat muscles, or varying the loudness), but in these instances also, final results will depend largely upon ear training.

THE EAR AS GUIDE AND TEACHER

The hearing mechanism serves as a guide during vocalization, regulating the pitch, intensity, and quality of the voice. Since, these are the basic vocal elements, you need to train the ear to recognize these factors in your own and others' voices.

Walter Lippmann has said,[1]

> Expertness in any subject is, in fact, a multiplication of the number of aspects we are prepared to discover, plus the habit of discounting our expectations. Where to an ignoramus all things look alike, and life is just one thing after another, to the specialist things are highly individual. For a chauffeur, an epicure, a connoisseur, a member of the President's cabinet, or a professor's wife, there are evident distinctions and qualities not at all evident to the casual person who discusses automobiles, wines, old masters, Republicans, and college faculties.

[1] Lippmann, W., *Public Opinion*, The Macmillan Company, New York, 1929.

These same observations hold as far as ear training is concerned. Once the ear has been trained to recognize the "evident distinctions and qualities," it can serve as an ever-present guide and teacher in correct sound production.

IMPROVING ABILITY TO HEAR SOUND DIFFERENCES

You may doubt that it is possible to make good ears hear analytically. What about the musician who develops an ear for perfect pitch or the railroad man who tests the wheels of his engine by tapping each of them with a hammer to see (or, rather, to hear) if they are sound? In most cases, it took training to develop these abilities.

The sensitivity of the hearing mechanism is as readily adjusted to sound particles as the seeing apparatus is to small particles of matter. You may have taken botany as a freshman and found on first entering the class that you had difficulty seeing the minute structures even though they had been magnified many times by the microscope. One explanation is that you did not know what you were looking for, but the main reason is that your eyes were not practiced in looking at such small structures. You had to look into the microscope many times before you were able to pick out the tiny particles readily. So it is with hearing; you will achieve about the same results at first as you attempt to train the ear. You hear the roar of the cannon, the shriek of the siren, or the babblings of a baby, but unless you have learned to listen objectively to the sounds about you, you will be unable to take the sounds apart and describe them. As the first step, you need to study the ear and learn how it functions, as well as to gain a clear understanding of the basic elements of sound. With this background, you will be able to proceed more intelligently with the entire program of ear training.

The hearing mechanism is the sensory end organ for hearing; it picks up the sound of your own voice as well as the sounds about you.

The three main parts of this mechanism are the outer ear, the middle ear, and the inner ear. The shell-shaped structure on the outside of the head (the auricle) is usually referred to as the "ear" and is said to "collect the sound waves." Actually, it has little or nothing to do with hearing. A much more important part of the *outer ear* is the auditory canal (external auditory meatus), a passageway that can be seen by looking into the auricle. This serves as a channel through which sounds pass on their way to the eardrum or tympanic membrane. The eardrum, a circular sheet of highly responsive tissue between the outer and middle ear, vibrates in response to pressures created by the sound waves.

The vibrations pass from the outer ear into the *middle ear* (or tympanic cavity)—a small air-filled chamber in the temporal bone—where they move along a chain of small bones which stretch across the tympanic cavity from its outer to its inner wall. These bones (the auditory ossicles) include the malleus, or hammer, which is attached to the eardrum; the incus, or anvil; and the stapes, or stirrup. The incus forms the connection between the malleus and the stapes. The

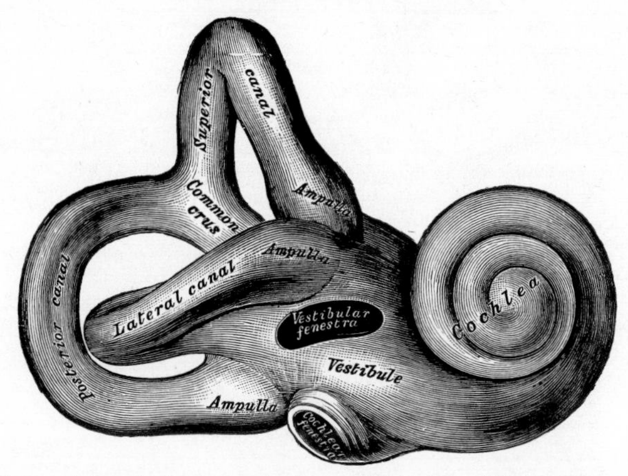

FIG. 1. The bony labyrinth, lateral view, right side. (*From Gray, Anatomy of the Human Body, 25th ed., Lea & Febiger, Philadelphia,* 1942.)

footplate of the stapes lies in the oval window in the wall of the tympanic cavity. It is here that the vibrations pass into the inner ear.

The *inner ear* stretches farther into the temporal bone and consists of a system of tubes and chambers known as the bony labyrinth (see Fig. 1). The central chamber of this labyrinth (the vestibule) opens into the spiral, snail-shaped cochlea and the semicircular canals which are responsible for balance. A corresponding system of delicate, interconnected membraneous sacs and tubes lies within the bony labyrinth. This is filled with a clear fluid called *endolymph* and is surrounded by a clear fluid called *perilymph.* A thin shelf of bone extends out from the wall of the cochlear canal and separates the cochlea into two parts, the *scala vestibulae* above and the *scala tympani* below (see Fig. 2). These two scalae communicate through a common opening at the upper end of the cochlea. The organ of Corti in the cochlea consists of modified cells extending the length of the cochlear duct and contains four lines of hair cells. The tectorial membrane, a leaflike structure, extends above the hair cells. The auditory nerve enters at the base of the cochlea, and nerve fibers extend out to the bases of the hair cells through canals in the bony shelf.

When a sound wave strikes the tympanic membrane, vibrations are transmitted over the chain of bones in the middle ear to the oval window. At this point, the perilymph of the vestibule and the scalae picks up the vibrations and passes them along to the hair cells of the

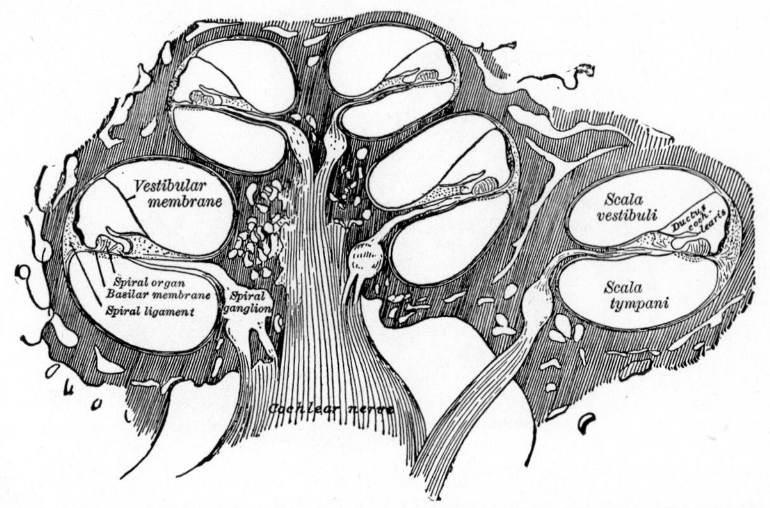

FIG. 2. Diagrammatic longitudinal section of the cochlea. (*From Gray, Anatomy of the Human Body, 25th ed., Lea & Febiger, Philadelphia,* 1942.)

basilar membrane, thus initiating impulses in the auditory nerve. This nerve carries the stimuli to the brain, where they are interpreted in terms of sound. The brain discriminates differences in quality, pitch, and loudness and has the power to translate the tones into thought symbols.

A PROGRAM FOR TRAINING THE EAR[1]

An acute ear—one that recognizes slight tonal differences—does not grow "like Topsy." You need to work at it. You must focus your atten-

[1] The program of ear training suggested here has as its purpose making the ear alert and discriminating and does not include the improvement of hearing acuity as measured in terms of percentage of hearing loss with the audiometer—a device used to study the amount of hearing possessed by an individual.

tion and listen to many voices in order to develop your full complement of hearing (or auditory) alertness.

The possibility that normal ears can be improved so that they hear better may seem out of the question when you first consider it, but before discarding the idea, look at the situation of those who are hard-of-hearing. It appears that they are able to improve their hearing ability. Louise M. Neuschutz[1] in her book, *How to Help Your Hearing*, tells how she set about sharpening the small remnant of hearing that she possessed. She listened to the radio and to the "small talk" of people about her and from her experience reached the conclusion that "The more residual hearing you possess the less time and effort will be required to educate yourself to utilize it to the best advantage. You will have to try to rouse it from its state of latency by systematic and persistent endeavor."

There is no exact dividing line between normal and partial hearing; the difference is only relative. People with normal hearing have more residual hearing than do those who are hard-of-hearing. In the hard-of-hearing the degree of auditory acuity is lessened; the auditory organs are not so sensitive as they are in the normally hearing person. For this reason, Mrs. Neuschutz' statement and suggestion regarding the utilization of the hearing faculty suit one group as well as they do the other.

Most people in college classes have normal hearing, but their ears are not alert; they do not listen. They must "practice listening" and "keep on listening with close attention" until they have discovered their fullest hearing potentialities. As one of this group, you need to take time to listen to the sounds about you. With practice, many will begin to hear the less obvious sounds for the first time. Awareness of the sounds will increase, and your ears will become more alert. Progress with this phase of the training should proceed concurrently with work to improve the attention factor and auditory discrimination. Part of the task will be to "take voices apart" and study their component elements just as you might, with experience, study an oil painting by examining the brush strokes, shadings, colorings, and composition. A course in art might give the training you need to make an intelligent analysis of a painting so that you can compare a Renoir with a Van Gogh or a Millet and tell *why* you prefer one over the other. So it is with

[1] Neuschutz, Louise M., *How to Help Your Hearing*, Harper & Brothers, New York, 1940.

your study of voices, but this time you develop auditory rather than visual alertness. The object of your study is vocal elements rather than a painter's techniques; now you examine the quality, pitch, and intensity elements of the voice rather than the brush strokes, shadings, and colorings of a picture.

Through your intensive ear-training program, you learn to break down the composition (or configuration) of vocal tones so that you are able to recognize, isolate, identify, and describe the component elements of your own and others' voices. Once this is done, you are prepared to correct your errors more readily and develop a pleasant, suitable speaking voice. It is not long until you are able to incorporate the new patterns into everyday speech with little or no conscious effort.

As you go about the task of making the ear more sensitive to sounds, you should pursue an active program that you carry out systematically. You will have to spend some time each day working to improve (1) the attention factor, (2) auditory alertness, and (3) ability of the ear to discriminate qualities, pitches, rates, and intensities.

Improving the attention factor. Although you may have perfectly normal ears and hear as much as the "average person," you probably have auditory ability that you do not use. You could "whet" this sense by improving your auditory alertness and training your ears to analyze the sounds they hear, but for most persons the first big job is the training of the attention factor.

To do this, you must do a great deal of listening, focusing attention on the tones and noises you hear about you. This will be a strange experience for many of you because you listen so little.

Usually sounds must be loud, unique, or directed at you personally; otherwise you do not hear them. And even though they may have one or several of these qualifications, they may go unnoticed. The chimes of Big Ben, the great hour bell attached to the "Westminister clock" in the Parliament clock tower, London, invariably attract the attention of the newcomers, but after the first few days have passed, these people seldom pay attention to the striking of the great clock unless they are interested in knowing the time of day. When, unexpectedly, you hear the sharp report of a gun, you make a sudden start, but after you accustom yourself to the sound, as, for example, at a skeet shoot or rifle meet, you cease to be startled by the noise, and eventually the firing may go on without your noticing it. The sounds may be lost because other matters get your attention. Frequently, unless you have some use for them in your thought and reaction pattern, they continue to escape your notice. Many persons perform in much the same manner in a conversation; they listen very little to what is said and how it sounds.

So few of us are good listeners that we are almost amazed to find someone who hears every word we speak. The author remembers a teacher he had in high school who always had a wealth of personal experience to offer on any subject on which she was speaking. One of the reasons she was so well versed was that she listened intently to everything that was said to her. Every youthful prattle received her keen attention, and like a pointer, she seemed to hear with her ears, eyes, nose, and, in fact, her whole being. No one could utter a single nonsensical word without receiving from her a sensible and sympathetic response. We would all be wise to emulate her ability to listen to what is said; then we would gain in knowledge and improve our latent powers of attention.

You should go about this first step in your ear-training program in a manner suggested by Mrs. Neuschutz.[1] "Keep on listening with close attention, practice listening at least one hour a day—and more, if possible." And since you intend to use your improved attentiveness in a voice-improvement program, you would be wise to focus your attention on how "what is said" sounds.

Exercises for improving the attention factor. The following exercises are suggested as means of improving your ability to focus the attention for longer periods of time than you do at present. Most of them should be used in practice periods outside class. Exercises 1 and 2 and, possibly, 3 and 4—depending upon availability of equipment—are adaptable for classroom use.

EXERCISE 1. Place a ticking clock—one which is heard easily—in a room in which there are no extraneous noises; listen to it intently for 2 minutes without wavering for a second. Gradually increase the time to 10 minutes.

EXERCISE 2. Place the same clock in a room in which there is considerable commotion; listen to it intently for 2 minutes in spite of disturbing factors. Gradually increase the time to 10 minutes.

EXERCISE 3. Tune in the Arlington time signal (via short wave) on your radio. Signals begin 5 minutes before the hour and continue until 5 minutes after the hour. Turn down the volume so that it is a little difficult for you to hear the sound. Focus your attention on the sound, and continue to listen as long as you can without allowing your attention to waver.

[1] *Ibid.*

EXERCISE 4. Tune in a speech on the radio, and listen to the content. Have someone else take notes, and let them quiz you on what was said. Try this exercise first on a quarter-hour broadcast and later on a half-hour program.

EXERCISE 5. Attend a lecture presented by a guest speaker at your school or a sermon at your church, listen to the ideas presented, but do not take notes. Then go to your room and carefully write out a complete outline of the content of what was said.

EXERCISE 6. Repeat Exercise 5, but this time write down all the anecdotes, descriptions, and personal incidents used to illustrate the speech.

Exercises for improving auditory alertness. Most of the exercises for improving auditory alertness can be practiced during unoccupied moments—while you are walking to classes or just relaxing. Exercises 7 and 8 are adaptable for use in class as well as in the individual program.

EXERCISE 7. Sit quietly in a room and listen to the sounds around you (those which are present in the room and those entering from outside). Have a pencil and pad ready, and make notations as to what sounds you hear. When your hearing becomes alert, you may even hear the sound of air currents as they pass through the window and door openings.

EXERCISE 8. Approach a mechanical clock and see at what distance you are first able to hear it tick. Repeat the process several times, trying to pick up the sound at a greater distance each time.

EXERCISE 9. Stand at an open window three or four floors up and try to hear the voices of couples and groups on the walks below.

EXERCISE 10. As you walk along the street, try to pick up the voices of people who are approaching you when they are at a distance of a 100 yards. Probably you will not be able to hear them when they are this far away, but continue to listen until you can hear them easily. Listen to their voices after they have passed until the sound dies out.

EXERCISE 11. When there is but one car on the street, listen to the sound the motor and tires make as it passes you; then continue to listen until you can hear it no longer.

DEVELOPING AUDITORY DISCRIMINATION. The work in auditory discrimination consists chiefly in listening to sounds and analyzing them on the basis of quality, pitch, and intensity (or loudness).

In the beginning, you can use any instrument or object you wish—for example, whistle, clarinet, drum, slapstick—as you produce the sounds you are studying, but later the major part of your study should be devoted to the analysis of voices.

Your early analyses should be devoted to isolating and identifying the three basic factors: quality, pitch, and loudness. You will not always find this easy—for example, since the quality obscures the pitch, a thin voice may create the impression that the pitch is high when it is average. In some instances, a throaty voice may cause the pitch to sound lower than it actually is. Sometimes, a weak voice will make the pitch seem high when it is below average. You need to be especially cautious about your analyses and try to avoid confusing the elements. Once your ear can spot quality, pitch, and loudness readily, you should further your ability to describe each of them in detail.

Exercises to improve your ability to discriminate quality, pitch, loudness, and rate. As suggested earlier, your first job in improving auditory alertness should be the isolation of the basic elements of sound. By practicing the following exercises, you should improve this ability and be better prepared to study voices. In some instances, the equipment needed will dictate whether certain exercises are practiced in the classroom, at home, or on the street.

EXERCISE 12. Tune in a regular program on the radio. Set the volume at average, and study the changes as you move the tone indicator from low to high. Then, without watching, have a member of your family change the adjustment for you. Listen carefully and tell him whether the dial is at the extreme low, the extreme high, or somewhere between.

EXERCISE 13. Listen to the sounds that various automobile horns make. Try to spot differences in quality. Be careful that you do not confuse pitch with quality.

EXERCISE 14. Listen to the various whistles that are blown in your vicinity. Compare their various qualities, but here again do not confuse quality and pitch. Make the same study of bells you hear.

EXERCISE 15. Have someone play five notes on the piano or some other instrument, one at a time, at slightly different pitches—for example, middle C, C#, B, middle C, and A#—with a 10-second pause between each note. Listen carefully, and make notations telling whether the last note was higher or lower than the one that preceded. Afterward, check with the player to determine whether your judgments were correct. With this as a basic exercise for developing pitch discriminations, you can work out several similar exercises. As you improve in ability, make the exercises increasingly difficult.

EXERCISE 16. Pluck a tuning fork, trying to remember the pitch. Pluck a second tuning fork of another frequency, and listen intently to the resultant tone. Compare the first with the second. Proceed in a like manner with several tuning forks of various frequencies, trying to accustom your ear to differences in pitch. After practice, have a friend assist you as you determine which of two pitches is higher.

EXERCISE 17. Arrange the tuning forks you have in order of their frequencies. Pluck each of them several times until you have memorized their frequencies and can name the number of double vibrations per second for each of them. Then ask a friend to test your memory of the sounds by plucking them at random while you turn your back and identify them.

EXERCISE 18. Obtain a matched set of glass tumblers, and pour various quantities of water into each of them. Graduations in pitch will be determined by the amount of water in each glass. Hit the glasses with a pencil, and note differences in pitch. After experimenting for a while, try to match their pitch with the pitch of the tuning forks you have.

EXERCISE 19. Tune in a regular program on your radio. Set the volume at average, and then have a member of your family change the adjustment, increasing and decreasing the intensity slightly ten separate times. Have him keep an account of the adjustments he makes. Listen carefully and make notations as to the adjustments you think he is making, but do not watch him. Afterward, compare notes. Repeat the exercise several times, and keep trying to improve your ability to discriminate slight differences in intensity.

EXERCISE 20. Use the metronome to develop your ability to discriminate variations in rate. Have someone set it going at a certain rate, say 100 ticks per minute. Listen to the ticking for 15 seconds, and then have your helper increase or decrease the rate slightly. Do not watch the adjustments. Then listen again for 15 seconds. Make your judgment, and then compare notes. Try this at several different rates.

ANALYSIS OF VOICES

The analysis of voices should be accomplished in the following manner: first, listen to voices and report what you hear in purely descriptive terms; second, evaluate a large number of voices and complete a critical report on each of them; finally, analyze and critically evaluate your own voice.

DESCRIBING VOICES. Having studied each of the basic elements of voice, you are better prepared to differentiate them as they are produced during speech. Continue to be careful that you do not confuse the elements.

EXERCISE 21. Listen to the voices of your classmates, and write a description of each of them.

EXERCISE 22. Attend a lecture, listen carefully to the speaker's voice, and make a report of what you heard.

EXERCISE 23. Listen objectively to the voices of members of your family, and prepare a written description on each member.

EXERCISE 24. Take a note pad with you the next time you go shopping. Listen to other shoppers as they place their orders. Let your memory and rough notes serve as a basis for your written description of several of the voices you heard.

CRITICAL EVALUATION OF VOICES. Once you have trained the ear in the manner suggested above, you are prepared to make evaluative and critical reports on voices. In this phase of the ear-training program you apply your ability to listen to the various elements and pass judgment on their auditory effect. Before you can do this effectively, you need to know how voices should sound.

How the voice should sound. In order to be considered normal, the general pitch level of the voice must be suited to the age and sex of the individual—neither too high nor too low. There is considerable flexibility; the pitch does not remain on one level but varies in accordance with the meanings and emotions that the speaker wishes to express. The tempo likewise changes as different thoughts and feelings are expressed. Sometimes it is slow; at other times it is quickened. Never does the rate of speaking compare with a company of prisoners doing the lockstep across the prison yard; it changes easily as the speaker expresses his ideas and emotions.

The quality (or *timbre*) should be resonant and free from noise if it is to be considered normal. Frequently, there are deviations in this attribute. For example, a voice may sound as though the speaker has his head in a chimney or down a rain barrel so that the vocalization is muffled. Another voice may lack clarity because there is, along with it, the sound of air escaping over partially closed vocal folds, a quality termed *breathy*.

Another unpleasant quality heard frequently has been called *nasal;* in this, there is an excess of nasal tone, that is, too much [aahn] in sounds which should be produced almost entirely in the mouth cavity. The speaker says, "Sprnninng hnnanns commmme," instead of a clear "Spring has come." The person with a "denasal" voice leaves out all the nasal resonance as he says, "Sprig has cub," and the vocal quality that results is as unpleasant as its opposite, the excessively nasal.

Some of the other timbre deviations are the *metallic*, *hoarse-husky*, *thin*, *hollow*, *harsh*, and *throaty*. The *metallic* quality is sharp and gives the impression of the rustle of sheet iron. The *thin* voice lacks the pleasing, resonant fullness that one hears in the normal voice.

Exercises for evaluating voices. Keep the remarks about how voices should sound in mind as you proceed with the following exercises.

EXERCISE 25. Using the form shown in Fig. 3, check the voices of all members of the class as they talk in ordinary conversation. After you have finished analyzing the entire class, put these analyses aside and make the same check as the members read a poem. Repeat the process while the class is giving public speeches, but do not compare your notations until all three forms of speaking are completed for the entire class. Then study the results on each individual. In many instances, they will be the same, but occasionally, differences in the basic elements will appear when a different form of oral presentation is used. For example, a nasal quality not normally present during conversation may be apparent when an individual is reading poetry, or the habitual loudness will increase or decrease during public speaking.

EXERCISE 26. Use the vocal-analysis form to make analyses of the voices of your family and friends, the radio announcer, your minister, a political speaker, and people on the street. You will get the best results if you will do this two or three times a day, 10 minutes each time, devoting your entire attention to the analysis.

VOICE RATING SHEET

NAME____

(Last) (First) (Middle)

SEX__________ HEIGHT__________ AGE______ OBSERVER__________

Quality		*Pitch*	*Intensity*
Breathy______	Hollow______	Extremely low______	Extremely weak______
Denasal______	Metallic______	Low______	Weak______
Flat______	Nasal______	Medium______	Average______
Falsetto______	Thin______	Above average______	Above average______
Hoarse______	Throaty______	Extremely high______	Excessive______
		Monotonous______	Monotonous______

Other comments: ______________________________

*Rating________________

* Make ratings from 1 to 5: 1, poor; 2, below average; 3, average; 4, above average; 5, good.

FIG. 3

ANALYSIS OF YOUR OWN VOICE. You do not hear your own voice as others hear it because the sound waves are being conducted through the bony tissues of the head as well as out into the surrounding air. The bodily parts through which the sounds must pass (bones, muscles, cartilages, connective tissues) tend to filter out some of the tones. This phenomenon would handicap you greatly in a voice-improvement program if it were not for the availability of various types of recording devices. With high-fidelity equipment it is possible to have a recording made that will be a fairly accurate reproduction of what others hear when you speak.

As you listen to a recording of your own or another's voice, you must remember that even with the best recording equipment certain qualities are introduced by the apparatus that result in distortion. These must be allowed for in your judgment of your voice. Probably one of the best means of evaluating a recording of your voice is to compare it with recordings made of another voice—a voice that you know and perhaps admire. Listening to your own voice should be prefaced by listening to the record of the other voice.

You may decide from your study of one of the transcriptions that the quality is too thin, the pitch is too high, or the intensity is weak. Perhaps the words come so slowly that your sentences lose their interest before they are finished. When you are able to make such deductions as these, you are on your way toward objective listening.

EXERCISE 27. Have a recording made of your own voice, and listen to it carefully. Ask yourself questions about it. Does the pitch rise at the end of sentences in which questions are asked? If it does not, make it do so in your next recording. Does the pitch vary as you speak sentences? Is the loudness the same all the time, or are there variations? Is the quality pleasant? If not, how would you classify it?

EXERCISE 28. As your work progresses, make additional recordings and study them in the same manner. Not only will you gain ear training, but you will have a measure of your progress. If you have not improved since your last recording, you will need to look for reasons, and finding them, you will be able to correct errors and get back to correct procedures.

Once you have made a recording, do not lay it aside. Listen to it many times and study it carefully; it will guide you toward improved vocalization.

One of your biggest obstacles to rapid voice improvement will be inability to practice alone unless you have adequately trained your ear. You may obtain superior results in class and in conferences with your instructor, but when you are without supervision, you may do poorly. Your ear must be capable of giving you the guidance needed when your voice teacher is not present to make corrections. As has been pointed out, your ear is your guide and teacher; it can serve these functions only with proper training. A good foundation in ear training not only will help to correct vocal faults and give you general voice improvement but will help you to avoid slipping back into old speaking habits once you have developed new and more effective speech patterns. Also, it will serve as an indispensable aid during practice periods.

Keep continually at your task of training the ear; improve (1) the attention factor, (2) auditory alertness, and (3) ability to discriminate between qualities, pitches, and intensities. Utilize this experience to produce better voice every time you speak.

PART THREE

MECHANICS OF VOCALIZATION

STIMULATING AND INTEGRATING VOCALIZATION

Progress in the voice training program is accelerated when the student understands the mechanics of voice production. He accomplishes the objectives of the course sooner and with less effort if he knows how the structures assist in voice production.

The speech process is most easily understood when the student proceeds step by step, studying first factors that arouse the vocal response, then what happens within, and finally what occurs during speech.

STIMULATION FOR SPEECH

External and internal conditions. The beginning of any speaking results from occurrences in the environment or from changes within. A person hears someone downstairs calling to him, and he yells, "I'll be down in a minute." He burns his finger as he attempts to light a bonfire, and he utters an audible "Ouch!" He recognizes an acquaintance as he walks along the street, and he says "How-do-you-do." In each of these situations, the vocal response is the result of a change of some sort that is perceived in the environment.

The stimulation does not always come from outside the body. Some inner condition may provoke a speech response. For example, he becomes hungry and asks the cook how long it will be before dinner is ready; or he holds his head askew to look around a lady's hat at a movie, the muscles of his neck become sore, and he complains to those present. The conditions inside the body in these two cases are responsible for the vocal utterance he makes.

Governing system. The fact that stimuli are received and appropriate responses made indicates that there is a governing system which coordinates the mechanism. This coordinating system is principally the nervous system.

The sensory apparatus (the part of the nervous system which has to do with the reception of stimuli) makes knowledge and understanding possible. Sensory endings (sense organs which are in close contact with the environment) pick up information concerning the shape, size, color, sound, intensity, distance, and other factors regarding objects and movements in the environment; the information is transmitted to the brain, where it is interpreted and from where a proper bodily adjustment is made.

The following situation in which a person speaks and a suitable vocal response is made can be used to illustrate how this integrating system works:

1. A person says, "Good morning!" The sound waves produced by his voice cause the tympani, or eardrums, of the listener's outer ear to vibrate. The vibrations pass through the middle ear to the inner ear, where the auditory nerve is stimulated. In other words, the stimuli are received at the periphery (outer surfaces) of the body by the sensory end organs (receptors) and the specific nerve involved in hearing is excited.

2. The impulses pass to the brain, and the listener becomes aware of the voice. The nervous stimulation is translated into thought symbols. Now what has been said comes to have meaning almost immediately.

3. Efferent (outgoing) impulses travel from the brain to various effector organs, for example, the muscles of the larynx, tongue, lips, and jaw.

4. The final responsive activity occurs in these effector organs, and the listener says, "Good morning."

This oversimplified outline describes the make-up of the reflex arc which forms the basis for most, if not all, nervous activity.

SENSORY STIMULATION

The first two steps occur in the peripheral nervous system, which receives environmental stimulation. This network consists of many fibers, some of which carry sensations from the skin, muscles, tendons, stomach, intestines, and other bodily parts to the central nervous system. These receptors are specialized and react only to certain stimuli. The auditory nerve responds to stimuli resulting from sounds; certain end organs and nerves respond to touch sensations; others in the muscles to stretch; etc. These sensory receptor mechanisms—as well as motor and mixed sensory and motor peripheral nerves—play an important role in voice and articulation training. They are responsible for the speaker's awareness of the activity of the tongue, lips, jaw, and other bodily parts involved in speech production. Receptors in the muscles assist in giving him awareness of hypertensions; skin receptors tell him where the tongue is contacting the palate or roof of the mouth as he produces the [s] sound. Without these he would find development of the new physical controls—so necessary for voice and articulation improvement—difficult, if not impossible.

The stimuli must be strong enough to excite nerve impulses. Very weak stimuli may fail to stimulate nervous activity; for example, the listener does not hear sounds that are produced in the environment unless the vibrations they produce are strong enough to set nervous impulses flowing in the auditory nerve. Many sounds are produced in the environment that are not heard for this very reason. These are known as *subliminal sounds*. When a slight stimulation causes a few fibers to become active so that the listener is able to hear the sounds very faintly, they are known as *threshold sounds*. A still stronger stimulation may cause all the fibers of the nerve to become active; now the stimulation is *maximal*. Once nerves are sufficiently stimulated, the individual fibers make a maximum response. In such an instance, the all-or-none law of nervous activity is in operation. This happens not only with hearing but with all other kinds of nervous stimulation—touch, pain, smell, hunger, muscle stretch.

HEARING. Hearing is probably the most important means of stimulation for speech. From the very outset this capacity is utilized by the individual, along with vision, as he learns to speak. After speech is developed, hearing becomes an important guide, and adults can use the auditory cues to help themselves correct improper habits and gain general speech improvement.

VISION. Vision is another sensory channel vital in the stimulation of speech. Like hearing, it plays a part in learning to speak as well as serving as an important guide after speech is developed. Infants learn much of their speech from seeing (as well as from hearing) their elders speak. This fact is responsible for the oft-quoted statement that "every adult is the child's teacher of speech."

The movements of the lips, tongue, and jaw are important because they serve as indicators of the sounds that are being spoken. When a speaker has a weak voice or fails to "project" his voice, these movements may be almost indispensable in interpreting what he is saying. The person who attempts to talk to a "mumbler" or a "word swallower" unconsciously reinforces his auditory perception with the visual. The deaf and the hard-of-hearing depend to a large extent upon vision as a means of stimulation for speech, since they cannot be reached easily through the auditory pathway.

Vision not only has these roles to play, but it serves as a gateway to stimulation for speech in other ways. It receives sensations from various distances, and frequently, occurrences in the environment that are seen are sufficient to bring about a speech response. For example, someone may see a child stumble in the path of an oncoming automobile and shriek "Stop!" A bridge player trumps his partner's ace, and seeing the error, the partner groans. Normal eyes are equipped with sets of muscles that move them simultaneously in one direction or another. The objects in the environment reflect rays of light, and these are brought to focus on the sensory end organs of vision (rods and cones in the retina).[1] The stimulation of the nerve endings results in nervous impulses which are transmitted through various relay stations to the optic nerve and to the brain. Because the eyes perceive light, form, color, depth, and distance, this sensory channel becomes vital as (1) a gateway to the learning of speech, (2) a guiding factor after speech is learned, (3) a means of general stimulation for speech, and (4) a help in relearning speech.

Other sensory capacities. Hearing and vision are the sensory capacities most vital to the speech process, but others play their part. Thirst, hunger, taste, touch, smell, appetite, and muscular sensibility also are gateways to the general stimulation for speech. Each of these has its specialized end organs in various parts of the body, and frequently, when they are acted upon by some energy change, a conscious or an unconscious speech response occurs.

Thirst, hunger, and appetite. Dryness in the pharynx will cause the sensation of thirst, and the individual may ask for water.

Sensations of hunger, caused by contractions of the walls of the

[1] For a complete description of the eye, see Kimber, D. C., C. E. Gray, and C. E. Stackpole, *Textbook of Anatomy and Physiology*, 9th ed., pp. 543–557, The Macmillan Company, New York, 1938.

stomach, are the result of stimulation to the nerve fibers that are distributed to the mucous membrane. The pangs of even light hunger are frequently sufficient to bring forth an utterance of distress. The rather pleasant sensation of appetite that is the result of stimulation to the sensory endings for taste and smell often causes the utterance of a phrase of satisfaction.

Taste and smell. Taste buds scattered over the upper surface of the tongue, soft palate, and other parts of the oral cavity and the special nerves of the sense of smell located in the nose likewise serve as means of stimulation for speech. They elicit a vocal response according to how they are stimulated. The taste of lemons or sulphur and the smell of castor oil can bring forth some very anguished utterances, while fried chicken, ice cream, hot mince pie, and a sizzling T-bone steak cause exclamations of pleasure.

Touch and muscular sensibility. The surface of the skin has scattered over it thousands of minute sensory endings that receive different qualities of touch sensations, for example, pressure, cold, heat, and pain. These organs are responsible for many of the comments people make. A person accidentally grasps the handle of a hot flatiron or cuts a finger. The vocal result may be an oath of some sort or an "Ouch!"

In like manner, muscular sensibility often brings about a vocal response. Specialized sensory endings in the muscles give information as to their condition and position. This sense and the touch sensations are vital to speech, especially where the tongue is concerned, because they serve as important guides during this activity.

DIRECT ROLE OF SENSORY CAPACITIES IN SPEECH TRAINING

All the sensory organs are gateways for speech stimulation, and as such, they play an indirect part in speech production, but certain capacities play a direct part. Those most important in voice and articulation training are hearing, vision, touch, and muscular sensibility. All these capacities serve as guides and teachers in accomplishing the goals set forth in this text.

Through vision, you may watch for signs of hypertension in the lips, jaw, and throat as you produce vocal tones. Watch yourself in a mirror as you practice the exercises, and you will be able to see the muscles of these parts tighten when they should relax; for example, muscles about the throat may stand out prominently and draw the "voice box" upward toward the mandible, or jaw bone. If they were relaxed, the larynx would remain in its normal position, lower in the throat. This sensory capacity can be helpful as you work to improve articulation and pronunciation. By watching the lips, jaw, and tongue, you learn to alter the movements of these mechanisms. Seeing mistakes, like hearing them, helps to correct errors and accelerates the retaining program.

Increased awareness of the touch sensations is especially helpful in improving articulation because of its importance in making you aware of tongue contacts that occur during the production of speech sounds. Muscular sensibility can serve the useful purpose of assisting in your work with abdominal breathing, and combined with touch, it can help in obtaining "openness" as you adjust the mouth and pharynx to improve vocal resonance.

Like hearing, which was discussed at length in this and the preceding chapter, these sensory capacities can give valuable assistance in improving voice and articulation.

INTEGRATING MACHINERY

After the end organs have been stimulated and before a vocal, or any other, response is made, an extremely well-coordinated process of nervous integration occurs within the body. In fact, anything a person does—speak, run, turn up his nose, or grunt—is the result of some sort of sensory stimulation, plus the activity of the nervous system with its many parts and pathways.

The whole arrangement has been compared[1] with a central clearinghouse or generalissimo's headquarters. Messages are received at stations all over the body (sensory end organs) which are transmitted through lines of communication (afferent nerve paths) to other stations. Some of these messages are passed on to the generalissimo's headquarters for action, while others can be handled by officers of lower grade. An example of the latter is the simple reflexes, which involve only the stimulation, the passage of the impulse through the afferent pathway—the spinal cord—the passage of the impulse to the responding mechanism, and the responsive action. In the case of these reflexes,

[1] Carlson, A. J., and V. Johnson, *The Machinery of the Body*, 2d ed., p. 394, University of Chicago Press, Chicago, 1941.

the "generalissimo" is not consulted; the information does not reach his headquarters and he is not aware of what has happened, although he indirectly influences the action. Occasionally, he is made aware of the information that has been received, and as a result, he and his staff have some jobs to do. Then this part of the organization goes to work,

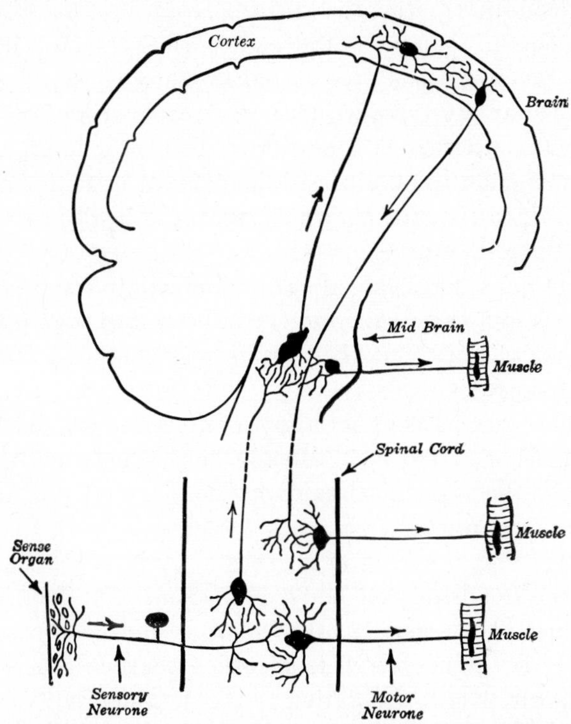

FIG. 4. Connections of the first, second, and third levels. The arrows indicate the direction of the nerve impulses. The area between the two lines at the top of the brain represents the cortex. *Note:* The three levels referred to reactions at the first level, the simple reflexes; reactions at the second level, involving the brain stem and cerebellum; and reactions at the third level, cerebral cortex. (*By Gates, from Kimber, Gray, and Stackpole, Textbook of Anatomy and Physiology, The Macmillan Company, New York,* 1938.)

"operating perfectly automatically according to the rules and principles which have been inherited from predecessors or acquired by experience." The information that is sent through outgoing channels (the efferent pathways) depends upon the information that was received, and the result is an adjustment that will put the bodily parts in a better position in relation to the environment (see Fig. 4).

To put it in other words, the stimulations of the sensory endings in the ear, eye, nose, tongue, throat, skin, etc., are transferred from sensory end organs to conduction pathways in the spinal cord. After they reach the cord, they pass to the cerebrum, and the brain becomes aware of the change that has occurred in the environment. Then, on the basis of concepts learned or inherited from its forebears, the body makes a response. Sometimes the action occurs almost immediately. Other times the sensations "are stored as many concepts, and may be called into play at any time, without an external stimulus."[1] When the response occurs, whether it comes immediately or later, the nervous impulse travels from the brain, out the efferent or motor pathways in the spinal cord, to the muscles which move the bodily parts—the jaw, the tongue, the arm, etc.

The stimulations that bring about an immediate response are simple reflexes. The impulses travel from the sensory end organs to the cord and out to muscles without there being any conscious control of the muscular response.

NERVOUS MECHANISMS. The large bodily parts which are involved in this integrating action have already been suggested; they are the spinal cord and the brain. The major divisions of the brain are the brain stem and the cerebrum.

The smallest unit involved in nervous activity is the neuron, which consists of the dendrite, cell body, and axon. The dendrites receive stimulation from the axons of other neurons and from external parts. The cell body is the nerve cell from which the two processes extend. The axon transmits the stimulation to the next neuron.

Spinal cord. The spinal cord, located in the vertebral column, is important for two reasons: (1) it is a center for reflexes, and (2) it is a conduction area for the passage of nervous impulses. Fibers in the posterior columns (those toward the back) of the cord serve as passageways for nervous impulses which lead up to the higher paths and centers. Fibers in the lateral (side) and anterior (front) columns lead from the higher centers down and out to the muscles.

Brain stem. Above the cord is the brain stem, which serves many important speech functions. Sensory and motor impulses pass through here en route to and from the brain. It is also an important reflex center and plays a vital part in the coordination of bodily movement for such

[1] Kimber, Gray, and Stackpole, *op. cit.*, p. 524.

activities as running, walking, swimming, and speaking. It is composed of the medulla, the cerebellum, and midbrain.

An automatic center for respiration, which sends impulses out to the muscles of breathing at regular intervals during ordinary quiet breathing, is located in the medulla. Ordinarily, the rhythmical activity of this center results in relatively even inhalations, but the rate may change as a result of sensory stimulation of one kind or another. Such occurrences as the sight of one's sweetheart, a slap in the face, or a scream in the dark may result in a marked acceleration of the rate of breathing, and, because of connections between the medulla and other parts, changes result in the rate of the heartbeat.

The center for the coordination of muscle movements is located in the cerebellum. If you will study yourself objectively as you speak, you will see, from the coordinated movements of the tongue, lips, jaw, soft palate, and other parts involved, how important the functions of this part of the nervous system become as you express your thoughts and feelings.

Centers that receive sensory stimulation from the ear, eye, tongue, skin, and other parts of the head are located in the midbrain. There are also motor centers here that send nervous impulses to the muscles of the larynx, soft palate, tongue, lips, and other parts during speech.

Cerebrum. Speech or language is part of a complex function which Henry Head has called *symbolic formulation and expression.* This process occurs in the cerebrum, the large bulk of tissue located in the skull just above the brain stem.

The cerebrum is divided into two halves, the right and the left hemispheres (see Figs. 4 and 5). These are convoluted by infolding grooves, or sulci, and outfolding gyri and are enveloped by a thin gray mantle called the cerebral cortex. Beneath this cortex are numerous interconnecting, ascending and descending pathways which connect lower centers and the periphery (that is, the outer surfaces) of the body with the cortex. Sensations that have traveled up the afferent pathways to the brain are conducted to sensory areas which receive and control the sensations.

This portion of the nervous system has its highest development in man, being responsible for all the higher mental processes. In addition to speech, it is responsible for thought, memory, intelligence, and the emotions. It is an integrating center exerting a degree of control over the lower centers of the nervous system. Almost all incoming impulses

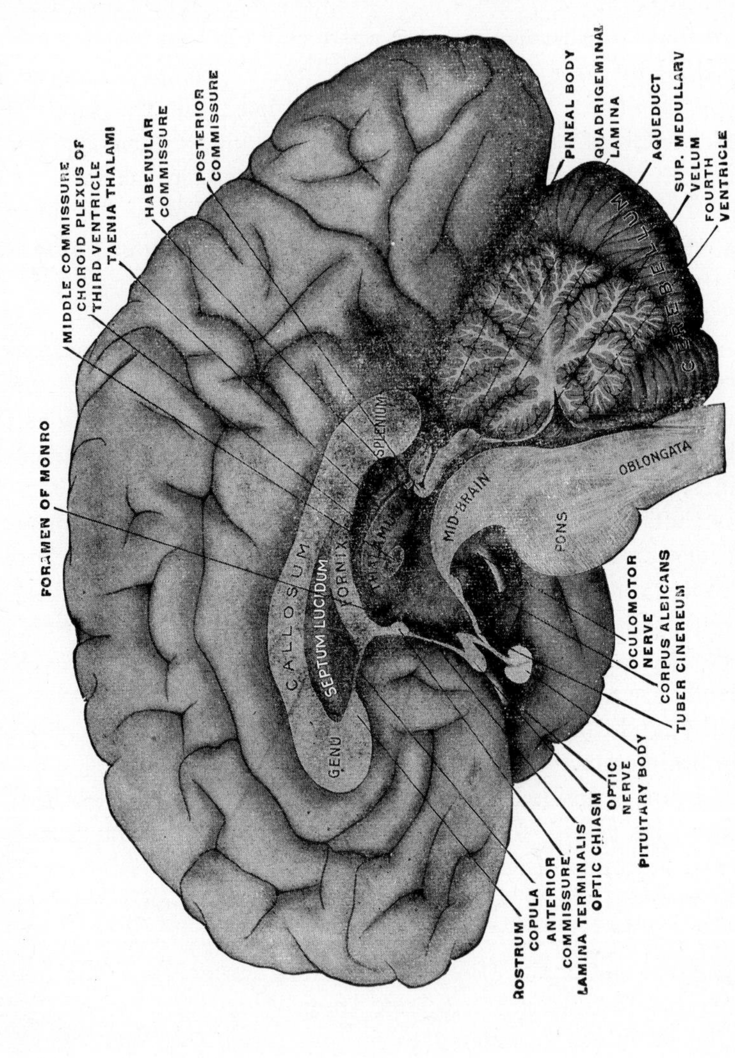

FIG. 5. Mesal aspect of a brain sectioned in the median sagittal plane. (*From Gray, Anatomy of the Human Body, 25th ed., Lea & Febiger, Philadelphia,* 1942.)

reach the cortex, and most outgoing impulses start there. The cortex functions to excite as well as to inhibit activities in the lower centers.

CEREBRAL ACTIVITY DURING SPEECH

The cerebrum goes into action every time a person speaks. Sensory stimulations are received there. Then the sensations are organized into word images. Next, through association fibers, sensory impressions are transferred to the parts involved in expression. Preparation of the words for utterance follows. Finally, motor stimulation for speech occurs, and the muscles involved in vocalization and articulation (the muscles of the larynx, tongue, soft palate, jaw, and lips) begin to move as speech is produced. All this preparation for utterance is dependent upon the action of the nervous system, mainly the cerebrum.

OTHER INTEGRATING SYSTEMS

The central nervous system is the most important of the integrating mechanisms for speech, but in spite of all its capabilities, the nervous system "is not the only integrating machinery of the body." The glands of internal secretion produce hormones (their secretion), and chemicals are produced as a result of respiration and other factors that "function significantly at one point or another to gear the parts of the machine to one another."[1] The blood stream carries the chemicals and distributes them throughout the body. These, especially the hormones, play a vital part as coordinators for speech.

SUMMARY

After the sensory end organs have been stimulated, the impulse passes to muscles or glands. Between these two occurrences, one of several things may happen to the nervous impulses that have been set in motion as a result of changes in the environment. The stimulation may result in a simple reflex activity involving the sensory neuron, a central neuron in the spinal cord, and a motor neuron. It may become more complicated than this and extent up into the brain stem, or it may become still more complicated so that it involves the cerebrum. The smallest unit involved in this nervous activity is the neuron with

[1] Carlson and Johnson, *op. cit.*, p. 395.

its dendrites, cell body, and axon. The grosser parts are the spinal cord, the brain stem and cerebellum, and the cerebrum. The spinal cord and brain stem serve as reflex centers and as passageways for sensory and motor impulses. In addition, the brain stem—mainly, the cerebellum—serves to coordinate bodily movement, and the medulla, which is part of it, contains the center for the automatic stimulation of the breathing muscles. The cerebrum is responsible for such higher mental processes as thought, memory, intelligence, and speech. The last process has been localized as to function so that, when we speak, the process of integration of nervous impulses follows somewhat this pattern:

1. Sensory stimulations are received and for the first time we become consciously aware of the changes in the environment.
2. The sensations are organized into word images.
3. Sensory impressions are transferred to parts involved in expression through association fibers.
4. The words are made ready for utterance.
5. Stimulations are sent from the motor area for speech to the muscles of the lips, tongue, jaw, soft palate, larynx, etc.

Systems other than the central nervous system serve to integrate all the activities of the body, including speech. These have to do mainly with the body chemicals as regulated by the glands of internal secretion and respiration.

5

RESPONDING MECHANISMS

After stimulation has been received from one source or another so that logically the next act is speech, nervous impulses travel from the brain to the muscles involved in vocalization and the first physical act occurs. Air is taken into the lungs. Then, for speech, the air in the lungs is forced out through the trachea and set into vibration as it passes over the vocal folds. It becomes "the water that makes the mill wheel go 'round," an activating force essential to speech. It is the source of energy for vocalization. The tones produced as the result of vibration of the vocal folds are modified and amplified by the resonating cavities (principally the pharynx, mouth, and nose) and then formed into specific speech sounds by movements of the lips, tongue, jaw, and soft palate.

Some of the structures involved in speech serve more than one purpose. The larynx, for example, is a passageway for air during respiration, it is the focal point for vocalization, and it seems to provide some resonance. Its chief purpose in speech, however, is to change the expiratory air stream into tones through the vibration of the vocal folds. The mouth functions as the part of the human mechanism chiefly responsible for articulation and at the same time is an important resonator. The nose is a passageway for air and also serves as a resonator. So it is with the other mechanisms involved in speech production. To avoid confusion, the structures and cavities will be discussed in connection with that part of the speech process (respiration, vocalization, resonation, or articulation) with which they are most closely allied.

RESPIRATION

DEFINITION. Respiration (or *breathing*) is a biological function concerned primarily with maintaining life in the organism and secondarily as a force assisting in the production of vocalized sounds. It consists of two phases: *inhalation* and *exhalation*. Inhalation, sometimes referred to as *inspiration*, causes air to flow into the lungs, supplying the body with oxygen. Exhalation (or *expiration*) causes the air—laden with carbon dioxide and other waste products—to flow from the lungs.

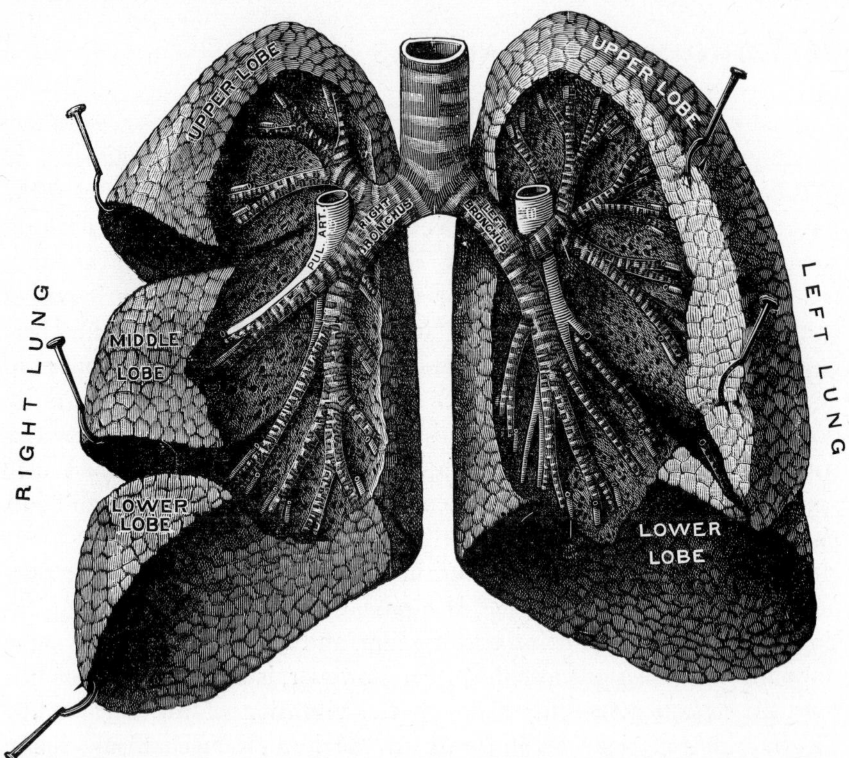

FIG. 6. Bronchi and bronchioles seen from front. Parts of the lungs have been cut away to expose the air tubes. (*From Gray, Anatomy of the Human Body, 25 th ed., Lea & Febiger, Philadelphia,* 1942. *With special permission Masson and Cie, Editeurs, Paris, France.*)

STRUCTURES INVOLVED. For inspiration, the air passes through the nose, down through the pharynx, larynx, trachea, bronchi, and into the lungs; expiration reverses the route. The bodily structures thus most directly and exclusively involved in the breathing process include the trachea, lungs, and their surrounding tissues (rib cage and breathing muscles).

Trachea. The trachea (see Fig. 6), a tube about 4½ inches in length, extends down from the larynx into the chest cavity. At its lower extremity, it divides into two bronchi which extend into the right and the left chest cavities.

Lungs. The lungs are a spongy mass of tubes and air cells covered with elastic tissue (see Fig. 6). Like sponge rubber, they are inert except for their elasticity. The lung on the right side of the body is divided into three large parts (lobes), while on the left side it is divided into two parts, leaving space for the heart. The lungs are conical in shape and conform to the inner wall of the thorax.

Bony framework. The bony framework of the chest consists of twelve pairs of ribs; the sternum, or breastbone; and the vertebral column, or backbone. All the ribs unite by flexible joints to the vertebral column. The first seven (upper) ribs are connected directly to the sternum. Each of the next three ribs is connected to the rib above by means of cartilage. The two lower ribs have no connection toward the front of the body. Each of the ribs slopes downward on either side of the vertebral column, and they gradually increase in length from the top rib down to the seventh and then decrease in length to the twelfth. Because of the flexibility of the connections of the ribs with the vertebral column at the back and with the sternum at the front, the entire rib cage is movable in order to increase or decrease the size of the thoracic cavity. Furthermore, because of the slope, length, and cartilaginous attachments of the ribs, the thoracic cage increases in its side-to-side and front-to-back dimensions when it is lifted upward; thus, enlargement of the chest cavity occurs in all dimensions simultaneously.

Muscles of breathing. Muscles attached to the ribs and sternum cause the chest to increase and decrease in size during respiration. During inspiration the intercostals, levatores costarum, scaleni, sternocleidomastoid, trapezius, and pectoralis major and pectoralis minor (see Figs. 7 and 8), which are attached to the bony framework, take an active part in increasing the size of the chest.

The diaphragm, a large sheet of muscle separating the chest from the abdomen, forms the floor of the chest and the roof of the abdomen. If the fingers are placed at the point of the angle just below the sternum, or breastplate, and then moved along the lower edge of the ribs all the way around to the spinal column, they follow approximately the line of attachment of this muscle. Then if the diaphragm is visualized as being somewhat igloo-shaped and rising from these points of attachment upward into the chest cavity and toward the center of the body, this important breathing muscle will be easily understood.

During exhalation, the chest becomes smaller. While gravity and the elasticity of tissues account for some decrease in side-to-side and front-to-back dimensions of the bony framework of the chest, more active exhalation requires the use of the rectus abdominus, external oblique,

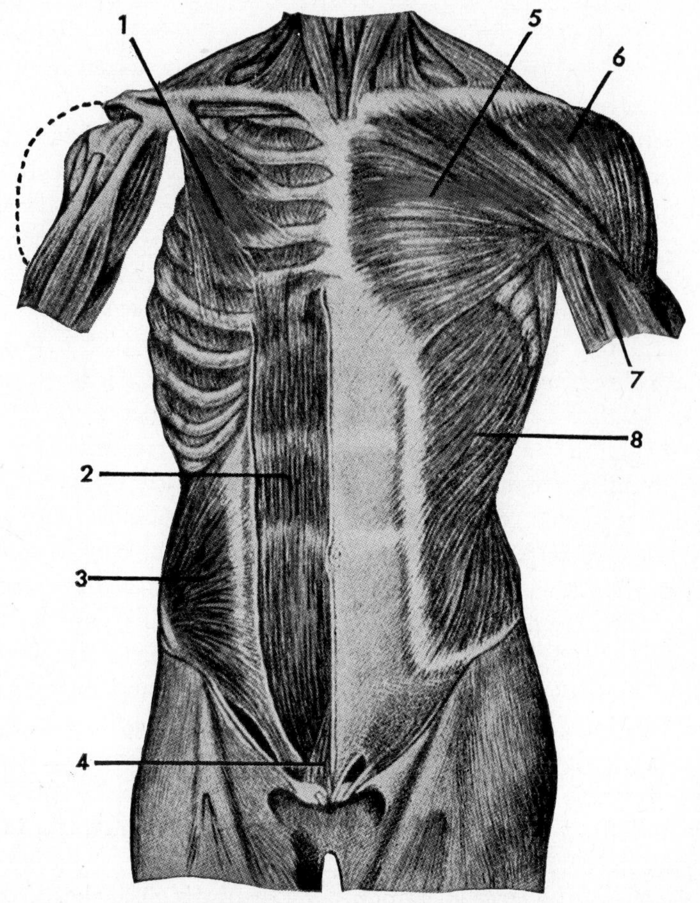

FIG. 7. Muscles of the abdomen. 1, pectoralis minor; 2, rectus abdominus; 3, internal oblique; 4, pyramidalis; 5, pectoralis major; 6, deltoid; 7, biceps; 8, external oblique. (*From J. K. Young, Handbook of Anatomy, 8th ed., F. A. Davis Company, Philadelphia,* 1936.)

internal oblique, transversus, serratus posterior inferior, and quadratus lumborum.

BREATHING PROCESS. When it is time for a new breath, nervous impulses travel from the respiratory center in the medulla of the brain stem to the muscles of the back and chest. During quiet breathing, the nervous impulses flow from this center at regular intervals (average rate, 17 respirations per minute; range 12 to 20 per minute). The muscles of breathing, through their contractions and relaxations, cause the ribs to move out to the side and the sternum to move upward and forward, increasing the volume of lung space. At the same time, the

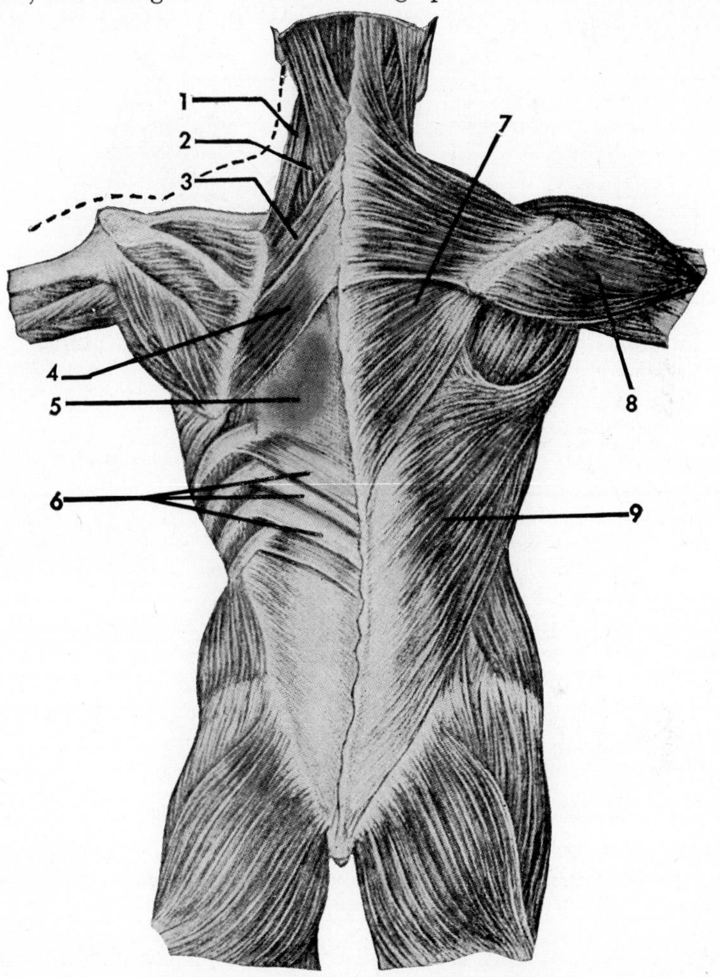

FIG. 8. Muscles of the back. 1, levator scapulae; 2, splenius; 3, rhomboideus minor; 4, rhomboideus major; 5, lumbar fascia; 6, serratus posterior inferior; 7, trapezius; 8, deltoid; 9, latissimus dorsi. (*From J. K. Young, Handbook of Anatomy, 8th ed., F. A. Davis Company, Philadelphia,* 1936.)

diaphragm contracts and in so doing changes from a relaxed, dome-shaped muscle to one which is slightly flatter. H. H. Bloomer discovered, in his roentgenographic study of the mechanics of respiration, that the average range of movement for the diaphragm in normal respiration is about 33 millimeters.

Active and passive nature of the breathing process. On inhalation, the diaphragm contracts slightly, flattening the dome-shaped muscle. Since the diaphragm is the floor of the lung chamber, its descent on contraction has the effect of increasing its vertical diameter. Simultaneously, the external intercostal and other muscles that control the sternum

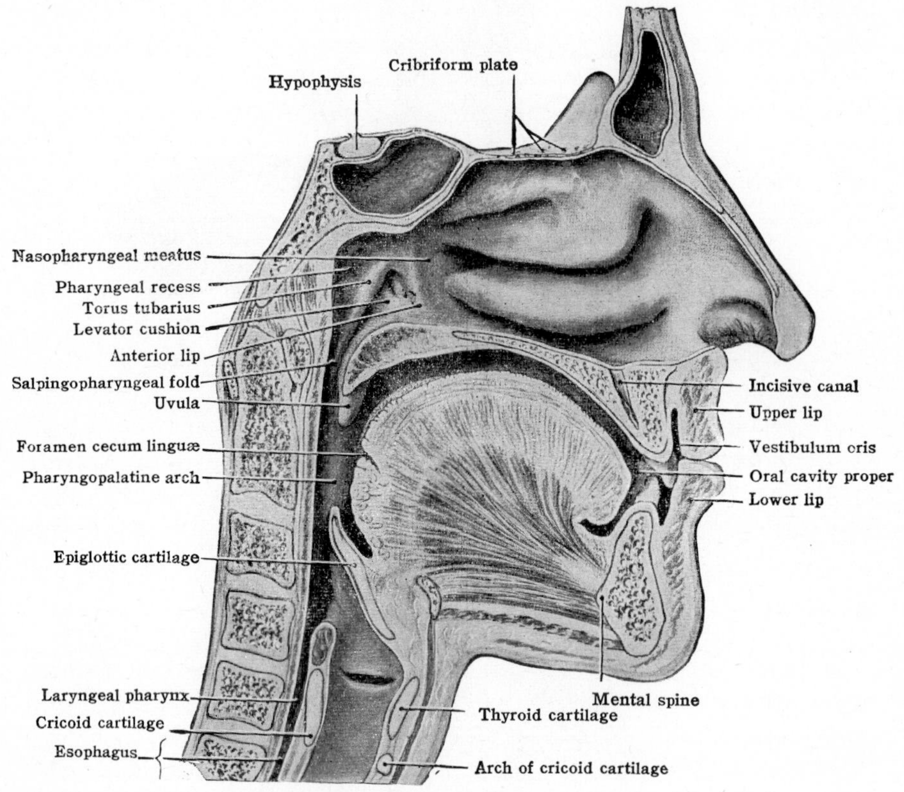

FIG. 9. Sagittal section of the head, through nose, mouth, pharynx, and larynx. (*From Morris, Human Anatomy, 10th ed., The Blakiston Company, Philadelphia,* 1942.)

and ribs contract, raising the entire framework of the chest. This contraction expands the lung cavities in all horizontal directions, slightly raising the upper chest, and the air outside the body flows in to maintain equal pressure.[1] Since the air passages terminate in the lungs, this movement of air results in an inflation of the lungs.

[1] The air that is taken into the lungs is under pressure (approximately 15 pounds per square inch). It moves in and out because of equalization of pressures between the outside air and the air within the respiratory tract.

In passive exhalation the chest walls and lungs resume the position occupied by them at the beginning of inhalation. The muscles that have been in a state of contraction during inhalation relax, and the lung tissue which has been distended shrinks. The decrease in the size of the chest is facilitated by the force of gravity upon the bony thoracic cage and the elastic recoil of the skeletal parts of the cage, the lung tissues, and the viscera (stomach and intestines) under the diaphragm.

BREATHING DURING SPEECH. The outflowing stream of air is employed for speech purposes and is subject to great variation as it passes from the lungs, over the vocal folds, and through the pharynx, mouth, and nose. During phonation, the rate of the expiratory output is less than in ordinary expiration because the vocal folds are brought together, or nearly so, impeding the passage of air. The accenting of words modifies expiration because continuous active control over the air pressure causes variations in the force of utterance. This pressure is probably regulated by the following factors: muscles active in exhalation and control over openings in the laryngeal and oral passages.

In singing, public speaking, and reading aloud, the amount of air required to speak (or sing) a sentence may exceed that of normal exhalation; therefore, more air is required. In such a case, the speaker may use reserve air in the lungs.

VOCALIZATION

In speech, the expiratory air stream from the lungs serves the purpose of setting the vocal folds into vibration. It is generally assumed that this vibration results in the tone produced during vocalization.

STRUCTURES INVOLVED IN VOCALIZATION. The vocal folds with their surrounding structures—the cartilaginous, muscular, and connective tissues of the larynx—are chiefly responsible for vocalization.

Larynx. The larynx (see Figs. 9 to 13) is commonly called the "voice box"; its protuberance, the "Adam's apple." In a degree, this is a "box" in that it is hollow and surrounded by walls of cartilage. When the thumb and the index finger of one hand are placed over the larynx, they are touching the thyroid cartilage, which is rounded in the female but quite pointed and prominent in the male. When the thumb and finger are moved down about half an inch, they are brought near the cricoid cartilage, which is in the shape of a signet ring and lies at the top of the trachea, or "windpipe." The enlarged signet portion lies toward the rear and serves as a base for two pyramidal-shaped cartilages called *arytenoids*. The vocal folds or cords are attached to these at the rear and to the interior surface of the thyroid cartilage toward the front. The epiglottic cartilage extends backward from the mid-line of the interior surface of the thyroid cartilage and serves to guard the entrance to the larynx.

The larynx opens into the pharynx above and the trachea below. Muscles within the larynx (intrinsic muscles) perform the function of closing the upper portion of the larynx during swallowing, regulate the size of the glottis (the opening between the vocal folds), and increase and decrease the tension in the vocal folds during vocalization.

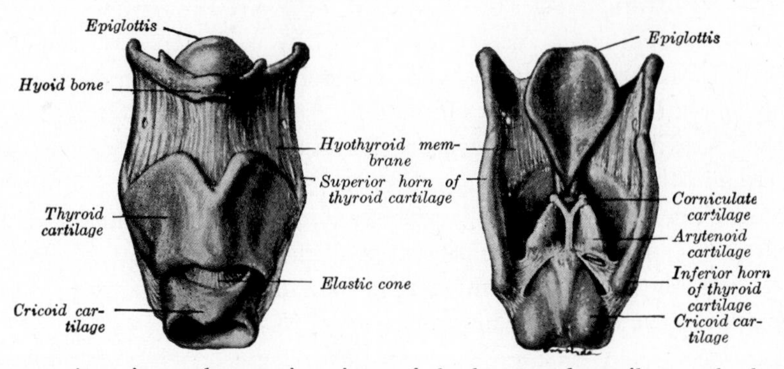

FIG. 10. Anterior and posterior views of the laryngeal cartilages, the hyoid, and some of the connecting membranes and ligaments. (*Callander.*) (*From C. Marshall and E. L. Lazier, An Introduction to Human Anatomy, 3d ed., W. B. Saunders Company, Philadelphia,* 1947.)

Vocal folds. The vocal folds (sometimes called, *vocal cords*, *vocal lips*, or *vocal bands*) stretch from mid-line points on the inner surface of the thyroid cartilage to the arytenoid cartilages. Just above the two vocal folds are the false vocal folds. The glottis opens widely during inspiration and narrows during expiration. During speech the air passing between the vocal folds causes the vocal folds to move in a complicated manner, producing vocal tones.

THEORIES OF VOCALIZATION. As yet the exact manner in which the vocal folds vibrate during vocalization has not been decided by investigators.[1]

[1] An excellent picture of movement of the vocal folds has been prepared by the Bell Telephone Laboratories. This film is entitled *High Speed Motion Pictures of the Human Vocal Cords* and is available on a loan basis.

There are several theories regarding the manner in which the tones are produced during vocalization. One is the "puff theory," which states that the vocal folds let out small puffs of air which set the resonators pulsating. Another, the "harmonic theory," holds that the vocal folds themselves vibrate, causing a weak tone to be produced which is amplified in the cavities above the vocal folds. This activity,

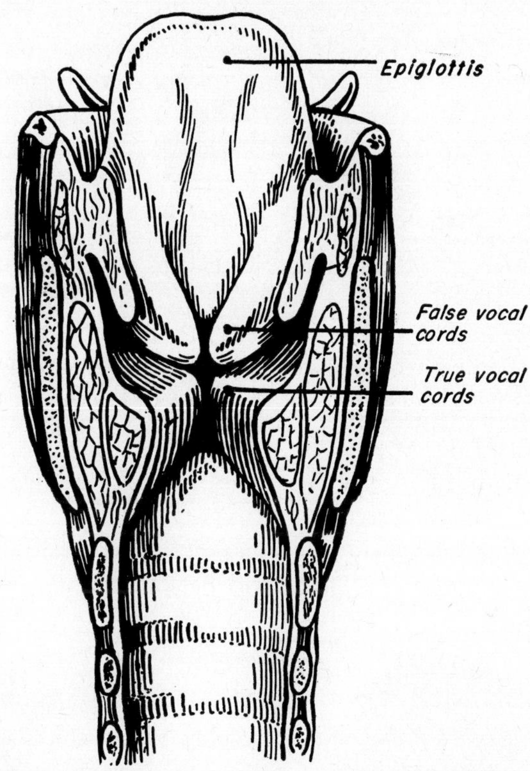

FIG. 11. Transverse section of human larynx. (*From Houssay et al., Human Physiology, McGraw-Hill Book Company, Inc., New York,* 1951.)

plus whatever other movement of the folds occurs, is spoken of as *vibration.*

VOCAL-FOLD VIBRATIONS AS DETERMINERS OF PITCH, LOUDNESS, AND QUALITY. The rate of vibration determines the pitch and, possibly, to some extent the quality of the tone produced.[1] The more rapidly the vocal folds vibrate, the higher the pitch of the voice will be, and naturally, the more slowly they vibrate, the lower the pitch.

[1] G. O. Russell, in *Speech and Voice,* p. 162 (The Macmillan Company, New York, 1931), discusses the effect the structure of the vocal folds has on vocal quality.

The amount of energy behind the vibration of the vocal folds determines the loudness or intensity of the sound produced. The amount of air taken into the lungs to supply the source of energy for vocalization

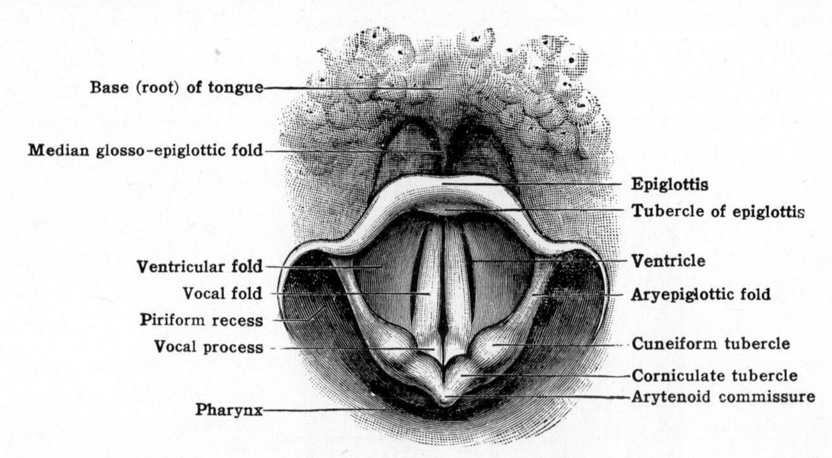

FIG. 12. View of interior of larynx as seen from above during vocalization. (*From Morris, Human Anatomy, 10th ed., The Blakiston Company, Philadelphia,* 1942.)

is not important, but a steady air stream is vital for efficient use of the voice.

Most singing teachers spend considerable time training their students to control breathing so that they will be able to supply the energy

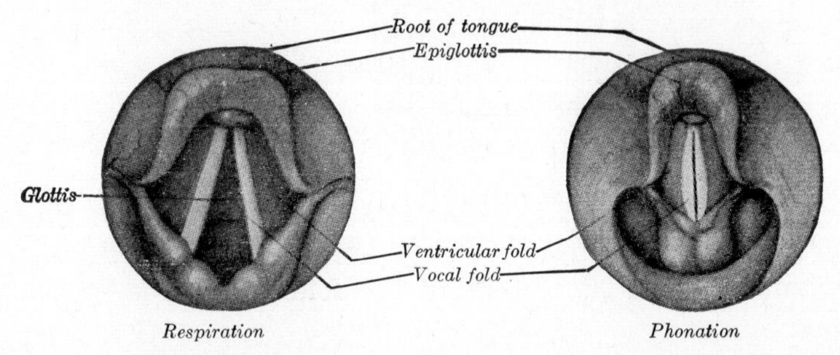

FIG. 13. The position of the vocal folds during respiration and phonation. (*Callander.*) (*From C. Marshall and E. L. Lazier, An Introduction to Human Anatomy, 3d ed., W. B. Saunders Company, Philadelphia,* 1947.)

required for sustained tones and long phrases while they are singing. Singers usually employ the abdominal respiratory type of breathing. It is just as important to have an adequate supply of energy while training the voice for speech. The manner in which you should go about this is presented in Chap. 8.

RESONATION

The tone produced—if there is a tone produced[1]—at the larynx is weak and lacking in quality, but in the resonators it is greatly amplified and enriched.

STRUCTURES INVOLVED IN RESONATION. The upper part of the larynx, the pharynx, the mouth, and nose are considered the important resonators for speech. The larynx was described under vocalization.

Pharynx. The pharynx is the common passageway for air and food directly behind the nose and mouth and includes the cavity back of the tongue (see Fig. 9). This space is sometimes divided into the upper, middle, and lower pharynx. The portion back of the nose is called the *nasal pharynx;* the portion behind the mouth, the *oral pharynx;* and the lower portion, the *laryngeal pharynx.* A small portion of the back wall of the pharynx can be seen behind the uvula (the small nub on the lower border of the soft palate) and the base of the tongue. The soft palate separates the nasal pharynx from the mouth cavity.

Nose. The nose consists of the external and the internal portions (see Fig. 9). The external nose consists of cartilage, covered on the outside with skin and on the inside with mucous membrane. The openings into the external nose are called *nostrils.* The internal nose is the cavity directly behind the external nose through which the air passes on its way to the pharynx. From the bridge of the nose back through the internal nose is a structure called the *septum,* which divides the external and internal nose into two separate passageways. In some instances, this structure is deflected to the right or to the left. When the condition is pronounced, the passageway may be blocked or partially closed. Under such conditions breathing may be difficult and the vocal tones nasalized or denasalized.

Mouth. The mouth (see Fig. 14) is divided into the vestibule and the oral cavity proper. The vestibule can be identified by placing the tongue tip outside the teeth but inside the lips and moving it about so that it touches the outer surface of all the teeth. Now retract the tongue, close the jaws, and move the tongue about, and you will identify the oral cavity. You will observe that it is bounded on the sides and front

[1] According to the "puff theory" the vocal folds would not produce any sound.

by the teeth and gums, to the rear by the soft palate, above the hard palate, and below by the tongue.

The mouth serves a dual purpose during speech. It is an important resonator as well as the center for the formation of specific speech sounds.

CAVITY RESPONSE TO VOCAL-FOLD VIBRATION. The cavities of the larynx, pharynx, mouth, and nose respond to the vibrations of the vocal folds in somewhat the same manner as the jug does to the lips of an efficient player. The lips themselves make very little noise, but because of the force, the air in the jug begins to pulsate and a loud tone

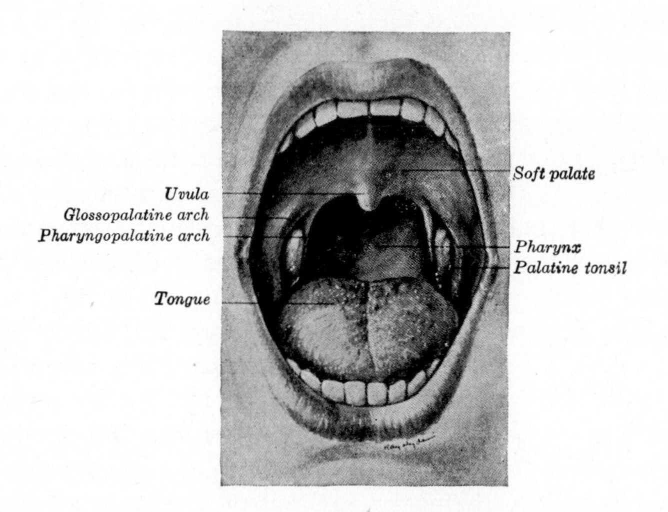

FIG. 14. The mouth. (*Callander.*) (*From C. Marshall and E. L. Lazier, An Introduction to Human Anatomy, 3d ed., W. B. Saunders Company, Philadelphia,* 1947.)

is produced. The jug is the resonator in this case, just as the upper part of the larynx, the pharynx, the mouth, and the nose are the resonators during vocalization. The player's lips are the vibrators during jug playing, while the vocal folds are the vibrators during vocalization. The air column, of course, is the same in either case.

There are differences between the jug and the human mechanisms that make for differences between the pitch, intensity, and quality of the sounds produced by each. For example, the jug has only one opening, while the human resonators are tubes with openings at each end.

The openings differ in diameter and length, and the resonators themselves differ in size, shape, and texture.

Larger cavities make a more effective response to lower rates of vibration, while smaller cavities respond best to higher rates of vibration. The length of the neck of the opening also plays its part in the response of the resonator.

INFLUENCE OF CAVITY WALLS ON VOCAL TONES. Although the walls of a cavity and any connected parts vibrate along with the air in the cavity and help to reinforce and amplify the sound, the space within the cavities is not their only important feature. Their texture helps to determine the quality of the resultant tone. According to G. O. Russell,[1] soft surfaces "mellow" the high partials, or piercing quality, in the tone and may "deaden" it; hard surfaces accentuate the high partials and make the tone "bright," or what is described as "resonant" or "clear" and "ringing." You will see later how the adjustment of the resonators serves to improve the quality and the loudness of vocal tones. In many instances, alterations resulting in greater "openness" during vocalization help to correct deviations in vocal quality and increase the loudness.

ARTICULATION

The tone produced at the larynx is changed into specific sounds as a result of the movement of the articulators—the lips, jaw, tongue, and soft palate. These mechanisms make contacts and adjustments which results in the s's, o's, m's, and t's and all the other sounds that are produced during speech. The hard palate, with its gum ridge, and the inside surfaces of the teeth are important walls where the movable parts may make contacts during articulation.

STRUCTURES INVOLVED IN ARTICULATION. Anatomical structures involved in articulation include the lips, jaw, tongue, and soft palate and the inner surfaces of the teeth, gum ridge, and hard palate.

Lips. The mouth opening is altered by combined adjustments of the lips and jaw. Consisting of skin, muscles, connective tissue, and mucous membrane, the lips are highly flexible and can be moved into numerous positions essential to articulate speech.

The *orbicularis oris* and the *risorius* muscles play a prominent part in the movement that occurs at the lips. The *orbicularis oris* surrounds

[1] Russell, *op. cit.*

the mouth and is responsible for rounding and pouting movements of the lips. The risorius is the smile muscle and retracts the corners of the mouth.

As the boundary of the mouth opening, the lips play a part in chewing and sucking as well as in the formation of the consonant and vowel sounds.

Teeth. The teeth, like the hard palate, serve as important surfaces during articulation; *e.g.*, on the [s] sound, a thin stream of air is directed over the cutting edge of the lower front teeth, causing the "noise" that has come to be recognized as the [s] sound.

Normally, there are thirty-two teeth in the mouth of the adult, sixteen uppers and sixteen lowers. The teeth are embedded in the alveolar or gum ridges of the upper and lower jaws. The alveolar processes can be identified by moving the tip of the tongue over the surfaces just above the upper teeth and just below the lower teeth.

Hard palate. The hard palate serves as an important surface against which the tongue makes contacts during speech. It consists of bone covered with mucous membrane. This structure forms the roof of the mouth cavity and is bordered by the gum ridge in front and at the sides. Attached along its rear border is a flexible curtain called the *soft palate*, or *velum*.

Soft palate. This structure is attached to the tongue by the glossopalatine arch and to the side wall of the oral pharynx by the glossopharyngeal arch. The movable tip at the mid-line of its free border is called the *uvula*. During speech, muscles within the soft palate contract to raise the structure backward and upward toward the back wall of the pharynx, thus closing the nasal recesses during the utterance of the oral vowels and consonants.

The *isthmus of the fauces*, which is very closely allied with the soft palate, forms the opening between the oral cavity and the oral pharynx (see Fig. 14). The boundaries of the isthmus are the soft palate above, the undersurface of the tongue below, and the glossopalatine arches at the sides. These arches extend from the tongue to the soft palate. Just back of these arches are similar pharyngopalatine arches which extend from the pharynx and soft palate. Both pairs of arches consist of muscles with mucous membrane covering.

Muscles which have their origins in the soft palate and pass through the glossopharyngeal arches and other muscles from the pharynx and larynx function in lowering the soft palate and raising the pharynx and larynx. Muscles having their origin in the soft palate and passing through the glossopalatine arches to the tongue draw these arches together, pull the sides of the tongue upward and backward, and draw the sides of the soft palate forward.

Tongue. The tongue is a flexible organ consisting of muscles, glands, and connective tissue. It is attached to the hyoid bone at the base. At the rear it is attached to the epiglottis and to the soft palate (by means of the glossopalatine arches). A median fold of mucous membrane called the lingual frenulum connects the undersurface of the tip of the tongue to the floor of the mouth.

This member consists chiefly of muscles. Located within the tongue are four sets of intrinsic muscles: the superior and inferior longitudinal, the transverse, and the vertical. The extrinsic muscles of the tongue extend into the tongue from other origins—the chin, the hyoid bone, the base of the skull, the soft palate, and the larynx.

The intrinsic muscles are responsible for the many precise movements involved in the articulation of the speech sounds. This system of muscle fibers makes it possible to raise the sides, point and flatten the tongue, and curl the tip either upward or downward. The extrinsic muscles assist in the actions of the intrinsic muscles and function to raise and lower as well as to protrude and retract the tongue. The basic biological purposes of the tongue are (1) moving the food about in the mouth during chewing, (2) forcing the food to the back of the mouth during swallowing, and (3) serving as an important sensory gateway for taste, touch, and pain.

PRODUCTION OF VOWELS AND CONSONANTS. Vocalization, resonation, and articulation are so closely allied that it is difficult to determine where one leaves off and the other begins. It can be said, however, that the vowels are determined by the shape and size of the resonating cavities while the consonants are largely noises made with the lips and tongue as they make contacts with the teeth, gum ridge, hard palate, and soft palate. As the [s] sound is made, the teeth touch lightly and the sides of the tongue rise so that there is a shallow groove down the middle of the tongue which allows the air to pass between the tongue and the palate. The stream of air passes along this groove and over the lower teeth. The lips are drawn back. The passage of air between the teeth causes a noise to be produced which has come to be recognized as the [s] sound. On [t], the teeth and lips are apart. The tip of the tongue rises and makes contact with the hard palate at the gum ridge.

The back of the tongue is low in the mouth. As the tip is pulled away from the palate, an explosive sound is created which is known as the [t] sound.

These sounds have been described as isolated sounds. In speech, the articulators move in the same patterns as when the sounds appear in spoken words, but, of course, the sounds vary somewhat when they are combined with other sounds in sentences. Frequently, a particular sound is made easily when it is isolated, but when it is combined with another sound—for example, [s] with [o]—the [s] becomes defective.

SUMMARY

Speech is the result of coordinated and integrated action of the bodily mechanisms—muscles of respiration, larynx, pharynx, tongue, lips, jaw, etc.—involved in breathing, vocalization, and articulation. The first step in the speaking process is the inhalation of air. This is followed by vocalization, which occurs during the expiratory phase of respiration. The tone produced at the larynx is amplified by the resonators, and speech sounds are formed as a result of the highly specific movements of the lips, tongue, jaw, and other parts.

Normally, the bodily parts work together smoothly during the utterance of words and sentences and the speaker is not aware of their activity. But as he sets out to improve voice and articulation, the body parts receive his attention because they are the "machinery" used in producing speech. Almost from the very start of the program, he must develop conscious control over them as he develops new speaking habits. Frequent reference is made to these mechanisms during the course, and the student will find it helpful to have a clear picture of them and to know how they work together to produce speech.

PART FOUR

MAKING PHYSICAL PREPARATION FOR VOCAL ACTIVITY

LEARNING TO RELAX

Relaxation plays a vital role in voice production. If muscles are tense, they cannot make the intricate movements of speech nor can they move with the precise timing which is so important for good voice and clear articulation.[1] This was shown rather clearly in the case of a young lady with a high-pitched voice. She had been working on voice production for several months and had seemed to be able to free all her muscles from tension, yet she was not actually relaxing the muscles of her jaw and throat. After she had taken exercises for freeing this part, she could speak with greater ease and the pitch of her speaking voice was lower.

RELAXATION AND MUSCLE TONUS

Relaxation defined. The word "relaxation" refers to relative degrees of tonus in the muscles involved directly or indirectly in speech. The term does not imply complete relaxation, but as a training device, the student is advised to relax as completely as possible at the outset of the program.

Muscle tonus. The skeletal muscles which move to produce speech are in a state of sustained, partial contraction. This condition is known as *tonus* and is caused by a continuous flow of impulses from the brain to the muscles. The string of a harp when correctly tuned has normal tonus—if it is tightened, the tonus increases; if it is loosened, the tonus decreases. The muscles of a living person are never completely relaxed. The arm at rest at the side of the body is bent slightly, indicating that it is not entirely relaxed. Muscle tonus is always present, making "com-

[1] Dr. J. H. Muyskens of the University of Michigan has said, "Speech results from muscles moving, glands secreting, and nerves being innervated."

plete relaxation" an impossibility. This same condition is present in the muscles involved in phonation and articulation.

MUSCLE SENSE. Motor nerves transmit impulses from the brain to the muscles which cause the muscles to contract. Some of the fibers carry impulses which cause the tonic contractions described above; other fibers carry stronger currents which cause the muscles to effect movements of bodily mechanisms. Sensory fibers connect the muscles with the sensory centers of the brain and thereby report the state of tension in the muscles. For example, when the arm is held out to the side at shoulder height for a period of time, tensions increase in certain muscles and, because of the sensory fibers, awareness of increased tension in the muscles is carried to the brain. When the arm is allowed to drop to the side, the difference in the degree of muscle tension is also communicated to the brain through the sensory fibers. The same conditions of hypertension and relative relaxation can be felt when the muscles of the tongue, jaw, lips, and other parts involved in speech are tensed and relaxed.

MUSCLE ACTION

To prepare for the work on bodily relaxation, the student needs to understand the concept not only of tension in the muscles but also of tension between agonist and antagonist muscles as against a balance of tension and relaxation.

The skeletal muscles are paired so as to produce movements of the parts of the body. An antagonistic relationship exists between opposing muscles so that, when one of the muscles contracts, the other relaxes. Phonation and articulation, like all other bodily acts, result from the coordinated movement of many muscles working together and not from the isolated action of a single muscle.

During contraction, the movable point of attachment (insertion) of the muscle is drawn toward the fixed point of attachment (origin). In any movement, individual muscles may function in different ways. They may serve as prime movers, antagonists, fixation muscles, and synergists. The prime movers, as a result of active contraction, produce the actual movement that occurs. The antagonists relax to allow the prime movers to cause the movements. On other occasions, the prime movers may become the antagonists and the antagonists may become the prime movers and thereby cause the reverse movement. Fixation muscles make one of the attachments of the prime mover firm so as to exert force on the other attachment. Synergists control the position of the intermediate joints and inhibit any extraneous movements.

MUSCLE ACTION IN SPEECH. The precise movements of the lips, tongue, and jaw as they produce the consonants and the vowels and the vocal folds as they produce the tones require the coordinated action of groups of muscles moving together in this manner. Definite combinations of muscle action adjust the articulators as each sound is produced. For example, during the production of the vowel [o], the muscle surrounding the mouth (the *orbicularis oris*) rounds the lips, the tongue flattens, and mouth opens about ¾ inch. Accurate and well-timed movement of groups of muscles determines the quality of results obtained when this sound is produced. When the [o] is just one of the many sounds in a word or sentence and hundreds of such adjustments are necessary, the importance of the coordinated action of the groups of muscles with varying degrees of tension and relaxation becomes all the more obvious.

Since tension of the prime movers (agonists) and relaxation of the antagonists are essential in the process of muscle action, it is obvious that there must be a proper balance of tension and relaxation between these two groups of muscles during speech. General hypertension and failure to exert the balance of tension and relaxation in the antagonistic muscles involved in voice production often pose the biggest problem in proper voice production.

EFFECTS OF HYPERTENSION

When muscles involved in speech are hypertense, they lack freedom of movement and vocal utterance is impeded. As a result, the speech sounds and the vocal tones become distorted.

The student must develop the right amount of tonicity to become proficient in speech. If there is hypertension when there should be a degree of relaxation, results will not be satisfactory. The beginning tennis player plays a poor game because he has not learned to put the right amount of tension in the right muscles as he makes his serves and returns. The same is true of the beginner in ballroom dancing. When the neophyte tennis player, dancer, football player, golfer, or baton twirler learns to tense certain muscles and relax others in the "proper degree," his techniques and proficiency improve. In a degree, speech production is comparable, except that most people have spoken for years and they must unlearn some bad habits. They can do this best if they will start by learning to relax all the muscles as completely as possible. Sometimes the old hypertensions persist. For example, a person may become so accustomed to tensing the muscles involved in vocalization during speech that it seems almost impossible at first to eliminate the habit. These hypertensions can be relieved only through the continuous practice of relaxation exercises over a long period and through constant effort to free the muscles during everyday speech.

PROGRAM FOR DEVELOPING VOLUNTARY CONTROL

The muscles involved in speech production are small and not usually subjected to voluntary control, but you can learn to relax them. In order to be successful you need to make persistent use of effective procedures. You should start with the large muscles of the body in the beginning, because it is easier to relax big muscles than small ones. Relaxation goes from big to small. Certainly, you would be unable to free the small muscles of the larynx, throat, and jaw if you could not relax the muscles of the arms, legs, and trunk. You will find that the relaxation exercises are arranged with this concept in mind—you learn to relax first the large muscles, then the smaller muscles. Basically, you need to learn how to develop the power to withdraw tension from the voluntary muscles of the body.

WITHDRAWING TENSION FROM THE MUSCLES

You will have to go about your task in a manner to which you are not accustomed. Usually, when you are told to do something, you go about it in an active way. You work at it. You start some of your muscles moving. For example, when you move toward a chair or "tune in" at the radio, you begin to work. You do something. In other words, you create muscle tensions. In like manner, when you are told to relax, you are likely to go at it in the usual way; that is, you work at it. You will have to discover that what you really should do is *nothing*, because relaxation is the opposite of work. It is passive rather than active, and what you need to do to relax is to release tensions rather than create them.

You can develop this ability to release tensions. It is merely a matter of learning how to "let go" so that the stiffness leaves the muscles. If you can do this, you have mastered relaxation.

THINKING OUT ALL THE STIFFNESS. In many cases it will not be necessary to learn to relax. Far easier means than conscious-control exercises are available to those who do not have to learn. It is largely a matter of learning to "think out" the stiffness or to "let go" the muscular tension.

EXERCISE 29. If you must learn to relax you should first practice the conscious-control exercises. First, hang the arms at the sides and consciously stiffen and relax the hands several times; then, continue through the other exercises suggested.

When you can sense muscles moving, the next step is to distinguish differences in muscle tension. After you become adept at increasing and decreasing the tonicity, you are ready for the last stage in the developmental process. At the drop of the hat, you ought to be able to "think out" all the stiffness.

APPROACHING RELAXATION THROUGH PHYSICAL EXERCISE

Your success in voice improvement will depend in large part on the physical controls you will develop during the early stages of the course. Just to read the text is not enough. You must learn these controls through participation in active physical exercises. As you practice the following exercises, work with these thoughts in mind:

1. You are doing the relaxation exercises to develop the ability to create and release tension in the muscles of the trunk and extremities.
2. You must learn to "let go" the muscular tension instantaneously and thoroughly.
3. You must develop this ability before you proceed to the next assignment.
4. In order to accomplish these objectives, you must have regular daily practice periods, two or three each day.
5. You should practice at times when you are rested.
6. You should practice vigorously.

SOME EXERCISES FOR LEARNING HOW RELAXATION FEELS. Before you begin a program for developing the ability to relax, you must realize what relaxation is and how it feels. You can make this discovery in various ways. For example, you may clench your fist and hold your arm and forearm up at an angle so as to make the muscles of your arm and shoulder bulge. After you have held your arm in this position for several seconds—20 or 30—you will feel the pull and notice the quivering that results from the hypertension. From this, you become mentally aware of how extreme tension feels. Now if you withdraw the tension, the arm falls to the side, and although you still sense some tonus in the muscles, they feel comfortable in their freedom from strain and hypertension.

The following exercises are designed to further your ability to recognize how relaxation actually feels so that eventually you will know when you have learned to relax the muscle.

EXERCISE 30. As a preliminary experience, stiffen your hands, hold them tense for a few moments, then let the stiffness go. As you do this, some of the muscles of the forearm become tense, but as the stiffness leaves the muscles of the hands, the muscles of the forearms relax and the hands drop to wherever gravity takes them.

EXERCISE 31. As a second experience, stiffen any other part of the body and then let all the stiffness go. In doing this you have merely tensed and then relaxed the muscles. Now as you stand or sit or lie on a couch or on the floor, stiffen all the muscles of the body, then relax.

These experiences will prove that you can achieve control over the voluntary muscles.

CONSCIOUS-CONTROL EXERCISES. The conscious-control exercises that follow have been designed to develop a feeling of muscles moving and an awareness of differences in muscle tension. Through their practice you should increase your ability to relax the degree of tension in the muscles. As you perform each of the following exercises, try to sense the differences in tension in various muscles and be careful to put just enough energy into the movement to have it performed efficiently, taking heed not to tense muscles that are not involved in the act. Muscles that are not holding the body erect or are not involved in the performance should be relaxed. There should be a minimum of tension in the muscles that are carrying out the movement.

EXERCISE 32. Take a good standing position, letting the arms hang down at the sides. Then keeping the arms straight, raise them slowly in front. As they are brought up, feel that the movement is controlled. Be careful not to overtense any of the muscles involved, and move slowly. When the arms are straight in front, begin to move them out to the sides. Now slowly bring the arms straight forward again. Then let them move slowly to the sides of the body as they were in the first position. The forearms and wrists should lead the movements. As you practice the exercise, you should become progressively more graceful and the performance should require less effort. Do the same thing with the right arm only. Turn the head and eyes slowly to the left as the arm is moved out to the side. As the arm is brought to the front, slowly turn the face forward. Do the same, using the left arm only.

EXERCISE 33. Now raise the right arm slowly in front, the palm of the hand turned down and the arm straight. When the hand is at shoulder height, bend the elbow and bring the hand slowly toward the left shoulder and, at the same time, slowly turn the head to the right. The muscles of the forearm move at the same time as those which are used in the head movement. After the fingers have touched the left shoulder and the head is turned as far as possible to the right, start bringing the hand up to the front again. At the same time slowly turn the face forward. Repeat these conscious movements of the head and the right arm and then slowly lower the arm to the side. Do the same thing, using the left arm.

Run through this series several times in an attempt to develop a feeling of muscles moving. Each time control the motion so that it is slow and even, being careful to exert no more energy than is required to produce the movement.

Use the same procedure while you do a variety of things in this "slow-motion" way, remembering to make all movements smoothly and steadily. Walk about the room very slowly, setting first one foot down, then the other. Pick up chairs; turn lights on and off; lean over and roll and unroll rugs; change the positions of the pillows on the davenport, accomplishing each action so slowly that the performance seems to require many minutes. Try to make your movements seem to be like those of a runner shown in slow-motion pictures. Practice will increase your ability to sense differences in degrees of muscle tension and will result in consciously controlled muscle movements.

The tightrope walker is able to perform his death-defying stunts largely because of his ability to exert the right amount of tension in his muscles. Indeed, all poise results from the rhythmical movement with which muscles work together when they are neither too tense nor too flaccid.

The consciously controlled movement suggested by these exercises should lead the way toward relaxation. It should also develop poise.

EXERCISES FOR SENSING DIFFERENCES IN MUSCLE TENSION. In order to become able to cause your muscles to pass from an active to a relatively passive state in a few seconds, you must learn to increase and decrease muscle tonus "at will," so that the very instant you think about becoming relaxed, you are immediately in a state of relaxation. Since it is easier to achieve relaxation in certain muscles, the beginning may well be made with the extremities, trunk, and neck. The exercises which follow take you through active and relatively passive phases of muscle tension.

EXERCISE 34. Take a good standing position, letting the arms hang down at the sides. Breathe deeply as you bring the arms slowly up to the thrust position. Hold the air in the lungs as you clench the fists tightly. Now relax the hands and arms, and allow them to fall to the sides as you release the air.

EXERCISE 35. (*Active.*) Take a good standing position. Bring the arms slowly around to the front so that the backs of the hands are toward the mid-line of the body. Bring them up so that the thumbs drag along the vest buttons and continue up past the nose and high into the air. Rise onto the toes, stretch, and feel the tension throughout the body. (*Passive.*) Quickly let the tension go and sink to a squat, so that you are seated on your heels, your arms are hanging down with your hands touching the floor, and your trunk and shoulders are slouched forward. Hold this position while you count 10 seconds. After you have done this a few times, you will notice that, although you have exhaled, your lungs do not refill with air until you begin with the next active step. (*Active.*) Rise slowly, first straightening the knees, then bringing the hips forward and the shoulders back, so that, when you have finished, you are back in a good standing position.

If the exercise is executed correctly during the passive stage, the muscles will be free from most of the tension and you will sink rapidly to the standing-squat position. During this part of the exercise you learn to feel relaxation.

Execute the exercise slowly and feel the movement of the muscles. Remember that in order to achieve complete relaxation you must be able to recognize differences in muscle tension.

The above should be followed by an exercise that is very similar.

EXERCISE 36. (*Active.*) Proceed to the stretch again, but do not rise onto the toes. Hold the arms aloft for several seconds, and notice the tension. Hold them close in. (*Passive.*) Let them "fall" through the mid-line.

During this exercise be careful not to pull away or to stiffen the arms during the passive stage.

EXERCISE 37. (*Active.*) Move the arms from the side to extend straight outward like the wings of an airplane. After standing thus for several seconds you will begin to feel tension in the arms and shoulders. (*Passive.*) When you feel this tension, drop the arms to their original position.

EXERCISE 38. (*Active.*) Bring the arms from the sides up so that they extend straight out in front at shoulder height, and hold them there for several seconds. (*Passive.*) Let them fall loosely to the side.

EXERCISE 39. Take a good standing position with the arms straight down at the side. Now allow the trunk and head to fall forward so that the hands are nearly touching the floor. With the back muscles, swing the arms from side to side. Do this several times, then rise to the erect position.

EXERCISE 40. Stand up straight and still like a glass statue. Gradually relax, and fall limply to the floor.

EXERCISE 41. When the arms are relatively free from tension, swing them loosely at the side by making the trunk turn, bringing first the right shoulder and then the left shoulder forward.

Execute each of these exercises three or four times before proceeding to the next. In all these exercises the forearm should lead the movement. This is the "natural" way, which has been described by Delsarte as "the wrist leading." It is the muscles of the forearm which bring the wrist forward. The hand muscles are relaxed, and the hand follows the wrist. When the mind has the intention of pointing, the fingers tense and the index finger points.

You should be careful to use just enough energy to bring about smooth, easy movement. Do not seem to hurry. The action must not be a series of jerky movements; it should appear as it would in a slow-motion picture. By this time you will have learned to recognize differences in degrees of muscle tension. When you know you are relaxed, you have made your first step.

RELAXING THE TRUNK AND EXTREMITIES

The average person will find that portions of his body will occasionally become tense. This is true even though the individual is not "nervous." For example, when he is walking rapidly to keep an appointment, some of his muscles are unduly strained; or when he is writing an examination against time, he clasps his pen tightly and all his hand and arm muscles are tense. Instead of allowing his muscles to be free for rapid movement, he actually is holding them "stiff" and is using far greater energy than is necessary for the activity. Furthermore, it is likely that he does not perform his work so efficiently as he would if he had the ability to do the job without putting into it any more energy than is necessary for successful accomplishment. The best results are had when there is just enough tonicity in the muscles to accomplish the task in the time allotted. Under these circumstances there is no hypertension.

At times such as these, you need to be able to "let go" the tension in one area and then proceed with your work. When one portion of the body is tensed, either permanently or temporarily, you need to analyze conditions and find out where the tension lies, then include in the relaxation program exercises designed to relax the part involved. The following exercises are included for this purpose.

ENTIRE TRUNK. Lie on the back, arms at sides.

EXERCISE 42. Contract the knee muscles, raising the heels off the floor, and release.

EXERCISE 43. Contract the hip muscles vigorously enough to draw the hips up from the floor, and release. Repeat for the waist, chest, and head.

Lie in prone position with arms at sides.

EXERCISE 44. Raise leg up, knee straight, keeping head on floor and abdomen in, and drop. Repeat for hips, waist, chest, and head.

UPPER TRUNK. Stand erect, arms stretched above head and feet 12 inches apart.

EXERCISE 45. Fully extend arms and body, stretch, then release all muscles and fall forward, body bending at the waist, knees slightly bent, head forward almost between knees, arms trailing on floor. Bob several times. For this bob, the muscles about the waist pull the body slightly up; then as you release the muscles, you relax and let the body fall back to original position. Come to a standing position slowly and repeat.

WAIST. Stand with feet apart, one a little ahead of the other for balance.

EXERCISE 46. Bending at the waist, fall forward and bob several times down and up with arms, shoulders, and neck relaxed. Bend sideways, keeping hips forward, head and arms relaxed. Bob several times. Bend backwards, arms and head falling back, hips forward. Bob several times. Bend on opposite side, and bob. Repeat until you can make this movement a rotation of the waist on the hips.

LEGS. Stand with one hand on a table. (This support may be dispensed with after a few days of practice.)

EXERCISE 47. Swing leg forward and back, swinging it from the hip and keeping the body erect, hips forward. The leg is relaxed. In the forward swing, the knee is bent, the lower leg and foot hang loosely. In the backward swing, knee bends and lower leg and foot kick up and backward toward the hip.

EXERCISE 48. Follow this with the extended leg swing, in which knee and leg are perfectly straight and tensed, toes pointed.

ARM AND SHOULDER. Take a good standing position.

EXERCISE 49. Raise the shoulder, and allow the elbow to turn up. Arms should swing out at the side. Make the elbow lead first, then the wrist, until the arm is horizontal with the body. Release the arm, and allow it to drop to the side.

ARMS. Take a good standing position, arms stretched above head, palms facing.

EXERCISE 50. Swing arms down in half circle to side. Let them swing through and come up in back, completing the circuit. Elbows should be straight, with arms making as wide a circle as possible. Let the weight of the arms and hands carry the arms around. Reverse the swing, arms going back and coming forward to complete the circuit. Keep the body position normal, and swing the arms; the head does not jerk back and forth.

HANDS. Take a good standing position.

EXERCISE 51. Bring the forearms up in front so that they are at right angles to the body. Relax the hands, and shake them vigorously using the forearms.

RELAXING THE THROAT, JAW, AND TONGUE

Many students develop hypertensions in the muscles of the throat, jaw, and tongue because they do not know how to coordinate the muscles involved. They tend to place stresses and strains in wrong places, and their vocal efforts result in unpleasant, inefficient, or unhygienic vocalization. Somehow, if they have any hypertension at all, they tense the muscles involved in vocalization. Consciously or unconsciously, they act on the assumption that, because tone is produced at the larynx, they should "work for voice" in the throat area. As a result, they soon place the burden for vocalization here and fail to use other sources of vocal power—muscles of the abdomen and diaphragm. Through disuse in voice production these latter muscles lose their overlaid function of assisting as motive forces in speech. The muscles directly involved in vocalization are called upon to bear the entire burden of speech, and because in most cases this burden is too great for these small muscles, hypertensions develop and vocal difficulties and unhygienic habits of vocalization result.

The vocal folds which produce sound are membranous muscles attached to other muscles. These, in turn, are attached to still other muscles, and so on; therefore it is apparent that, the more flexible the body is, the more flexible and pleasing the voice will be.

Since speech is a reflection of the entire personality, it is almost self-evident that you need to make all the muscles of the body usable, coordinately or "in tune."[1] You must learn to achieve the proper degree

[1] Rasmussen, Carrie, *Speech Methods in the Elementary School*, p. 23, The Ronald Press Company, New York, 1945.

of relaxation in the muscles involved directly in speech and utilize other muscles which assist in the process (see Chap. 7).

Muscles used directly in speech are small and are not usually subjected to voluntary control. The persistent use of exercises for freeing them will be necessary in order to achieve the relatively passive state required for their efficient functioning.

NECK. The muscles in the front part (anterior) of the neck require more attention than the larger, back (posterior) muscles. Head-rotation exercises serve the purpose very well.

EXERCISE 52. First, relax the head and trunk forward, bending at the waist, and rotate the trunk clockwise at first for several turns, then reverse. Roll the trunk, and at the same time allow the head to roll around on the shoulders, with the jaw and the neck relaxed. The head should roll like a ball in a bowl.

EXERCISE 53. Second, take a good standing position. Allow the head to fall forward so that the chin rests on the chest. Be sure that the posterior muscles of the neck and the muscles of the jaw are relaxed. Hold the chest up; roll the head to the right side, back, on around to the left side, then down in front. Repeat this a number of times; then reverse the movement, keeping the face, jaw, and throat muscles relaxed.

EXERCISE 54. Let the head fall forward; bob it up and down four times in succession. (To bob, use the muscles in the back of the neck and slightly pull the head erect, then release the pull and let the head again fall forward.)

EXERCISE 55. Repeat, letting the head fall to both sides and then back, bobbing four times in each direction. When the head is back, the jaw falls open and relaxes. Repeat, bobbing only twice in each direction. Repeat, bobbing once in each direction.

EXERCISE 56. Entire rotation of head on the shoulders, keeping the muscles as relaxed as possible.

SOFT PALATE. The yawn is frequently suggested as an exercise for opening and relaxing the throat. A yawn gives the "feel" of what is desired.

Yawning, a reflex activity, in itself will not accomplish the purpose you have in mind. You must also develop voluntary control over the soft palate.

EXERCISE 57. Stand before a mirror with a light focused into your mouth, and practice moving the soft palate. When you are able to lift it easily, try pulling it toward the back wall of the pharynx and then relaxing it. You should be able to accomplish this in a short period of time. The same technique may be used in freeing the sides of the throat from any excess tension.

JAW. One usually encounters much difficulty in learning to relax the jaw. You should be able to allow the jaw to drop as easily as you drop the arm. In beginning the practice, take a good standing or sitting position. Hold the chest up well. Lower the head forward; relax the neck and, as far as possible, all the muscles of the face, including those which are active in the movements of the jaw; toss the head straight back, allowing the mouth to fall open. Repeat this several times. With each succeeding attempt the mouth should fall open farther. Be careful not to force the jaw down; the muscles should be passive in order to obtain satisfactory results. When you feel that you have made some progress without moving the head back, let the jaw fall of its own weight.

EXERCISE 58. Later lie on your back, and draw your knees up, keeping your heels flat. Keep your chest up. In this position you will find that jaw relaxation comes easily.

EXERCISE 59. Stand or sit erect. Relax the jaw, and throw the head back. Now bring the head forward to its normal position, counting slowly from 1 to 5 with the jaw relaxed.

EXERCISE 60. After some practice with these procedures, stand erect and place the thumbs beneath the chin. Try moving the chin down and up. If you encounter resistance, go back to techniques suggested earlier. Try the head rotation again.

EXERCISE 61. When you really have learned to relax the jaw, try voicing [ah]; as you do, you will find that there is a change in the vowel sound with each movement of the jaw. Keep the throat open for the [ah] sound, and continue voicing as you move the jaw down and up. Do this several times, keeping the jaw free from tension. Later try speaking a sentence, for example, "This is a fine day," "May all your days be happy days," or "The sky is clear this afternoon," and at the same time keep the jaw muscles relaxed.

As you continue moving the jaw in this manner, you will find that your articulation will not pass the censors, but if you are able even to approximate the desired end and still keep the jaw muscles relaxed, you are well on the road to success. Do not stop when you feel that you have learned to free the muscles. Continue to practice consistently until you have obtained a high degree of control and can speak the sentence clearly, making all the movements accurately, but with sufficiently relaxed muscles.

BACK OF TONGUE. Any attempt to relax the tension in the back of the tongue should be accompanied by complete relaxation of the muscles of the jaw.

EXERCISE 62. Start by opening the mouth and forcing the tongue forward. Hold. Now relax the tensions and let the tongue come back to its usual position. Hold this and allow the tongue to rest flatly. Say *ah*, observing how the tongue lies relaxed on the floor of the mouth. Now observe what happens as you make some sharp movements with the tongue, keeping the throat open and relaxed. Your tongue will probably move into some of the final consonant positions so that you produce such words as *ah—t* and *ah—d*.

EXERCISE 63. Hold the tip of the tongue down with a tongue depressor or spoon. Raise the back of the tongue high in the mouth. Relax the tongue into its normal position. Continue five times.

FACE AND LIPS. Massage is one means for obtaining relaxation of facial muscles. Pressure from the fingers relaxes the tension, and the muscles remain relaxed until they are stimulated from within.

EXERCISE 64. To accomplish relaxation voluntarily, first tense the muscles in the same way that you stiffen the hands, then release the tension. Retain the relaxed condition for a longer period of time than you tense the muscles. Sit in front of a mirror and release the muscles of the face for a period of 15 seconds, stiffen the muscles of the face for 5 seconds, and then relax the muscles for 15 seconds. Gradually increase the length of time during which the muscles are relaxed. Carry out the same type of activity to obtain relaxation of the lips.

For general relaxation every muscle must be free from excess tension. Ability to relax the muscles of the throat, jaw, and tongue is especially important in speech, but it will usually be found that exercises specific to these parts must be practiced before relaxation is accomplished.

THE RELAXATION PERIOD

When you know what relaxation really is and are able to free all the muscles from stiffness at will, you are ready for the relaxation period. In the beginning, it is more desirable to lie on a cot during this time. Later, you may sit erect.

SUPINE POSITION. Lie on a cot or on the floor with the face upward, and place the arms parallel with the body. Be prepared to use at least 8 minutes for this exercise. Beginning with the toes, think of the various portions of the body—the legs, hips, trunk, shoulders, arms, hands, fingers, neck, and face—and feel that every part is free from tension. During this time "think out" the stiffness.

You may not be able to accomplish this at first; in fact, when you begin to think about the muscles, you may even become more tense.

In this event, you will need to try some other approach. Apply an opposite technique, consciously stiffening each part and then as consciously letting all the stiffness go. For another approach forget about the parts and think of some quiet peaceful scene. As you think of a leaf or a feather floating on a still breeze, rest easily, and after a few moments, as you become aware of muscles again, you will find them free from excess tension. You should derive great satisfaction from this accomplishment.

SITTING POSITION. When a cot is not available and the hard surface of a table or the floor does not invite you, you might resort to a chair. Choose one that is comfortable, with room enough for your hips to be well back and your shoulders held forward. Let your hands drop into your lap and your head fall forward a little. Then think of the various portions of the body and feel that there is complete relaxation in each part.

Feel that the muscles that hold you erect are free from hypertension, and relax all facial muscles. Yawn if you need to. Think of a quiet scene, and feel the calm that comes from visualizing a peaceful picture. Forget your worries and cares, and remain in this position for several moments. You will probably be thinking of nothing at all. Indeed, you may go to sleep and remain so for a short period of time.

It is sometimes illuminating to have another person assist you at this point to see if you are relaxed. You might have your roommate or a member of your family lift an arm or a leg and let it fall, gravity alone determining the downward movement. Let him push your head from side to side to test whether it turns easily on its axis. It should if the muscles of the neck are relaxed. Be sure you do not offer any resistance. If you are relaxed during these tests, each part should move freely and easily with no inhibitions.

EXERCISE 65. When you are completely relaxed, raise the head, open the eyes, inhale, and release an audible sigh. Repeat several times.

EXERCISE 66. Maintaining general relaxation, inhale and vocalize a soft, sustained [ha] sound. Be careful that you do not make any effort to produce the sounds. Repeat several times. Applying the same principles, vocalize each of the vowel sounds softly without effort. Now speak short phrases such as, "Many, many moons ago," "Never, never again," "May was a beautiful month," and "Now is the time to go." Be careful that you do not tense the muscles of the throat, jaw, lips, or tongue as you speak the words. Until you can retain the proper degree of muscular tonicity without tensing, you may distort the sounds so that they give the impression of careless articulation.

AIDS TO RELAXATION

PICTURES. Before you start your period of relaxation, look at a peaceful scene which stimulates relaxation. When you are free from tension, let your mind dwell upon it. Later, without turning to the original, you should be able to recall "at will" the picture image.

DESCRIPTIONS. Secure relaxation by having the person assisting you describe, or yourself read, a description of some peaceful scene.[1] When you are so completely relaxed that you have forgotten the physical part of yourself, recall the impressions that came to you as you were reading or listening.

PHONOGRAPH RECORDINGS. Some find that soft music helps in achieving relaxation during the early stages. Several compositions which usually have this effect during the rest period have been listed in Appendix C.

The condition of tissues of the body is affected by mental states, and vice versa. During the relaxation period, it should be possible to establish normal conditions for both the mind and the body if you free the entire body from tensions and think about peaceful music and quiet scenes. You should prepare yourself for the task at hand by spending a few minutes in relaxation and then carry over into your work this feeling of ease and freedom so that you will be more efficient.

PRACTICAL SUGGESTIONS

Exercises:

1. Find exercises which suit your needs.
2. Set up a relaxation program.
3. Follow directions carefully.
4. Plan group exercises with different members of your family serving as directors.

Time:

1. Set a regular time.
2. Execute procedures which require physical exercise before meals.
3. Have relaxation periods immediately after meals.

[1] Several descriptive passages are included in Appendix B.

4. Completely relax two or three times daily, at least 10 minutes each time. Have someone check up to see that you are really relaxed.
5. Relax in a near-by chair for short intervals several times daily.

Accessories:

1. Provide yourself with a cot.
2. Wear no tight clothing
3. Make use of phonograph recordings, pictures, poetry, and descriptive passages.

7

POSTURE FOR VOCALIZATION

Good posture prepares the body mechanism for action. It serves as a basis for poise and efficiency in walking, running, sitting, and standing and, in like manner, is vital in any type of vocal activity.

"Get set" tells the runner to put himself in readiness for the start of the race. As soon as he hears this command, he places the finger tips on the ground, digs in with the toes, raises the hips, and looks straight ahead. The gun snaps, and after a few steps, he is running at top speed. His starting posture and the way he carries himself help him to coordinate the movement of the arms and legs with the rest of the body as he races toward the goal.

The concert singer must also utilize principles of posture which increase his bodily efficiency. In some instances, he assumes a position resembling that of the Atlas who spreads his muscles on the platform at a carnival sideshow and challenges anyone in the audience to five rounds of rough-and-tumble. The purpose of such a position, as far as the vocalist is concerned, may be to strengthen the muscles of the back so that they assist in enlarging the chest and help to give support for vigorous abdominal or diaphragmatic activity. This may not be true in every case, but the author does know that singers often assume the posture that seems most serviceable to them for singing.

Likewise, the person who wants to use his voice well during speech must give careful consideration to posture, for here again the body is in action.

GOOD POSTURE AND VOICE

The position of the skeletal parts can very easily hinder the movement of muscles that should be moving freely during speech. Since, as we have already pointed out, *speech is produced by muscles moving*, it is vitally important that proper skeletal adjustments be made for the activity. If you will look about, you will soon discover that very few people are aware of this or heed this elementary principle as they speak.

The positions assumed by speakers vary in many ways; they range from the slovenly slouch of the gunman's moll to the *rigor mortis* posture of the cadet lieutenant in a prep school. The slumping type may lower one of the shoulders, so that he looks as though he were carrying a bucket of coal in one hand and a feather in the other. He may allow both of the shoulders to slump forward so that his back takes on the appearance of a boy scout's travel pack. At the other extreme, the shoulders may resemble the squared shoulders of the scarecrow. The general varieties are numerous and in many cases tend toward one extreme or the other—they droop or they draw up. It is just as easy to have good posture. All you have to do is push the head up. This will pull the chin in, put the spine in proper shape, and lift the chest. As the ribs go up, the stomach should go in. If it does not do this, you should lift it in with the stomach muscles. Just the slight change—the head lifted a little higher—puts the body mechanism in readiness for better voice.

A GOOD, STANDARD POSITION

What you should strive for is an easy relaxed posture with the skeleton adjusted symmetrically so that the body is carried in perfect balance. A position that serves as a good, everyday standard and one that is acceptable for use in speech because it gives freedom for the efficient action of muscles required for easy vocalization, meets the following requirements.

1. The toes point straight ahead.
2. The knees are straight, without stiffness.
3. The weight is distributed evenly on both hips.
4. The hips are forward.
5. The trunk is in a vertical line with the legs.
6. The chest is relaxed.
7. The shoulders are extended out to the side.
8. The head is centered over the neck.
9. The crown of the head is held high.

If any one of these requirements were to be pointed out as most important, it would be the last. By lifting the crown of the head high, you tend to accomplish the other requirements for a good, standard position. The use of this particular approach to correct posture greatly simplifies the matter when, during the early stages of the voice training program, there are so many other requirements to keep in mind.

However, as you work with posture as a single item in the training program, you will be wise to check yourself on all items listed above and develop habits which make them a part of your usual standing and sitting habits.

When you meet all the requirements of the standard position, the body is prepared for the mechanical activity required for breathing. The muscles of the thorax and abdomen are free, and the principles of relaxation can be put to use readily during breathing and vocalization.

MAKE GOOD POSTURE A HABIT

Get in the habit of having an erect posture, whether you are sitting or standing. I remember vividly an army captain who was in charge of our R.O.T.C. unit. He had remarkably good posture as he stood before our company and gave orders. Inquisitive as teen-agers are, a bunch of us wondered if he was as straight in his barrack room as he was on the drill field. One of our group was designated to investigate. He manufactured a reason for calling on the captain after hours and found him writing a letter at his desk as straight as ever. His good posture was a firmly fixed habit. As speakers, we need to fix similar habits.

SOME MISTAKES TO AVOID

As you attempt to develop the type of posture suggested, you should avoid the mistakes made by beginners. Your weight should be placed directly over the ankle; it should not rest on the heels or on the balls of the feet. You should keep the knees free so that, if you wish to take a step, your legs can move easily; they should not buckle. You should keep the chest "at ease" and avoid the soldier-at-attention position. Your shoulders should rest easily at the side. Forcing them backward may cause tensions to be created in the muscles of the larynx, pharynx, and neck which result in tense vocalization; allowing them to droop to the front may pull on these muscles and, likewise, cause tensions. And although you lift the crown of the head slightly, the chin should not be thrust forward.

POSTURE DEPENDS ON BODILY BUILD

You may find that you cannot meet some of the specifications set up for the standard position because of your bodily contour. If this is the case, you should attempt to come as close to the requirements as your build will allow and carry over into all your activities the principles of easy balance afforded by the basic posture.

START WITH A POSTURE ANALYSIS

Before starting the improvement program, you should learn about your posture tendencies of the past and present and compare them with the requirements listed on page 79.

1. Get out the family album and study some of your photographs. What position did you take as the camera was snapped? Do you find that you consistently assumed a posture which deviated in some way from the standard? If so, was this due to poor habits or was it due to something you could not avoid because of bodily deformity or a crippled condition?

You can do something to improve your poor posture if it was caused by careless habits.

2. Dress in a tightly fitting bathing suit and have some pictures taken of yourself from the front, rear, and both sides in the standing position. Study the pictures to determine what problems you need to correct.

3. Study your posture in profile and full view before a full-length mirror. Check each of the items listed on page 79.

SOME TECHNIQUES FOR DEVELOPING GOOD POSTURE

When you know what your remediable problems are and are ready to develop postural habits which are in accordance with the suggestions given in the outline, practice the following exercises:

EXERCISE 67. Stand with your back to a wall—heels, hips, shoulders, and back of head touching the wall slightly. Raise the crown high, bringing the chin in. Hold the position as you step one pace forward. If you have done this correctly and have no bodily deformities, it will give you the standard position from which to work as you practice the breathing exercises.

EXERCISE 68. Stand in profile before a full-length mirror at least four times a day, and check the bodily parts from toe to crown. Through constant practice, get the proper mental picture of good posture and learn how it feels. Develop your muscle sense to the point where, if you allow the shoulders to droop or the hips to protrude behind, you become aware of the deviation and unconsciously make immediate corrections.

EXERCISE 69. Imagine yourself a five-star general reviewing his troops or a beauty queen at an Atlantic City pageant. Play the part, look the part.

EXERCISE 70. Walk back and forth in front of a full-length mirror, being careful to maintain good posture.

EXERCISE 71. After you feel that you have gained something from your work, have more snapshots taken of yourself standing in good posture. Study the results you have obtained through your practice by comparing the new pictures with those taken formerly.

EXERCISE 72. Have some motion pictures taken of yourself while you are walking. Have them taken from the side, the front, and the rear. Study them carefully, and try to improve the posture on the basis of your observations. After a few weeks repeat the process.

Carry the principles of good posture over into all you do, whether it is standing, walking, or sitting. Be especially careful to meet the standard of good posture every time you speak.

After you have developed an easy, relaxed position with the skeleton adjusted symmetrically so that the body is carried in perfect balance, you are ready to begin your work on breathing for vocalization.

BREATHING FOR VOCALIZATION

The supplying of the motive force—that is, taking in the air—is the first actual mechanical step in voice production. Utilization of the air stream is the second step. As the air flows from the lungs, it exerts a pressure beneath the vocal folds, producing the basic tones that are necessary for resonant speech. According to the more commonly accepted opinion, these tones are almost inaudible but later, as they pass through the throat, mouth, and nose, their intensity is increased many times.

The amount of air required to assist in the production of the sounds is small, yet it must be there doing its job effectively. Unless the air is used conservatively during vocalization, it will escape without producing tone or a *breathy* sound will be superimposed upon the tone. As a result, the voice will lack clarity and be unpleasant in quality. The pressure behind the air column should be firm and steady. If it is weak, the voice will be thin; it will lack the resonant tones which make it pleasant in quality and will be hard to hear. If the outflow of air is jerky, the voice will be spasmodic and will lack the forward movement that is characteristic of good speech.

You can avoid some of these deviations and improve the voice generally by learning to coordinate the breathing with vocalization. If you can coordinate both of these functions efficiently, there is greater possibility that you will produce a pleasant, resonant, speaking voice.

QUIET BREATHING

Ordinarily, you breathe without exerting voluntary control over the breathing process—the abdomen moves freely and coordinately with the chest. With each inhalation the lower ribs move out to the side, the abdominal wall moves forward, and the upper part of the chest expands. During exhalation the lower ribs move toward the center of the body, the abdominal wall moves inward, and the upper part of the chest moves downward slightly. The movements occur easily, with no forcing or straining.

BREATHING FOR SPEECH

When you are reading, conversing, giving a public speech, or singing, the number of times you take in air depends upon the breath needs as they relate to the phrasing of the spoken material. Most persons speak in short sentences as they converse and therefore take in a small amount of air at frequent intervals. But as they read, make a public address, or sing, they may take in larger amounts less frequently because some of the phrases are longer.

Some persons need to develop control over the breathing process so that they are better prepared to supply the force required for longer phrases. Others need control to give better support to the tones produced during speech. When breath control is needed, exercises which place emphasis upon the abdominal type of breathing are recommended.

"TYPES" OF BREATHING

Traditionally, breathing has been categorized into "types"—thoracic, abdominal, clavicular, etc.—and the layman has thought of these as different ways of breathing. Actually, the terms are simply names for slight variations in the activities of the different structures used in breathing. The chest, abdomen, and clavicles are all involved in breathing for speech. One person may believe that the abdominal muscles should be strengthened and the chest remain almost motionless. Another may combine the movement of both the abdomen and the thorax. Differences in opinion and practice have led to the development of the numerous "types" of breathing described in the text books.

THORACIC BREATHING. When the term *thoracic* breathing is applied to the respiratory process, reference is to movement of the thorax. The mechanical aspects of this type of breathing are those described for ordinary quiet breathing.

ABDOMINAL BREATHING. Abdominal breathing means the movement of the abdominal wall to make room for or allow the descent of the diaphragm on inhalation. The reverse occurs during exhalation. The term may be misleading, and therefore it should be pointed out that the air goes into the lungs located in the thorax and not into the abdomen. This form of breathing has been designated as *abdominal* because the emphasis is upon the movement of the wall of the abdomen—primarily above the belt line—with only a slight movement of the thoracic cage.

In abdominal breathing, the abdominal wall moves forward toward the belt with each inhalation. Upon exhalation the chest remains erect and the abdominal wall moves inward and upward in the direction of the spinal column.[1]

Use of abdominal breathing by singers and speakers. Most trained singers use abdominal breathing because experience has proved to them that it is a serviceable approach in singing. With the expiratory phase controlled, they are able to sustain vocal tones for longer periods. Having used this form both in singing and speaking, the author finds that some of its advantages can be applied in speaking.

If it is learned sufficiently so that it can be applied without conscious effort, abdominal breathing can be helpful when the voice is used for extended periods before large audiences and when oral presentations require long phrases, *e.g.*, in the reading of legal documents, certain poems, and plays.

Practice of abdominal breathing in the voice training program. A common practice in voice training is to create a firm pressure below the air column to improve loudness and projection. The procedure has its values. The author has found the approach to be especially suited to certain students, in cases where the voice is weak, thin, and poorly projected.

Advantages of abdominal breathing. Abdominal breathing has certain advantages and disadvantages. When the chest is held easily erect and the abdomen is moving freely, the possibility of increased tension in the area of the larynx is lessened. The abdominal muscles are far removed from those of the larynx, and voluntary contraction of these muscles is a relatively easy matter once the form has been practiced. There is little danger that abdominal effort, which is made to exert pressure on the expiratory air column, will cause hypertensions in the muscles involved in vocalization if this form of breathing is properly controlled. In some instances, it may be found desirable as a starting point in the voice training program. Later, the position can be relaxed

[1] The phrase "diaphragmatic breathing" is used occasionally. When used, it means *abdominal breathing*, since activity of the diaphragm on inhalation demands corresponding activity of the abdominal group.

and the chest (especially the lower portion) allowed to move coordinately with the abdominal wall.

Disadvantages of abdominal breathing. Although this type of breathing is conventional and traditional, it has certain disadvantages. Unless a proper attitude is established toward its use, it is apt to become a stunt or trick. As the student attempts to contract the abdominal walls, he may increase tensions which adversely affect the easy, coordinated flow of air required for vocalization.

CLAVICULAR BREATHING. In *clavicular* breathing, the upper portion of the rib cage and the clavicles rise and fall during respiration. Only a small amount of air is used in vocalization, and as stated previously, even though the amount of air required for vocalization is not important, this type of breathing may affect the voice adversely. It tends to create hypertensions in muscles which bear directly on vocalization, resulting in weak, thin tones. The small amount of air taken into the lungs is used quickly and frequent inhalations are required, or as is often the case, the speaker is forced to use the reserve air in the lungs and hypertensions result. The frequent inhalations cause the rhythm to become jerky, and the speaker is unable to speak long sentences smoothly.

Clavicular breathing tends to create tensions in the muscles of the neck and throat. As a result, tones are apt to be thin, shallow, unsteady, and "breathy" and phrases are not timed to suit the thoughts the speaker wishes to express.

ABDOMINAL-THORACIC BREATHING RECOMMENDED FOR USE DURING VOCALIZATION. The speaker may use thoracic breathing, abdominal breathing, or the two combined. Generally, however, the best results are obtained by the abdominal-thoracic type. The approach closely resembles quiet breathing as described on pages 48–49 and requires little or no retraining on the student's part. When it is used properly, the coordinated movement of the chest and abdomen results in a steady flow of air from the lungs and there is less danger of creating adverse tensions. Hence this recommendation is made for its use during vocalization.

BREATHING EXERCISES

EASY BREATHING. In all the following exercises take the standing position suggested in Chap. 7 and be careful to keep the throat and jaw relaxed. Allow the thorax and abdomen to move easily.

EXERCISE 73. Inhale. Hold the breath for an instant, and then have an assistant count to draw out the expiration. Repeat several times. If no assistant is available, use a watch with a secondhand to take the place of the counting. Hold the expiratory phase for 5 seconds at first, then increase the time to 7 seconds, 9 seconds, 11 seconds, etc. Execute the exercise in the same manner; this time hum the [m] and then the [n] sound. Next, produce a whispered [ah] sound. Follow with the sustained and vocalized [ah] sound. In like manner, sustain the [o], [e], and [i] sounds.

EXERCISE 74. Applying the same principles, speak sentences. Start with short phrases and gradually increase the length. Use such sentences as:

1. He is here.
2. He is here now.
3. He is here now, and we can go.
4. He is here now, and we can go if we care to.
5. The dog is friendly.
6. The dog is very friendly.
7. The dog is very friendly and smart.
8. The dog is very friendly and smart, and he knows tricks.
9. The dog is very friendly and smart, and he knows many tricks.
10. The man is gone.
11. The man is in the village.
12. The man drove his car to the village.
13. The man drove his car to the village to get some flour.
14. The man drove his car to the village to get some flour and sugar.
15. We were there.
16. We were there until five o'clock.
17. We were there until five o'clock, and then we left.
18. We were there until five o'clock, and then we went to the play at the Ring Theater.

EXERCISE 75. Stand with good posture, inhale, count from 1 to 4; pause and inhale, count from 5 to 8; pause and inhale, count from 9 to 12, etc.

EXERCISE 76. Stand with good posture, inhale, count from 1 to 6; pause and inhale, count from 7 to 12; pause and inhale, count from 13 to 18, etc.

EXERCISE 77. Speak the following sentences, pausing and inhaling at the places indicated by the slanted line:

1. / The sky is blue / the grass is green / and the sun is shining brightly.
2. / The man walked in loneliness / he had no friends / or enemies.
3. / Drive like mad / the bridge will go down any minute now.
4. / Walk slowly, young man, / there is much to see while you still have your vision.

EXERCISE 78. Apply the principles of combined abdominal and thoracic breathing as you read the practice selections at the end of the chapter.

As soon as you are able to employ the principles suggested for combined abdominal and thoracic breathing, you should begin to use them every time you speak. As you practice the exercises given in the following chapters, you should be careful to apply (along with the principles of posture, relaxation of throat and jaw, and general relaxation) the principles of breathing.

CONTROLLED BREATHING. If it is necessary that controlled breathing be developed to eliminate vocal faults, emphasis should be placed upon the abdominal type of breathing mentioned earlier. Steps in this process are as follows:

1. Establish a posture suitable for abdominal breathing.
2. Exercise to learn the abdominal type of breathing.
3. Combine abdominal breathing with vocalization.

Exercises for abdominal-breathing posture. It is helpful to precede the work in abdominal breathing with exercises which establish a standard posture suited to this form of breathing.

EXERCISE 79. In order to get the erect position, stand with the heels, hips, shoulders, and back of head against a doorpost. Step away, but continue to maintain the erect posture.

EXERCISE 80. After you have assumed the straight position, attempt to tone up the muscles of the upper and lower portions of the back. Try to flatten the back, yet keep the muscles of the front of the body relaxed and free from tension. At first you may have difficulty in strengthening the muscles of the back. To "get the feel" of what is needed, find a strong wall in your home, place your palms against the wall, and push. Keep the muscles of the face and the front part of the neck and chest free from tension. Feel strength in the muscles of the back of the neck and shoulders and the lower portions of the back as you apply the pressure.

EXERCISE 81. If you have a large dumbbell or similar object in your home (a kitchen chair will serve the purpose as well), you can use it to help you obtain the same controls. Place the dumbbell on the floor. Stand in an erect position above it. Allow the trunk to relax forward. Do not bend the knees. Grasp the bar, and lift slowly. Feel the muscles in the small of the back slowly contract at first, and then feel the tension fairly run up the back as you slowly rise to an erect position.

EXERCISE 82. After you have learned to strengthen the back muscles and yet keep the muscles of the anterior (front) part of the trunk and neck relatively free from tension, try to use this ability as you raise the rib cage and extend the lower (floating) ribs out to the side. Pull the abdomen in and up, and try to feel that the strength that you are now able to sense in the upper portion of the back is helping to hold the rib cage up and that the strength in the lower portion of the back is helping to pull the lower ribs out to the side.

Be careful to keep the muscles of the throat free from tension and to avoid hoisting the shoulders as you attempt to raise the rib cage. These problems seldom arise if the crown of the head is held high and the muscles of the back are strengthened.

In summary, the techniques for developing abdominal breathing and posture for abdominal breathing are:

1. Take a good standing position, holding the crown of the head high.
2. Strengthen the muscles of the back.
3. Raise the entire rib cage, and extend the lower ribs out at the side.
4. Pull the abdominal wall inward (toward the spinal column) and upward.
5. Inhale through the mouth, opening the mouth and throat cavities.
6. Allow the abdomen to move away from the spinal column as the air is taken in, but keep the chest up.
7. Now bring the abdomen inward and upward again, exerting pressure by means of the abdominal muscles beneath the thorax as you exhale. Continue to hold the chest high, but allow for some inward movement of the lower ribs.
8. Repeat the steps in the same manner with each inhalation.

Abdominal breathing exercises. Proceed with the abdominal breathing exercises with the chest up and the abdominal wall above the belt level moving freely.

EXERCISE 83. Lie on the back, place one hand on the abdomen and the other on the chest. Inhale, allowing the abdomen to move upward. Release the breath, and feel the abdomen sink. The chest should move only slightly during this exercise. Inhale and exhale several times.

EXERCISE 84. Take a good standing position with the chest up and the abdomen in. Place one hand on the chest and one hand on the abdomen, then:

1. Inhale slowly, hold, exhale slowly.
2. Inhale slowly, hold, exhale quickly.
3. Inhale quickly, hold, exhale slowly.
4. Inhale quickly, hold, exhale quickly.
5. Pant.

Repeat each phase several times. Be careful to hold the chest erect throughout the exercise, allowing only the abdomen to move.

EXERCISE 85. Practice abdominal breathing as you walk along the street, inhaling during four paces and exhaling during four paces. After you have worked at it using four steps, change the count to three. Next, change the count to two, then one. Now change to five steps, six, and then seven.

Abdominal breathing combined with vocalization. When you have developed an easy control over this type breathing, combine it with vocalization. Be careful in all these exercises to keep the muscles of the throat and jaw relaxed.

EXERCISE 86. Apply abdominal pressure as you sustain each of the following sounds: [ah], [o], [e], [i], [m], and [n].

EXERCISE 87. Applying the same principles, speak such sentences as:

"No, I won't do that."
"The sky is blue today."
"He built his life for the service of his fellow man."
"Dream only a little in the time that you have; do much."

After you have worked with the abdominal type of breathing for some time and have it coordinated with easy vocalization, you are ready to relax the position recommended for abdominal breathing. Now you can use the combined abdominal and thoracic breathing.

PRACTICE SELECTIONS

Inhale at the / as you speak the following sentences aloud:

/ How are you today?

/ Do you plan to stay home tonight? / Or, are you going to a movie?

/ I was very pleased to meet the young man. / He was both pleasant and well-mannered. / His friendly attitude will help him to go a long way.

/ I wonder if the world would not be better off if its big decisions, especially those concerning wars, were made by its young men. / Or, better yet, by their mothers.

/ The man complained constantly about governmental actions on the national, state, and local levels. / When I asked him if he had been to the polls on November 7, he said, "No." / I was surprised that he showed no indication whatever of embarrassment or concern.

/ I have always felt that men fall into two categories: / those who live positive, constructive lives / and those who do nothing but spend their time criticizing and belittling the works of the "doers." / Of course, criticism is helpful and necessary, but it is unfortunate that we have so few people in the former category and so many of the others.

Apply the principles of breathing as you read the following prose selections aloud. The length of sentences and punctuation will determine the breath needs.

ECHOES FROM THE WORLD WAR (An Explanatory Note), *Edwin Markham* [From *Gates of Paradise* by Edwin Markham, Doubleday Company, Inc., New York, 1924. Copyright, 1920, Edwin Markham.]

I am a man of peace: war, in general, is one of the huge madnesses of men, and it can be cured only by the divine forces of love and justice. Nevertheless, in a world ruled by self-interest, it is necessary sometimes—in hours of supreme crisis—for a nation to rise full-armed in defence of her existence and the existence of human rights. A nation not willing to defend her existence deserves to perish. Still we must work for peace. Sometime war will be seen to be antiquated and barbaric. It will cease like duelling and other ancient follies. If war does pass away under the light of political wisdom, it will pass away under the sense of humour, the sense of the absurd. . . .

From "Letters to His Son," *Earl of Chesterfield* [*Letters to His Son* by the Earl of Chesterfield, published in the Universal Classics Library, M. Walter Dunne, Washington, 1901.]

Speaking and Writing, clearly, correctly, and with ease and grace, are certainly to be acquired by reading the best authors with care, and by attention to the best living models.

I hope you employ your whole time, which few people do; and that you put every moment to profit of some kind or other. I call company, walking, riding, etc., employing one's time, and upon proper occasions, very usefully; but what I cannot forgive in anybody is sauntering, and doing nothing at all, with a thing so precious as time, and so irrecoverable when lost.

Virtue and learning, like gold, have their intrinsic value: but if they are not polished, they certainly lose a great deal of their luster; and even polished brass will pass upon more people than rough gold.

Take warning then by them: choose your pleasures for yourself, and do not let them be imposed upon you. Follow nature and not fashion: weigh the present enjoyment of your pleasures against the necessary consequences of them, and then let your own common sense determine your choice.

There is time enough for everything, in the course of the day, if you do but one thing at once; but there is not time enough in the year, if you will do two things at a time. The Pensionary de Witt, who was torn to pieces in the year 1672, did the whole business of the Republic, and yet had time left to go to assemblies in the evening, and sup in company. Being asked how he could possibly find time to go through so much business, and yet amuse himself in the evenings as he did, he answered, there was nothing so easy; for that it was only doing one thing at a time, and never putting off anything till to-morrow that could be done to-day. This steady and undissipated attention to one object is a sure mark of a superior genius; as hurry, bustle, and agitation are the never-failing symptoms of a weak and frivolous mind.

I really know nothing more criminal, more mean, and more ridiculous than lying.

PRACTICE AND APPLICATION OF PHYSICAL CONTROLS

The habits developed during the early years of life become more and more fixed with the passing of the years. If, during childhood, you stood in a stooped position, walked with a shambling gait, or continually pouted the lower lip, the chances are that you will continue to commit the same grotesquerie unless you realized your fault and corrected it before it was too late.

Fortunately your body possesses a degree of plasticity which enables you to change posture, walk, facial expressions, and other forms of activity even after you have reached your twenties or thirties—yes, even your forties.

Flexibility is relatively great during childhood but diminishes gradually with age. It is easy to implant new habits in the young child, but as he gets older, the task becomes more and more difficult. Fortunately, however, the statement "You can't teach an old dog new tricks" is not entirely true. Older people as well as dogs can learn "new tricks," but they must work harder than youngsters and pups. They must be careful to apply their new acquisitions consistently over a longer period of time if they hope to make the habits permanent. Their job is not an easy one. They must be willing to give the problem at hand many hours of attention and effort.

OLD HABITS FOR NEW

SELF-EVALUATION AS A FIRST STEP. You must recognize poor habits and be willing to make changes if you hope to improve. Early in the program you need to study your speech habits objectively and evaluate yourself fairly. The ear-training program plays a vital part in this process. Once you can hear monotony, nasality, thinness, or whatever your faults may be, you are psychologically prepared to go to work and make the necessary changes. Until then, it is probable that your habits will remain unchanged. This part of the voice training program will take time; in fact, you may be halfway through the course before you are fully aware of your problems. Nevertheless, as you work with ear training, you can learn something about how the mechanisms function. At the same time, you can progress with the physical controls which have been discussed: developing your ability to relax generally, learning specific relaxation of the muscles which are closely allied with speech production, improving posture, and developing control over breathing.

CLEAR-CUT CHANGES NECESSARY. You cannot expect to eliminate faults that have been implanted deeper and deeper as the years have gone by without making distinct, clear-cut changes. You need to go all the way at first, making large alterations rather than small ones. It is much like lighting a campfire. If the wind blows out your match, you do not strike all your matches in the same way, allowing the wind to continue to defeat your efforts. You change the position of your hands, or you face in another direction. You get improved results in the speech-training program by making definite changes in the way you speak. If you continue in the same old way, you tend to make old habits permanent.

POSITIVE ACTION ESTABLISHES NEW HABITS. General relaxation, specific relaxation, posture, and breathing have been discussed as basic controls, and exercises have been suggested for their development. These controls and exercises are positive in nature. They aim to help you build new and correct habits. Nowhere has the suggestion been made that you try to avoid former mistakes or to "break" old habits. Practice and application of these controls cause the bad habits to disappear. Once you have become proficient in the use of the controls, you have laid the foundation for improved vocalization. After that, they serve as a sound basis for all your work in speech training. By putting them to use every time you speak, your voice improves generally and, in some instances, specific problems (which are treated fully later in the text) disappear.

PRACTICING THE EXERCISES

PRACTICE CAREFULLY. Naturally, you must be careful to practice the prescribed exercises correctly. If you did not follow directions carefully, you might ingrain wrong habits and deter progress or cause harm to the voice. Therefore, you should study each exercise until you are sure you understand it and then follow out each detail very carefully as you practice.

You may find it helpful to have another interested person work along with you so that together you will attain a clear understanding of purposes and procedures. One person can assist the other in working with the ear training program; in checking the state of relaxation, posture, and breathing; and, later, in listening to and criticizing the vocal sounds. What is just as important, two working together help to motivate work on the program.

PRACTICE PRINCIPLES WHICH REQUIRE MOST ATTENTION. Occasionally you will find that proficiency in just one of the principles, for example, general relaxation, will do much to accomplish the improvement you are seeking. More often, however, it is advisable to start at the beginning of the program and follow through in the manner outlined in the text. Of course, it is not necessary to spend a great amount of time working on exercises in which you are already proficient. If you do not need to work on one of the principles, you should go on to the next. But when you are ready to put them all together, you must be careful to include all those which are discussed in these pages. As soon as you have achieved some success with one principle, hurry on to the next, and then as you work with the new one, go back and review the old. After you have completed the program once, go back through it many times, attempting to fix the new habits firmly. You should try to combine each principle with all the others so that they integrate to produce a pleasant, suitable, well-projected speaking voice.

Your progress with the principles should move forward rapidly. It will, if you work with and live with the program, trying hard to achieve mastery of each of the principles in a very short time.

In order to make rapid progress with your voice-improvement program you should:

1. Practice exercises that develop the controls most needed to improve your voice generally as well as to correct specific problems.
2. Understand the mechanics of and the reasons for the control you are attempting to develop.
3. Keep the purpose of the exercise you are doing clearly in mind as you practice, and be careful never to commit errors that will defeat the purpose.

4. Arrange a practice schedule and follow it conscientiously. Three or four 10-minute practice periods each day would be satisfactory during the early stages of the program. Later, you should increase the amount of time because, as you proceed, you will add new procedures and you will need to review the exercises you practiced earlier.
5. Apply the principles (the purposes behind the special techniques or exercises) every time you speak. If you do this consistently, you will eventually reach a point where you will begin to apply them unconsciously. You will then be well on the road to permanent improvement.

PART FIVE

DEVELOPING BASIC ELEMENTS

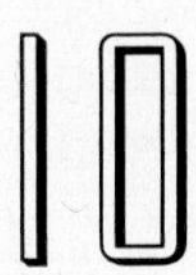

IMPROVING VOCALIZATION

The voice training program thus far has dealt mainly with training the ear, studying about the mechanics of vocalization, and making physical preparation for vocalization. Although the student has been doing some vocalizing in connection with this training, he has not paid attention to producing a voice that meets with high standards of vocalization. At least, this aspect of the program was not stressed.

Greater stress is placed upon the production of a pleasant, adequate, effective speaking voice from this point on, but at the same time, the student is encouraged to continue to develop the discriminatory ability of his ear and further his control over relaxation, posture, and breathing. Now he should make a greater effort to use the controls he has developed and improve his voice as he practices vocal exercises and speaks in various situations. In other words, his two goals—general voice improvement and the correction of vocal faults—are brought to a sharper focus, and his every effort is toward improving the basic elements of voice.

GOALS FOR IMPROVED VOCALIZATION

General voice improvement. The student's goals for general voice improvement should be to:

1. Find the pitch best suited to his vocal equipment.
2. Develop adequate loudness.
3. Learn to initiate and sustain a clear, vibrant tonal quality without effort.
4. Develop full vocal resonance.
5. Improve the variability of the pitch and loudness so that meanings and feelings are expressed more effectively.

As he accomplishes these specific ends, his voice will show over-all improvement and he may even correct specific vocal faults. However, in some instances, this latter accomplishment may require extra work.

CORRECTION OF VOCAL FAULTS. The student should eradicate vocal faults which require special attention concurrently with his work on the general voice-improvement program. The faults which may be present can be analyzed into the following categories:

1. Defects of pitch.
   a. The pitch is too high or too low.
   b. The pitch element is monotonous.
2. Defects of loudness.
   a. The voice is weak in intensity.
   b. The voice is overloud.
   c. There is monotony of the loudness element.
3. Defects of quality.
   a. The voice sounds throaty, coarse, heavy, hoarse-husky, or hollow.
   b. The voice sounds thin, breathy, harsh, metallic, or whining.
   c. There is excessive nasality, or there is an absence of nasal tones on the [m], [n], and [ng] sounds (denasality).

When general procedures do not eliminate individual problems, conferences with the instructor will be required in addition to classroom work. The time set aside for these consultations will be devoted to furthering the ability of the student to recognize his problem and to showing him how he can correct it. Each time the student achieves desirable results in correcting his faults, the instructor will call the student's attention to the success. The voice problem will disappear as the frequency of the student's successes increases. Once his ear has become accustomed to hearing his improved voice and new habits become fixed, he will no longer need to work with the specific problem. He should, however, continue to strive for general voice improvement.

PROCEDURES FOR IMPROVED VOCALIZATION

Various approaches will be used to improve the student's ability to use his voice. Some instructors will concentrate upon specific vocal exercises to achieve the goals of the program; others will rely upon conversations, speeches, and readings to accomplish this purpose. In most instances, however, a combination of vocal exercises and the speaking experiences is used to achieve improved vocalization.

In this course the attention of the student should be on making general voice improvement and correcting specific vocal defects rather than on oral interpretation of the literature he is reading, his ability to give a public speech or to become an effective conversationalist. Although he may make secondary gains in these latter skills as he proceeds with voice and articulation training, he should not allow such matters to detract from reaching the goals of the course.

All efforts should be directed toward utilizing the ear training, developing knowledge of the mechanisms involved in vocalization, and establishing the physical controls. In all speaking situations as well as in class recitations and activities, students should strive for a pleasant, adequate, suitable voice, which is free from distracting and unpleasant deviations.

11

IMPROVING THE PITCH

A college junior who wants to make a career of radio announcing in spite of his high-pitched voice rushed into the office recently. When he got his breath, he said, "I just heard that if I took a teaspoon of honey every morning for a period of a year my voice would be lowered by an octave. Is it so? Would it be that easy?" The answer was "No." The author explained that first the student must discover the pitch for which his vocal equipment was best suited and then strive to fix the new level into his habit patterns. Accomplishing his goals would require extensive ear training, practice of suitable exercises, and continuous application over a long period.

Most students in the voice training course will have average to good voice as far as the pitch element is concerned and will require only general improvement. A few will need to improve pronounced pitch defects and will require special consideration.

Principal factors in general improvement of the pitch element include the following:

1. Determining the appropriate pitch level.
2. Making this pitch level habitual.
3. Developing adequate pitch variability.

Such specific defects as extremely high or low pitch and monotony require specific techniques, but the approaches suggested for general improvement serve as the basis for their correction.

GENERAL IMPROVEMENT OF PITCH

The voice has an efficient pitch range just as an automobile has an efficient driving-speed range. Some of us discover that we get best performance out of our car when we are traveling at a speed of 45 miles per hour. Another car may do better at 50 or 65 miles per hour. So it is with the voice. One person's vocal mechanism operates more efficiently at one pitch level than at another. Defective vocalization results when an unsatisfactory pitch level is used.

DETERMINING APPROPRIATE PITCH LEVEL. The pitch range customarily used during speech is called the *habitual pitch level*. This range may be narrow or broad, but in any case it consists of those pitches which are used most frequently by the speaker. Early in the program, you must determine whether the habitual pitch level you are using is suited to your vocal mechanisms. If it is not, then discover the "proper" pitch level and either raise or lower your pitch accordingly.

In this text, the appropriate pitch level is called the *structural pitch level* because, for any individual, the mechanisms involved in vocalization determine in large part what the pitch level should be. Although it is usually stated that the pitch is determined by the rate of vibration of the vocal folds, the basic determining factors in pitch range are the length, mass, tension, and elasticity of the vocal folds. As anyone who is familiar with musical instruments understands, the longer and heavier the vibrating string, the lower the pitch, and vice versa. When the string is tightened, regardless of its length and thickness, the pitch is raised. The vocal folds, because of their elasticity, present a more complicated picture. The mass and length of the fold change with each change of muscular tonicity, so that when tension is increased, the mass becomes thinner and the folds become longer. At the same time, the thyroarytenoid muscles that are embedded in the folds contract, decreasing their elasticity. These factors seem to be working in opposition when an attempt is made to analyze them, but actually there is a balance between the factors which results in the variety of pitches produced during vocalization. As the term is used here, *structural pitch level* refers specifically to the basic structural factors—length, mass, tension, and elasticity—which determine pitch and make for individual differences in pitch level and range.

These structural conditions, plus such other factors as air pressure below the vocal folds, imitation of other voices, emotional disturbances, strain, and nervous hypertension, play a part in determining the pitch level and often cause the habitual pitch level to be too high or too low.

Some speakers attempt to raise or lower the pitch level of the voice without making a careful check to discover exactly what structural pitch level is suitable to them. In the belief that a low voice is better for the male, some men attempt to use their lowest pitch, forcing a bass voice. Their results are seldom successful. After they have lowered the pitch to this depth, they have no lower pitches to use and variability below the average is impossible. They are already at "rock bottom." To get best results, they should find the structural level suited to their vocal equipment and then learn to vary the pitch around this average. The person who speaks at a pitch level which is too high is often unable to speak at higher pitches because he is at the top of his range. By speaking at an inappropriate pitch level, the possibility of variety is lessened and the quality and often the intensity of the voice are affected adversely.

USE OF SPOKEN SOUNDS TO DETERMINE STRUCTURAL LEVEL. To find the pitch level that is best suited to your individual mechanism, carry out the following directions:

1. Take a good standing position, inhale, and speak an [ah] sound as you would ordinarily produce it.
2. Speak [ah] at a slightly higher pitch, and make a subjective estimate as to whether or not it came easily.
3. Go back to the original pitch, and make comparisons.
4. Speak [ah] at a slightly lower pitch.
5. Try [ah] again at the original pitch. Did you find the [ah] at the lower pitch easier to produce than the original [ah]?
6. If the original pitch came with less effort, then you should adopt this as the average and build the variations around it.
7. If you found that the higher or the lower pitch was more satisfactory, then you should make further tests.
8. Assuming that you found that the lower [ah] came more easily than the original [ah], try an [ah] at a still lower pitch and compare results again. In like manner, if the higher pitch was more satisfactory than the original, try for an even higher pitch and make comparisons.
9. Continue this procedure until you have found the pitch at which you speak the [ah] sound most easily, then use that pitch as the average sound around which you develop your pitch range.

THE 25-PERCENTILE TEST. Fairbanks[1] gives us specific instructions as to the procedure to be followed in finding the structural (termed *natural*) pitch level:

Estimate your *natural pitch* as follows. Sing down to your very *lowest* tone. Letting this tone be *do* of the musical scale, sing up the scale to your *very highest tone including falsetto.* Repeat this several times to be sure that you

[1] Fairbanks, G., *Voice and Articulation Drillbook*, Harper & Brothers, New York, 1940.

are covering your maximum range. Count the notes as you go. Research has shown that, following these instructions, superior speakers have average total singing ranges including falsetto of approximately 22 to 24 notes, or 18 to 20 musical tones. Refer now to the table on the calculation of natural pitch level, and locate your highest note by number in column 2. The value opposite this in column 3 is the *number of musical tones* in your total singing range. Now move directly across to column 4, which tells you in musical tones approximately how far your *natural* pitch level lies above your lowest tone. In other words, this last value is a measure of your natural pitch level in musical tones above the lowest note of your range. In case you have access to a piano you can locate exactly the various pitches used in this process.

Count the notes as you sing up the scale, but in using the table to calculate the pitch level, count from the top of the table down, thus going from 1 in the second column to 12, 18, 23, or whatever your highest note may be. You will then read across the page from this highest number.

FIXING THE STRUCTURAL LEVEL. Once the structural pitch level has been determined, efforts should be made to establish it as the habitual pitch level. The following patterns should be used as guides for practice. Raise and lower the pitch as you count, being careful to stay within an easy pitch range.

DEVELOPING PITCH VARIABILITY. The voice that moves along with the humdrum "plunk" of a flat wheel fails to express the nuances of thought and feeling that are required for satisfactory communication. The student whose voice gives this impression must realize that, if words and sentences vary in pitch, loudness, and rate in accordance with their significance, they convey meaning to the listener. It is his responsibility to see that they do this as he reads or speaks in any situation. Unless variations are present, the listener does not discover the finer implications and the shades of feeling behind the words.

Exercises 88 to 94 have been designed to develop flexibility of pitch. Early in the training program, any attainments with this factor will seem strange to the student, and he will find difficulty accustoming himself to the changes. For all practical purposes, however, he should exaggerate the pitch variations at first and then gradually taper off to normal communicative variations. Eventually, the ear will become accustomed to the new acquisitions and the strangeness will disappear.

After spending considerable time with the exercises suggested above, he should practice varying the pitch as he reads poetry and prose and

CALCULATION OF NATURAL PITCH LEVEL IN TONES ABOVE LOWEST NOTE BY DETERMINING 25 PER CENT OF TOTAL RANGE. From Fairbanks, G., *Voice and Articulation Drillbook*, Harper and Bros., 1940.)

Name of highest note	*Number of highest note*	*Range in musical tones*	*Natural pitch level in tones*	*Name of natural pitch level*
do	1	0		
re	2	1.0		
mi	3	2.0		
fa	4	2.5		
so	5	3.5		
la	6	4.5	1.1	re
ti	7	5.5	1.4	re
do	8	6.0	1.5	mi
re	9	7.0	1.8	mi
mi	10	8.0	2.0	mi
fa	11	8.5	2.1	mi
so	12	9.5	2.4	fa
la	13	10.5	2.6	fa
ti	14	11.5	2.9	fa
do	15	12.0	3.0	so
re	16	13.0	3.3	so
mi	17	14.0	3.5	so
fa	18	14.5	3.6	so
so	19	15.5	3.9	so
la	20	16.5	4.1	la
ti	21	17.5	4.4	la
do	22	18.0	4.5	la
re	23	19.0	4.8	la
mi	24	20.0	5.0	ti
fa	25	20.5	5.1	ti
so	26	21.5	5.4	ti
la	27	22.5	5.6	ti
ti	28	23.5	5.9	do
do	29	24.0	6.0	do
re	30	25.0	6.3	do
mi	31	26.0	6.5	re
fa	32	26.5	6.6	re
so	33	27.5	6.9	re
la	34	28.5	7.1	re
ti	35	29.5	7.4	re
do	36	30.0	7.5	mi

gives extemporaneous and impromptu speeches. He would be wise to read materials that have not been memorized formerly, as there is a tendency for him to fall into old habits and use previously learned pitch patterns.

Exercises in pitch variation. The common expression "Well, did you ever?" has entirely different meaning and emotional content when the last word is lowered in pitch than it does when the pitch is raised or remains the same.

Some sentences you utter are far less commanding when you speak them at one pitch level than they are when you raise or lower the pitch on the last word. Speak the words, "Bring it back now," all at the same pitch. Try the same sentence, lowering the pitch on the word "now." Note the difference in meaning.

Improvement in pitch variation can be achieved through practice of the following exercises:

EXERCISE 88. Practice the patterns shown below several times, raising and lowering the pitch within an easy pitch range.

PITCH

High								
		2				6		
Average	1		3		5		7	
				4				8
Low								

High								
Average	1						7	8
		2				6		
			3		5			
Low				4				

High				4				
			3		5			
		2				6		
Average	1						7	8
Low								

High			3					
		2						
Average	1							8
							7	
				4		6		
Low					5			

High								
Average	1				5		7	8
		2		4		6		
			3					
Low								

High					5			
				4		6		
							7	
Average	1							8
		2						
Low			3					

EXERCISE 89. Speak each of the following sentences several times, using a different pitch pattern each time. For example, you might say, "Why did you leave so early?" using these patterns:

Why
did you leave
so early?

leave early?
Why did you so

you
Why did leave so
early?

Be careful that you achieve variety as a result of pitch changes and not through added loudness or pause. For practice purposes overemphasize the pitch differences as you read aloud.

You mean you haven't seen that show?
What time is it?
Where are we going?
Why did you do it?
Did he go?
How could you ever do a thing like that?
At what time do you think we should leave?
How many are there?
Do you think he did it?
Is it very far to the stadium?
Have you ever seen anything as unusual as this?
Are you fellows going out tonight?
Who dreamed up that idea?
When will this ever stop?
How many times must I tell you no?
Will you, or won't you do it?
Are you going to drive me home tonight?
How are you?

EXERCISE 90. Raise or lower the pitch as you utter the last word in the following sentences:

Come back.
Hello there.
Stay here.
Don't go.
Work fast.
Stand still.
Slow down.
Quit it.

Go back.
About face.
Squads right.
Forward march.
Give now.
Don't step.
Hold still.
Come on.

EXERCISE 91. Vary the pitch of the voice around the structural pitch level as you utter the following exclamations:

Well, did you ever!
How right you are!
Oh, oh!
You don't say!
What do you know!
How awful!
I should say so!

Stop it!
Shut up!
Cut it out!
Don't!
Why?
Never!
I should say not!

EXERCISE 92. Vary the pitch in the manner prescribed by the location of the word or words on the scale:

Now
Average: is the time
to act.

Now
Average: is the time to act.

must
Average: We be vigilant.

right away.
Average: I want you to do it

no place
Average: There's like
home.

don't
Average: Susan, do
that.

Average: Susan,
don't do
that.

Average: Bring it back
now.

everything
Average: Drop this
minute.

not tell you
Average: I'll again.

Average: How
are
you?

EXERCISE 93. It would be very difficult to read the following passage without varying the pitch of the voice, especially if you tried to read it as a child might say it. Read it with abandon several times.

> I have a little shadow that goes in and out with me.
> And what can be the use of him is more than I can see.
> He is very, very like me from the heels up to the head;
> And I see him jump before me, when I jump into my bed.
> —ROBERT LOUIS STEVENSON, "My Shadow"

EXERCISE 94. Tell a young child some exciting stories, and you will find that the pitch of your voice naturally rises and falls in pitch as you express the ideas and emotions.

CORRECTING PITCH DEFECTS

The three approaches to pitch improvement are ear training, motor control of the vocal mechanism, and emotional readjustment. When the pitch difficulty results from improper vocal habits or poor auditory discrimination, it is first necessary to hear the deviation in the speaking voice and to admit to yourself that the voice is defective. A critical analysis should follow in order to determine exactly what is wrong. Listen to a recording of your voice. Are recurring patterns present? Is the pitch flat and monotonous? Have a paper and pencil available, and make notes as to exactly what problems require correction. It is helpful to have someone tell you about your faults, but it is still better to recognize them yourself. Discover your mistakes, and then go about developing the new motor controls necessary for eliminating the problem.

When the pitch is defective because of emotional causes, you should feel free to consult your speech teacher. He can assist you in straightening out problems that are causing you worry, frustration, and nervous hypertension. In most instances, he is the sort of person who merits your confidence and is willing to sit down and talk your problems over with you. Just telling him about yourself and your problems will do much to relieve the pressures that unfortunate experiences have built up within you. Once you have talked out the problems or, perhaps, have confessed thoughts and actions about which you have guilty feelings, you will feel relieved. You will have placed the major part of your burden on his shoulders. As emotional readjustment proceeds, your teacher may help you still further by suggesting how you can carry your new confidence into your voice training program.

Normally, the pitch of the voice is lowered during adolescence in both men and women. In males, the change occurs suddenly and is striking in character; in females, the transition takes place over a longer period of time and is less noticeable. If the change in voice does not occur and the individual passes into adulthood with the voice he had as a child, an abnormality exists in the speech which should be corrected. This applies to men especially. In some cases, the individual with this condition should see a specialist and consider the possibility of receiving glandular therapy.

In cases where the pitch is extremely high as a result of poor vocal habits, some of the techniques which have already been suggested would be suitable for improving the voice. For example, easy vocalization was the main basic principle used in the case of a young man who was enrolled in the author's clinic some time ago. He was eighteen years of age and was just entering college. His voice was so high-pitched that, when he telephoned to arrange for an appointment, he created the impression that a young girl was calling. But when he gave his name, the mistake was realized. He had been an operator on the telephone exchange in his home town, and people who did not know him thought that the operator was a girl. He could speak in a low pitch, but since the high pitch was easier for him to produce and far more comfortable, he seldom used the lower range. He was referred to a physician, who studied the larynx and made the following report: "Examination essentially negative. I believe that with practice and training he will be able to speak at a lower range."

TO CORRECT EXTREMELY HIGH PITCH. When high pitch results from worry, nervous hypertension, and emotional disturbance, the basic condition should be corrected before any effort is made to improve the voice through vocal exercises. In some instances, considerable work with general relaxation exercises (see pages 64 to 71) will help to establish proper conditions for voice production at the lower pitch range. However, if there is a deep-seated emotional or personality disturbance, the approach to the problem should be toward reducing anxieties and building self-confidence. These problems may require the help of a specialist.

When the problem is due to poor vocal habits, as, for example, those learned from the imitation of poor speech models, the approach will be toward building new speech habits, learning and applying improved control of the breathing, and throat relaxation. Exercises which accomplish these purposes are especially appropriate because, with the throat relaxed and free from hypertensions, the proper pitch level can be established without forcing the change. The exercises on pages 71 to 74 should be practiced in order to improve this aspect of vocalization.

In all cases, a careful check should be made to determine structural pitch level and the ear-training program should have progressed so that the trained ear can assist in establishing the new level.

TO CORRECT EXTREMELY LOW PITCH. The person with an extremely low pitch should discover his optimum and vary his voice around this pitch. In some cases, the extremely low voice will be the optimum pitch for the individual. When such is the case, no attempt should be made to raise the pitch. Frequently, the individual who uses this range is proud of his low voice and objects to having it raised. He prefers a flat, rock-bottom voice that can vary toward the upper pitches only to one that can rise above or fall below an easy average pitch. From the standpoint of satisfying the requirements for good voice, an easy average pitch is to be preferred because it makes possible the expression of meaning and feeling through adequate variation.

The person who wishes to raise the pitch level should improve projection. He must be careful to avoid the throaty quality; he can do this by speaking the sounds clearly and distinctly. In some cases, he will need to tone up the muscles slightly during speech.

TO CORRECT MONOTONY OF PITCH. An absence of variation in the pitch element causes the voice to be monotonous and uninteresting. To correct this problem, the student should practice Exercises 88 to 94.

In any pitch irregularity, the student should (1) find the pitch which is suited to his vocal mechanism, his age, and his sex and then (2) vary the voice around the average so that it expresses his meanings and feelings adequately. Throughout the program, he should strive to produce tones in pitches that will be pleasant to the ears of the listener.

PRACTICE SELECTIONS

FOR CORRECTING EXTREMELY HIGH PITCH

TO THE DRIVING CLOUD, *Henry Wadsworth Longfellow* [From *The Complete Poetical Works of Henry Wadsworth Longfellow.* Copyright 1902, Houghton Mifflin Company, Boston.]

Gloomy and dark art thou, O chief of the mighty Omahas;
Gloomy and dark as the driving cloud, whose name thou hast taken!

Wrapped in thy scarlet blanket, I see thee stalk through the city's
Narrow and populous streets, as once by the margin of rivers
Stalked those birds unknown, that have left us only their footprints.
What, in a few short years, will remain of thy race but the footprints?

How canst thou walk these streets, who hast trod the green turf of the
prairies?
How canst thou breathe this air, who hast breathed the sweet air of the
mountains?
Ah! 't is in vain that with lordly looks of disdain thou dost challenge
Looks of disdain in return, and question these walls and these pavements,
Claiming the soil for thy hunting-grounds, while down-trodden millions
Starve in the garrets of Europe, and cry from its caverns that they, too,
Have been created heirs of the earth, and claim its division!

Back, then, back to thy woods in the regions west of the Wabash!
There as a monarch thou reignest. In autumn the leaves of the maple
Pave the floors of thy palace-halls with gold, and in summer
Pine-trees waft through its chambers the odorous breath of their branches.
There thou art strong and great, a hero, a tamer of horses!
There thou chasest the stately stag on the banks of the Elkhorn,
Or by the roar of the Running-Water, or where the Omaha
Calls thee, and leaps through the wild ravine like a brave of the Blackfeet!

Hark! what murmurs arise from the heart of those mountainous deserts?
Is it the cry of the Foxes and Crows, or the mighty Behemoth,
Who, unharmed, on his tusks once caught the bolts of the thunder,
And now lurks in his lair to destroy the race of the red man?
Far more fatal to thee and thy race than the Crows and the Foxes,
Far more fatal to thee and thy race than the tread of Behemoth,
Lo! the big thunder-canoe, that steadily breasts the Missouri's
Merciless current! and yonder, afar on the prairies, the camp-fires
Gleam through the night; and the cloud of dust in the gray of the daybreak
Marks not the buffalo's track, nor the Mandan's dexterous horserace;
It is a caravan, whitening the desert where dwells the Camanches!
Ha! how the breath of these Saxons and Celts, like the blast of the east-wind,
Drifts evermore to the west the scanty smokes of thy wigwams!

FOR CORRECTING EXTREMELY LOW PITCH

FOR HARRY WHEN HE IS SAD, *Paul Engle* [From *American Song* by Paul Engle, Doubleday & Company, Inc., New York, 1934. Copyright, 1933, 1934, Doubleday & Company, Inc.]

Mark a ray of sunlight—take it
Between your hands and beat

Earth and yourself to break it
Gold on your face and feet.

Gather from the yielding land
Roots of purple thistle;
Go out in early dawn to stand
In clover fields and whistle.

Watch again the hovering swallow,
Under cloud and over sea,
Hurl its song into the hollow
House of hill and tree.

Trample your bare feet into
Bitter leaves of sorrel;
Wander all the valleys through
Where wind and water quarrel.

Pluck the glaring eye of sorrow,
Throw it from your mind,
Let the clean sunlight of tomorrow
Burn it staring and blind.

Loose on the barren mountain rocks
The scrawny goats of sadness;
Graze on the long green grass in flocks
The white sheep of your gladness.

FOR VARYING PITCH

OVER THE ROOFS, *Sara Teasdale* [From *Rivers to the Sea* by Sara Teasdale, by permission of The Macmillan Company, New York, 1927. Copyright, 1915, The Macmillan Company.]

I

Oh chimes set high on the sunny tower
Ring on, ring on unendingly,
Make all the hours a single hour,
For when the dusk begins to flower,
The man I love will come to me! . . .

But no, go slowly as you will,
I should not bid you hasten so,
For while I wait for love to come,
Some other girl is standing dumb,
Fearing her love will go.

II

Oh white steam over the roofs, blow high!
  Oh chimes in the tower ring clear and free!
Oh sun awake in the covered sky,
  For the man I love, loves me! . . .

Oh drifting steam disperse and die,
  Oh tower stand shrouded toward the south,—
Fate heard afar my happy cry,
  And laid her finger on my mouth.

III

The dusk was blue with blowing mist,
  The lights were spangles in a veil,
And from the clamor far below
  Floated faint music like a wail.

It voiced what I shall never speak,
  My heart was breaking all night long,
But when the dawn was hard and gray,
  My tears distilled into a song.

IV

I said, "I have shut my heart
  As one shuts an open door,
That Love may starve therein
  And trouble me no more."

But over the roofs there came
  The wet new wind of May,
And a tune blew up from the curb
  Where the street-pianos play.

My room was white with the sun
  And Love cried out in me,
"I am strong, I will break your heart
  Unless you set me free."

THE PARADOX OF TIME [Translated from the French by Austin Dobson, in Burton Egbert Stevenson, *Home Book of Verse*, Henry Holt and Company, Inc., New York, 1922.]

Time goes, you say? Ah, no!
Alas, Time stays, *we* go;
  Or else, were this not so,
What need to chain the hours,
For Youth were always ours?
  Time goes, you say?—ah, no!

Ours is the eyes' deceit
Of men whose flying feet
  Lead through some landscape low;
We pass, and think we see
The earth's fixed surface flee:—
  Alas, Time stays,—we go!

Once in the days of old,
Your locks were curling gold,
  And mine had shamed the crow.
Now, in the self-same stage,
We've reached the silver age;
  Time goes, you say?—ah, no!

Once, when my voice was strong,
I filled the woods with song
  To praise your "rose" and "snow";
My bird, that sang, is dead;
Where are your roses fled?
  Alas, Time stays,—we go!

See, in what traversed ways,
What backward Fate delays
  The hopes we used to know;
What are your old desires?—
Ah, where those vanished fires?
  Time goes, you say?—ah, no!

How far, how far, O Sweet,
The past behind our feet
  Lies in the even-glow!
Now on the forward way,
Let us fold hands, and pray;
  Alas, Time stays,—*we* go.

WEENG, *Lew Sarett* [From *Slow Smoke* by Lew Sarett. Copyright, 1925, Henry Holt and Company, Inc., New York, reprinted by permission.]

Hush! my baby, or soon you will hear
The Sleepy-eye, Wéeng-oosh, hovering near;
Out of the timber he will come,
A little round man as small as your thumb.
Swinging his torch of a red fire-fly,
Out of the shadows old Sleepy-eye,
With sound of a ghost, on the wind will creep
To see if a little boy lies asleep;
Over your cheeks old Wéeng will go,
With feet as soft as the falling snow—
Tip-toe. tip-toe.

Hush! my little one, close your lids tight,
Before old Sleepy-eye comes to-night;
Hi-yah! if he finds you are still awake,
He draws from his quiver a thistledown stake;
With an acorn for club he pounds on its butt,
Till Sleepy-eye hammers the open eye shut;
Then from his bundle he pulls out another,
Hops over your nose and closes the other;
Up and down with his club he will rap
On the open lid till he closes the gap—
Tap-tap. . . . . tap-tap.

If Wéeng-oosh comes at the end of this day,
And finds you asleep he will hurry away. . . . .
Do you hear him cry on the winds that blow?—
And walk on the earth as soft as a doe?—
To-and-fro. . . . . to-and-fro. . . . . .
Hi-yáh! he has crept away from my lap!
For he found my little boy taking a nap.
Oh, weep no more and whisper low,
I hear the feet of Sleepy-eye go—
Tip-toe. . . . . tip-toe.

LOOK TO THE LIGHTNING, *Gilbert Maxwell* [From *Look to the Lightning* by Gilbert Maxwell, used by permission of the publishers, Dodd, Mead & Company, Inc., New York, 1934. Copyright, 1933, Dodd, Mead & Company, Inc.]

I cannot die! I shall come back, I know—
Perhaps in the serene intelligence
Of flowers under snow;
Or maybe in the first breath-quickening sense
Of odour in the heather—
Some part of me will yet be blowing warm
Alive in April weather.
Something will speak to you out of a storm,
Something in rain and thunder;
But oh—do not be troubled if you rise
Out of your sleep in wonder:
Look to the lightning, love,—behold my eyes!

SONG OF THE LOTOS-EATERS, *Alfred, Lord Tennyson* [From "The Lotos-Eaters" by Alfred, Lord Tennyson, in *Selected Poems of Tennyson*, Macmillan Co., Ltd., London, 1947.]

There is sweet music here that softer falls
Than petals from blown roses on the grass,
Or night-dews on still waters between walls
Of shadowy granite, in a gleaming pass;

Music that gentlier on the spirit lies,
Than tired eyelids upon tired eyes;
Music that brings sweet sleep down from the blissful skies.
Here are cool mosses deep,
And thro' the moss the ivies creep,
And in the stream the long-leaved flowers weep,
And from the craggy ledge the poppy hangs in sleep.

Why are we weigh'd upon with heaviness,
And utterly consumed with sharp distress,
While all things else have rest from weariness?
All things have rest: why should we toil alone,
We only toil, who are the first of things.

Lo! in the middle of the wood,
The folded leaf is woo'd from out the bud
With winds upon the branch, and there
Grows green and broad, and takes no care,
Sun-steep'd at noon, and in the moon
Nightly dew-fed; and turning yellow
Falls, and floats adown the air.
Lo! sweeten'd with the summer light,
The full-juiced apple, waxing over-mellow,
Drops in a silent autumn night.
All its allotted length of days,
The flower ripens in its place,
Ripens and fades, and falls, and hath no toil,
Fast-rooted in the fruitful soil.

Hateful is the dark-blue sky,
Vaulted o'er the dark-blue sea.
Death is the end of life; ah, why
Should life all labour be?
Let us alone. Time driveth onward fast,
And in a little while our lips are dumb.
Let us alone. What is it that will last?
All things are taken from us, and become
Portions and parcels of the dreadful Past.
Let us alone. What pleasure can we have
To war with evil? Is there any peace
In ever climbing up the climbing wave?
All things have rest, and ripen toward the grave
In silence; ripen, fall and cease:
Give us long rest or death, dark death, or dreamful ease.

12

REGULATING LOUDNESS

Most people are unable to read lips; they must hear the voice to know what the speaker is saying. One requirement of the speaking voice is that it should be loud enough for the listener to hear what the speaker is saying. On the other hand, it must not be so loud that it blasts the ears of the listener. Often, a loud voice only calls attention to itself and is out of place. In many instances, the soft voice is far more suitable to the situation. There are times when the teacher, for example, needs to speak loudly, but the well-modulated voice is satisfactory most of the time. With it, he holds the attention of the children and conveys his thoughts to them with little effort. If he were constantly booming at them in a loud voice, they would tire of the blasting sound and, possibly, become irritated by it. If his voice were weak, it might not carry and he would fail to hold their attention. The same situation might exist in selling, preaching, and radio announcing. People in all walks of life would profit by becoming aware of the need for regulating the loudness of the voice so that it suits the needs of particular speaking situations. This awareness plus the ability to adjust the loudness level accordingly would go far in improving communication between the speaker and the listener.

If your voice is not loud enough, you should strive to make it louder through the practice of exercises for this purpose. Conversely, you should learn to decrease the loudness if the voice is overloud. Furthermore, you must learn the value of varying this basic element during speech. Variety in loudness, as well as in pitch and rate, assists in the vital process of communicating meaning and feeling to the listener and helps to hold his attention.

CAUSES FOR WEAK VOICE

Vocal characteristics are determined largely by the degree of tonicity in the muscles involved in vocalization. Since the muscles of the larynx, pharynx, tongue, and mouth work together in pairs and the various pairs of muscles coordinate in voice production, it is vital that a proper degree of tonicity be maintained. When the proper balance of muscle tension is not maintained, there is always the possibility of weak voice. Emotional disturbances of a temporary or continuing nature may decrease the loudness and firmness of the tones because of the effect of glandular changes on muscle tonicity; for example, the voice of the person who has been scolded or criticized may become weak, thin, and high-pitched. The psychopathic personality may come to possess a weak voice until the emotional problem is eliminated.

Structural disturbances in the larynx or pharynx such as enlarged tonsils may cause the voice to be weak. Similarly, organic conditions and any hypertensions which tend to inhibit the movement of the vocal folds or to decrease the size of the resonators may decrease vocal intensity. Interference by the false vocal folds is said to diminish the strength of vocal tones.

Because of his weakened condition and, in some cases, because of his demoralized state of mind, the patient in the sickroom seldom possesses a strong resonant voice.

Most frequently, weak voice is caused by poor habits of vocalization: improper use of the resonators, hypertension in the larynx, or improper use of the air stream.

PRINCIPLES TO APPLY FOR ADEQUATE LOUDNESS

You will have little trouble in producing an adequately loud voice if you apply the following principles of effective vocalization:

1. Forceful air column.
2. Open resonators.
3. Clear, resonant tone.

The careful application of the principles of breathing as suggested in Chap. 7 is vital as you attempt to control the loudness. A steady, firm pressure below the air stream seems to reinforce and thus assist in amplifying the tones.

The manner in which you take the air into the lungs as you inhale plays an important role also. By allowing the air to pass through the mouth on the inspiratory phase prior to speaking, you open the mouth and pharynx, with the result that the size of the resonators is increased. Now if you attempt to hold this openness by depressing the tongue so that it lies flat on the mouth, lifting the soft palate as far back as possible, and holding the oral pharynx fully open, you should be able to produce loud tones. With these conditions established, you should exert a steady pressure below the air column. The author believes that this is best accomplished through the use of abdominal breathing.

EXERCISES FOR INCREASING LOUDNESS

As you practice the following exercises, you should be careful to keep the muscles involved in vocalization relaxed and retain the controls suggested above: forceful air column, open resonators, and clear, resonant tones. There is always the danger of returning to the old habits of tensing the muscles of the larynx—especially the vocal folds—the pharynx, and the back of the tongue. As a result, the passage closes, defeating the purpose of the exercises. The resultant tones are harsh and, usually, higher in pitch. Such an approach to vocalization is unhygienic because of the strain placed on the intricate mechanisms producing the tones.

EXERCISE 95. Sustain an [o] sound after you have carefully prepared yourself for vocalization by inhaling through the mouth; holding the mouth, vocal outlet, and pharynx open; and exerting a firm, steady pressure below the air column. Repeat the exercise several times, making sure that there is no excess tension in the larynx.

Now utter some [o] sounds in succession, applying all the principles. Imagine that you are tossing balls of sound to the person at the rear of the auditorium.

EXERCISE 96. Give the following orders in a voice loud enough for a squad of twelve men abreast and 40 inches apart to hear:

(1) Parade (2) REST
(1) Eyes (2) RIGHT (3) Ready (4) FRONT
(1) About (2) FACE
(1) Hand (2) SALUTE
(1) Forward (2) MARCH
(1) Double time (2) MARCH
(1) By the right flank (2) MARCH
(1) By the left flank (2) MARCH
(1) Change step (2) MARCH
(1) Inspection (2) ARMS (3) LOCK (4) PIECES
(1) Inspection (2) ARMS (3) UNLOCK (4) PIECES
(1) Port (2) ARMS
(1) Present (2) ARMS
(1) Order (2) ARMS
(1) Right shoulder (2) ARMS

EXERCISE 97. Give these orders in a voice loud enough for four squads, one behind the other, at a distance of 40 inches between the ranks and with 40 inches between men abreast, to hear.

EXERCISE 98. Give these orders in a voice loud enough for four such organizations abreast to hear.

EXERCISE 99. Prepare a speech, and ask your audience to provide noise that will drown out your voice if you do not speak loudly. Apply the principles suggested, and make everyone hear you in spite of the extraneous sound. A siren can be used to provide the masking noise if one is available.

EXERCISE 100. Imagine that you are drowning, and cry out for help several times.

EXERCISE 101. Call to an imaginary person who is a half block down the street. Now increase the loudness so that he can hear you even though he is a full block away. You might use such sentences as: "Hey, wait for me"; "Hello there, Mary, how are you?" and "Goodbye, Bill."

TEMPERING THE LOUD VOICE

A few people are faced with the problem of having a voice that is overloud. When the problem exists, it can be a serious handicap. An interesting example of such a case is that of a salesman who telephoned the author immediately after one of his broadcasts on speech. The man wanted an immediate conference regarding his voice, so over a dinner that evening, the dynamic salesman—Captain Marvel in appearance—explained his trouble. As he talked, there was no sign of a difficulty. His pleasing, rich voice met all the requirements of the good voice and was well adapted to the "dinner at a hotel restaurant" situation. It was not until after the meal, while the man was attempting to sell the author on an idea, that there was any indication of the problem.

His voice gradually increased in loudness and raised in pitch as he carried on his discussion. His problem was this: in the excitement that came with his efforts to put over the item or idea he had to sell, the loudness increased and the pitch was raised so that the customer received the impression that the salesman was attempting to high-pressure him into buying something. The man did not want to make this impression because he knew the effects. But regardless of his attempt to control his voice, it betrayed him when he became excited and created impressions that brought the wrong kind of response on the part of the buyer. This not only was a problem of vocal control; it was a matter of keeping cool mentally and physically during the sale. If the man had been able to apply the principles of general and specific relaxation suggested in Chap. 5, and if he had trained his ear to perceive variations in intensity and pitch, he would have had no problem in his sales conferences with prospective customers.

The same controls apply in almost any case involving an extremely loud voice. However, in some the auditory guide might play a more important part than it did in the case of the salesman. A few persons become so accustomed to hearing their voices produced at an excessive intensity that the volume seems perfectly all right to them even though many of their listeners cringe at the blast. If they would make themselves aware of their loudness when it occurs, they would be able to bring the intensity level down to a plane suited to the occasion.

In general, the best criterion for determining how loud your own voice should be is the loudness of voice used by the group in a particular social situation. Of course, this would not be a good rule to follow in every gathering, because on some occasions all members of the group let their speech get out of control and their loudness exceeds the acceptable level for good taste.

As has already been suggested, a period of relaxation or just a thought about becoming relaxed will be sufficient to help decrease the intensity of the voice.

VARYING THE LOUDNESS

The problem of monotony in loudness can be avoided if you will work toward making appropriate variations of this basic element a part of your speech habits. Some exercises for this purpose follow:

EXERCISE 102. Speak an [ah] sound in order to discover a loudness which will serve as a good average for your speech mechanism; then use the following patterns as guides for varying the intensity of the voice. Vary the intensity *only* as you practice these exercises. Try to keep the voice at your average pitch as you vary the loudness.

1 2 3 4 5 6 7 8

1 2 3 4 5 6 7 8

1 2 3 4 5 6 7 8

1 2 3 4 5 6 7 8

1 2 3 4 5 6 7 8

1 2 3 4 5 6 7 8

EXERCISE 103. Count from 1 to 8, and let the size of the number indicate the degree of loudness.

EXERCISE 104. Repeat the above, using the [ah] sound instead of the numbers.

EXERCISE 105. Repeat, using the alphabet from *a* through *h*.

EXERCISE 106. Read the following sentences, varying the intensity appropriately:

Boomlay, boomlay, boomlay, boom!
Ye blocks, ye stones, ye worse than senseless things!
Run for your lives!
Stand up, speak up, shut up.
Drive hard, you will never make it.
Vulgar vultures; black, dirty vultures!
The waves rolled high, the wind blew hard!
Lift up your head, O ye gates: and be ye lifted up, ye everlasting doors.—*Psalms.*

As you work with the problem of loudness, you should develop ability to sense differences in this element and learn to adjust the loudness to particular social situations. Make your listener hear every word you speak. Yet do not be overloud. You will save yourself many repetitions, and you will spare your friends and acquaintances the embarrassment that goes with that oft-repeated phrase, "What did you say?" At the same time, you should strive for variation in intensity, for that, too, is an important factor in the expression of thoughts and feelings.

PRACTICE SELECTIONS

FOR DEVELOPING INTENSITY

FROM "THE PLEASURES OF HOPE," *Thomas Campbell* [*The Poetical Works of Thomas Campbell*, J. Crissy, Philadelphia, 1844.]

"Foes of mankind! (her guardian spirits say)
Revolving ages bring the bitter day,

When Heaven's unerring arm shall fall on you,
And blood for blood these Indian Plains bedew;
Nine times have Brama's wheels of lightning hurled
His awful presence o'er the alarmed world!
Nine times hath Guilt, through all his giant frame,
Convulsive trembled as the Mighty came!

"Nine times hath suffering Mercy spared in vain—
But Heaven shall burst her starry gates again;
He comes! dread Brama shakes the sunless sky
With murmuring wrath, and thunders from on high!
Heaven's fiery horse, beneath his warrior form,
Paws the light clouds, and gallops on the storm!
Wide waves his flickering sword, his bright arms glow
Like summer suns, and light the world below!
Earth, and her trembling isles in Ocean's bed
Are shook, and Nature rocks beneath his tread.

"To pour redress on India's injured realm,
The oppressor to dethrone, the proud to whelm;
To chase destruction from her plundered shore,
With arts and arms that triumphed once before,
The tenth Avater comes! at Heaven's command
Shall Seriswattee wave her hallowed wand!
And Camdeo bright! and Genesa sublime,
Shall bless with joy their own propitious clime!—
Come, Heavenly Powers! primeval peace restore!
Love!—Mercy!—Wisdom! rule for ever more!"

FROM "THE CAMPAIGN," *Joseph Addison* [From *The Miscellaneous Works of Joseph Addison*, edited by A. C. Guthkelch, George Bell & Sons, Ltd., London, 1914.]

Behold in awful march and dread array
The long-extended squadrons shape their way!
Death, in approaching terrible, imparts
An anxious horrour to the bravest hearts;
Yet do their beating breasts demand the strife,
And thirst of glory quells the love of life.
No vulgar fears can *British* minds controll:
Heat of revenge, and noble pride of soul
O'er-look the foe, advantag'd by his post,
Lessen his numbers, and contract his host:
Tho' fens and floods possest the middle space,
That unprovok'd they would have fear'd to pass;
Nor fen nor floods can stop *Britannia's* bands,
When her proud foe rang'd on their borders stands.

KING HENRY TO HIS SOLDIERS, *William Shakespeare* [From *King Henry V*, Act III, Scene I, in *The Complete Works of William Shakespeare*, World Publishing Company, Cleveland, Ohio, 1948.]

KING HENRY. Once more unto the breach, dear friends, once more,
Or close the wall up with our English dead.
In peace there's nothing so becomes a man
As modest stillness and humility;
But when the blast of war blows in our ears,
Then imitate the action of the tiger;
Stiffen the sinews, summon up the blood,
Disguise fair nature with hard-favour'd rage;
Then lend the eye a terrible aspect;
Let it pry through the portage of the head
Like the brass cannon; let the brow o'erwhelm it
As fearfully as doth a galled rock
O'erhang and jutty his confounded base,
Swill'd with the wild and wasteful ocean.
Now set the teeth and stretch the nostril wide,
Hold hard the breath, and bend up every spirit
To his full height. On, on, you noblest English,
Whose blood is fet from fathers of war-proof!
Fathers that, like so many Alexanders,
Have in these parts from morn till even fought,
And sheath'd their swords for lack of argument.
Dishonour not your mothers; now attest
That those whom you call'd fathers did beget you.
By copy now to men of grosser blood,
And teach them how to war. And you, good yeomen,
Whose limbs were made in England, show us here
The mettle of your pasture; let us swear
That you are worth your breeding, which I doubt not;
For there is none of you so mean and base,
That hath not noble lustre in your eyes.
I see you stand like greyhounds in the slips,
Straining upon the start. The game's afoot!
Follow your spirit, and upon this charge
Cry, "God for Harry! England and Saint George!"

FOR SUBDUING INTENSITY

CHILDREN'S KISSES, *Josephine Preston Peabody* [From *The Collected Poems of Josephine Preston Peabody*, Houghton Mifflin Company, authorized publishers, Boston, 1927. Copyright, 1927, Lionel S. Marks.]

So; it is nightfall then.
The valley flush
That beckoned home the way for herds and men,
Is hardly spent.
Down the bright pathway winds, through veils of hush
And wonderment.
Unuttered yet, the chime
That tells of folding-time;
Hardly the sun has set.
The trees are sweetly troubled with bright words
From new-alighted birds;—
And yet, . . .
Here,—round my neck, are come to cling and twine,
The arms, the folding arms, close, close and fain,
All mine!—
I pleaded to, in vain,
I reached for, only to their dimpled scorning,
Down the blue halls of Morning;
Where all things else could lure them on and on,
Now here, now gone,—
From bush to bush, from beckoning bough to bough,
With bird-calls of *Come Hither!*—
. . . Ah, but now,
Now it is dusk.—And from his heaven of mirth,
A wilding skylark, sudden dropt to earth
Along the last low sunbeam yellow-moted,
Athrob with joy,—
There pushes here, a little golden Boy,
Still-gazing with great eyes.
And wonder-wise,
All fragrancy, all valor silver-throated,
My daughterling, my swan,
My Alison!
Closer than homing lambs against the bars
At folding-time, that crowd, all mother-warm,
They crowd,—they cling, they wreathe;
And thick as sparkles of the thronging stars,
Their kisses swarm.

O Rose of being, at whose heart I breathe,
Fold over; hold me fast
In the dark Eden of a blinding kiss.
And lightning heart's-desire, be still at last!
Heart can no more,—
Life can no more,
Than this.

VERTUE, *George Herbert* [From *The Poems of George Herbert*, Oxford University Press, New York, 1913.]

Sweet day, so cool, so calm, so bright,
The bridall of the earth and skie,
The dew shall weep thy fall to-night;
For thou must die.

Sweet rose, whose hue angrie and brave
Bids the rash gazer wipe his eye,
The root is ever in its grave,
And thou must die.

Sweet spring, full of sweet days and roses,
A box where sweets compacted lie,
My musick shows ye have your closes,
And all must die.

Only a sweet and vertuous soul,
Like season'd timber, never gives;
But though the whole world turn to coal,
Then chiefly lives.

FOR VARYING INTENSITY

THE RED RIVER VOYAGEUR, *John Greenleaf Whittier* [From *The Complete Poetical Works of John Greenleaf Whittier*. Copyright, 1894, Houghton Mifflin Company, Boston.]

Out and in the river is winding
The links of its long, red chain,
Through belts of dusky pine-land
And gusty leagues of plain.

Only, at times, a smoke-wreath
With the drifting cloud-rack joins,—
The smoke of the hunting-lodges
Of the wild Assiniboins!

Drearily blows the north-wind
From the land of ice and snow;
The eyes that look are weary,
And heavy the hands that row.

And with one foot on the water,
And one upon the shore,
The Angel of Shadow gives warning
That day shall be no more.

Is it the clang of wild-geese?
  Is it the Indian's yell,
That lends to the voice of the north-wind
  The tones of a far-off bell?

The voyageur smiles as he listens
  To the sound that grows apace;
Well he knows the vesper ringing
  Of the bells of St. Boniface.

The bells of the Roman Mission,
  That call from their turrets twain,
To the boatman on the river,
  To the hunter on the plain!

Even so in our mortal journey
  The bitter north-winds blow,
And thus upon life's Red River
  Our hearts, as oarsmen, row.

And when the Angel of Shadow
  Rests his feet on wave and shore,
And our eyes grow dim with watching
  And our hearts faint at the oar,

Happy is he who heareth
  The signal of his release
In the bells of the Holy City,
  The chimes of eternal peace!

THE SISTERS, *John Greenleaf Whittier* [From *The Complete Poetical Works of John Greenleaf Whittier*. Copyright, 1894, Houghton Mifflin Company, Boston.]

Annie and Rhoda, sisters twain,
Woke in the night to the sound of rain,

The rush of wind, the ramp and roar
Of great waves climbing a rocky shore.

Annie rose up in her bed-gown white,
And looked out into the storm and night.

"Hush and hearken!" she cried in fear,
"Hearest thou nothing, sister dear?"

"I hear the sea, and the plash of rain,
And roar of the northeast hurricane.

"Get thee back to the bed so warm,
No good comes of watching a storm.

"What is it to thee, I fain would know,
That waves are roaring and wild winds blow?

"No lover of thine's afloat to miss
The harbor-lights on a night like this."

"But I heard a voice cry out my name,
Up from the sea on the wind it came!

"Twice and thrice have I heard it call,
And the voice is the voice of Estwick Hall!"

On her pillow the sister tossed her head.
"Hall of the Heron is safe," she said.

"In the tautest schooner that ever swam
He rides at anchor in Annisquam.

"And, if in peril from swamping sea
Or lee shore rocks, would he call on thee?"

But the girl heard only the wind and tide,
And wringing her small white hands she cried:

"O sister Rhoda, there's something wrong;
I hear it again, so loud and long.

"'Annie! Annie!' I hear it call,
And the voice is the voice of Estwick Hall!"

Up sprang the elder, with eyes aflame,
"Thou liest! He never would call thy name!

"If he did, I would pray the wind and sea
To keep him forever from thee and me.'"

Then out of the sea blew a dreadful blast;
Like the cry of a dying man it passed.

The young girl hushed on her lips a groan,
But through her tears a strange light shone,—

The solemn joy of her heart's release
To own and cherish its love in peace.

"Dearest!" she whispered, under breath.
"Life was a lie, but truth is death.

"The love I hid from myself away
Shall crown me now in the light of day.

"My ears shall never to wooer list,
Never by lover my lips be kissed.

"Sacred to thee am I henceforth,
Thou in heaven and I on earth!"

She came and stood by her sister's bed:
"Hall of the Heron is dead!" she said.

"The wind and the waves their work have done,
We shall see him no more beneath the sun.

"Little will reck that heart of thine;
It loved him not with a love like mine.

"I, for his sake, were he but here,
Could hem and 'broider thy bridal gear,

"Though hands should tremble and eyes be wet,
And stitch for stitch in my heart be set.

"But now my soul with his soul I wed;
Thine the living, and mine the dead!"

MEETING AT NIGHT, *Robert Browning* [From *The Poetical Works of Robert Browning*, Oxford University Press, New York, 1946.]

The gray sea and the long black land;
And the yellow half-moon large and low;
And the startled little waves that leap
In fiery ringlets from their sleep,
As I gain the cove with pushing prow,
And quench its speed i' the slushy sand.

Then a mile of warm sea-scented beach;
Three fields to cross till a farm appears;
A tap at the pane, the quick sharp scratch
And blue spurt of a lighted match,
And a voice less loud, thro' its joys and fears,
Then the two hearts beating each to each!

13

IMPROVING TONAL QUALITY

Vocal tones depend principally upon a steady flow of air for adequate loudness and upon freedom from hypertension in the laryngeal musculature for purity of quality.

During silence, the air stream flowing from the lungs passes between open vocal folds, but during vocalization, these folds vibrate at a rapid rate, producing sound. When the muscles of the throat and larynx are overtensed, the tones become unpleasant in quality—harshness, thinness, raspiness, and other qualities are introduced. When conditions are as they should be, the vocal folds are neither hypertense nor flaccid and the tones are pleasant at the beginning of voice production and during vocalization.

INITIATION OF VOCAL TONES

During practice periods and in ordinary speaking, you should use care in the initiation of tones; otherwise they will sound noisy and overloud to the ear of the listener. The delicately adjusted voice instrument is capable of loud tones with little or no effort on your part required. You must train yourself to free the mechanism from hypertensions and control the air stream in such a manner that effort used during vocalization comes from the lower chest and the abdominal region. You must avoid tongue, jaw, throat, and laryngeal hypertensions and be careful that you are not overenergetic in the initiation of tones. A relaxed mechanism is as essential at the start of vocalization as it is during speech.

VOCAL RESONANCE

At the outset of vocalization the sounds you produce are weak; they lack resonance and fullness. But almost immediately, the tone becomes amplified because it passes from the source (vocal folds) to the resonating chambers (the pharynx, mouth, nose, and others). Some persons tend to weaken the sound because they constrict the resonators. They need to learn to relax and open the passageway into the throat, mouth, and nose in order to increase the intensity of the tones.

Musical instruments are similar in many respects to the vocal equipment. The mouthpiece of the trumpet would produce a weak, thin sound were it not for the hollow metal horn in which it is placed. When the player blows into the inserted mouthpiece, this hollow portion of the instrument amplifies and adds resonance to the tones. In the human voice, the tone produced at the vocal folds would be weak were it not for the cavities of the nose, mouth, pharynx, and larynx. Like the metal cavity of the trumpet, these resonators serve to amplify the tones.

Flabby resonators do not respond to the tones as do resonators with firm, well-distended walls. The speaker who wishes to develop full resonance should open the throat and mouth during vocalization. Frequently, a voice will impress the listener as *throaty* or *mushy*. This may be caused by a tight or inactive jaw. The mouth does not open far enough to make complete use of the oral cavity as a resonator, and speech is muffled behind closed lips and teeth. In other cases, the *mushiness* may result from flaccid pharyngeal and oral musculature. The walls of the pharynx and mouth are not firmly distended, and these resonators are not used to capacity.

Another cause for *throaty* quality may be tensions which make the back of the tongue rise, causing partial closure of the opening between the pharynx and mouth. Sometimes, the tongue is thrust back into the upper pharynx. In either case, the tones are at least partially blocked and the "openness," so necessary for full resonant vocalization, is hindered. As a result, the voice becomes *throaty*.

Very little effort is required to produce a loud voice if the proper techniques are applied. Ordinarily, you increase the tension in the muscles of the larynx, pharynx, and jaw when you yell at someone across the street. As a result you constrict the most important resonators and hamper the movement of the vocal folds. You would get better results if you freed these muscles and opened the throat and mouth cavities. You need carefully to avoid tensions that raise the back of the tongue and decrease the resonance space in the pharynx and mouth. By doing this and allowing for the free movement of the vocal folds, you will be able to amplify and enrich the vocal tones.

Of course, you must eventually learn just how much relaxation you need in the throat, jaw, and tongue for efficient performance. At the outset, you should strive for as much relaxation as you can develop through working with the exercises listed in Chap. 5. You should speak the [hhhnnn], [m], [ah], [o], [nah], [no] sounds and the sentences, with the mechanisms thoroughly relaxed. While doing this, do not worry about the clearness of the enunciation. That will come later as you begin to put exactly the right amount of tonicity into the muscles involved in voice production.

EXERCISES TO OPEN THE PHARYNX. After ability to relax the lips, tongue, and jaw muscles has been firmly established, practice the following exercises to open the pharynx.

EXERCISE 107. Take a good sitting or standing position, open the mouth, and take a partial inhalation. Hold the air in the lungs for a few seconds, then exhale slowly, keeping the mouth and throat open.

EXERCISE 108. Repeat the above, but this time, instead of exhaling, sustain the [ah] sound, being careful to hold the mouth and throat open. Sustain the [o] sound with the throat open, the jaws apart, and the lips rounded.

EXERCISE 109. Cause yourself to yawn by opening the mouth and lifting the soft palate up toward the back wall of the pharynx. During the yawn, sustain a [ho] sound as the air flows from the lungs. Repeat, sustaining the [ha] sound.

Keep the muscles of the neck and jaw relaxed and the throat open while you read the passages at the end of the chapter.

BREATHING AND RESONANCE. The opportunity for opening the resonating cavities arises when the air is taken into the lungs prior to speaking or at the pauses during speech. Relax the jaw and open the mouth widely as you inhale. Normally the passageway will open to allow the air to enter. The glottis as well as the resonating cavities will open during the inhalation. Train yourself to retain this openness as you begin to speak.

EXERCISE 110. In practice periods, sustain the vowels [ah] and [o]. The steps are as follows:

1. Relax the jaw.
2. Open the mouth and pharynx as widely as possible.
3. Inhale through the mouth.
4. Retain the openness of the resonating cavities and the glottis.
5. Begin vocalizing the [ah] sound, sustaining the sound for 1 minute each time.

Use abdominal breathing, exerting a firm, steady force beneath the air column. The sound should get off to a smooth start. There should be no "break" or "glottal shock" as the tone is initiated. If the tone is noisy at the beginning, you have failed to keep the glottis open. Work with the exercise until you can start vocalizing without the break. Repeat the exercises using the [o] sound.

EXERCISE 111. When it is found that the [o] and [ah] sounds can be produced without glottal shock and constriction of the resonators, the [a] (as in d*a*y), [oo] (as in d*o*) and [e] (as in s*ee*m) should be practiced. The three vowels require less openness of the resonators and are slightly more difficult to produce without constriction. If the [o] and the *ah* are mastered first, however, and the same principles applied, little difficulty will be encountered with these sounds.

As has already been stated, the development of resonance depends in large part upon control of the breath stream. You would be wise to use abdominal breathing in early practice periods and then, as you speak, make a consistent effort to attain a regular rate of breathing and evenness of breath pressure. A firm support of the air column will do much to improve vocal resonance.

MAKING USE OF ALL RESONATORS. It has been said of Enrico Caruso that his entire body responded as a resonator when he sang. You can hardly expect such results during speech, but you should learn to make full use of the important resonators of the nose, mouth, pharynx, and larynx. Frequently, the cavities and surfaces of these parts of the body are not used to full advantage in the production of vocal tones. Properly directed effort can do much to accomplish this purpose, thereby amplifying the voice and at the same time enriching the tones. This phase of voice improvement calls for careful application of the vocal controls which have already been described.

Developing nasal resonance. Nasal resonance is necessary for normal vocal quality during the production of the [m], [n], and [ng] sounds. You should try to develop full nasal resonance as you practice the following exercises.

EXERCISE 112. Stand with good posture. Inhale through the mouth, and allow the abdomen to move forward. When the inhalation is completed, bring the abdominal wall in gradually and vocalize the [hhhnnn] sound. Air will escape through the nose as the [h] is produced, and the [n] will follow if the nasal outlet is kept open and the oral outlet is closed. You can accomplish the latter by raising the back of the tongue to the lower edge of the soft palate. Repeat the exercise until you are able to do it easily.

EXERCISE 113. Relax the jaw, touch the lips lightly, and hum an [m] sound. Keep the throat, jaw, and soft palate relaxed and feel the vibrating sensations in the nose.

Additional exercises for this purpose will be found on pages 142–143.

Developing oral resonance. You will have little difficulty with oral resonance if you have trained your ear to detect the difference between nasal and oral resonance and are careful to check for nasal vibrations by placing the forefinger to the side of the nose.

EXERCISE 114. Think the vowel [ah] as you go through the motions of producing the sound. In this exercise you are to just *think* the sound as you apply pressure below the air column and raise the soft palate.

EXERCISE 115. Follow by whispering the [ah] sound, being careful to apply the same controls.

EXERCISE 116. Make the vowel [ah] aloud, sustaining the sound. Avoid closing the vocal folds before starting to vocalize. If you have closed them, you will notice a slight "break" as the tone starts.

EXERCISE 117. Round the lips, and open the pharynx and oral cavity to their fullest extent. Lift the soft palate, and inhale through the mouth. Vocalize a sustained [o] sound.

EXERCISE 118. Open the mouth widely, and speak the syllables [ha], [ha], [ha], applying the same principles.

EXERCISE 119. Speak the following sentences and phrases, concentrating on oral resonance:

Good day.
How goes it?
I hope so.
How do you do?
Wait for us.

Have you tried?
The oval window is large.
Ask and it shall be given.
Opal does well in school.
Orval is over there.

Additional exercises for use in developing oral resonance will be found on pages 141–142.

DEVELOPING PHARYNGEAL AND LARYNGEAL RESONANCE. Open the pharyngeal cavity to its greatest capacity as you inhale prior to vocalization, and try to retain the openness. Avoid crowding the tongue back into the upper pharynx, and be careful that you do not allow the voice to become harsh and throaty as a result of hypertensions in the pharynx or larynx. The vocal folds should relax and move freely while the pharynx serves to reinforce the tone generated in the larynx. Special care should be taken to assure that the opening between the mouth and pharynx is fully distended. Partial closure of the passageway at this point due to the action of the tongue, pillars, and soft palate will tend to distort tonal quality and inhibit resonation.

The exercises suggested for working with oral resonance can be used to assist in the development of laryngeal and pharyngeal resonance.

CORRECTING DEFECTS OF TONAL QUALITY

As you proceed to work with defects of quality, you will realize that no two voices are exactly alike, because vocal mechanisms differ slightly in shape, size, and texture from individual to individual. Structural variations, plus some controllable factors that will be discussed later, cause certain partials or overtones to be accentuated more than others during vocalization, and this, in turn, determines whether the voice will be pleasant or unpleasant to listen to. One pattern may result in a voice that is raucous in quality, while another may result in one which is rich and resonant.

The qualities in voices vary in many respects. They can be classified according to type of quality and degree of severity, ranging between the extremely poor and the good. Some deviations in quality are easily recognized by the untrained listener; others are slight and can be spotted only by the person with the trained ear.

Defects of quality fall into three categories. They are:

1. The *throaty*, in which (with some exceptions) the lower overtones are prominent. The voice seems "down in the throat," and as it is produced, it sounds "mushy" in quality. It is not clear and well projected. Some of the empirical terms used in describing it are coarse, heavy, hoarse-husky, or hollow.
2. The *thin* voice, in which all the energy is in the fundamental tone or the higher overtones are prominent and there is a lack of resonance. Voices that are breathy, harsh, metallic, thin, or whining fit into this category.
3. The *nasal* and the *denasal*, in which the nasal resonance is disturbed. Sounds that are normally produced orally are nasalized, and the nasal voice results. The opposite is true of the denasal voice.

In many cases these defects will be eliminated if the work outlined in this text is completed and all the principles are applied consistently. In other cases, emphasis of one or another principle—for example, throat relaxation, tone production, or projection—will be required. Some will require special corrective devices.

THE THROATY VOICE. The voice that is deep in the throat does not meet the requirements for good voice because, in most cases, it is muffled and rough. It is not clear and well projected. Sometimes the throaty quality is caused by a temporary physical condition such as the common cold. In these cases, the huskiness disappears as soon as the structures become normal again. When the throatiness is, or has been, a more or less permanent condition, due to no organic disturbance, you should employ the following suggestions to get improvement.

Some general techniques for improving the throaty voice. Any type of throatiness, whether the term *coarse, heavy, hoarse-husky,* or *hollow* has been applied to it, usually requires improved voice production, with emphasis on a steady flow of the breath stream, open resonators, and clear, distinct articulation of the speech sounds.

Hypertensions which tend to close the pharynx or block the passageway from the pharynx into the mouth must be carefully avoided, and the inner walls of the resonators must have firmness without tenseness and relaxation without laxness. Considerable time should be spent in determining exactly what degree of tonicity is required to produce tones that are clear, resonant, and vibrant.

In some cases, the throatiness is due to the use of a pitch range unsuited to the vocal mechanism of the individual. A study should be made to determine whether or not the optimum or structural pitch is being used. If not, the student should find the range that is best adapted to him by carrying out the instructions given on pages 103–105.

Some techniques for treating specific problems of throatiness. When the voice has a *hollow* sound as though your head were in a cistern, emphasis should be placed on clear, distinct articulation. This will help to emphasize the higher tones. You must be careful to avoid becoming too precise. Form the speech sounds so that there is no doubt as to what you have said, yet do not become overarticulate.

In cases of *chronic hoarseness,* in which the disturbance seems to be due to a cause other than the common cold, advice of the physician or the speech pathologist should be sought. Singer's nodes, enlarged tonsils, or tuberculosis of the throat are some factors which may cause this irregularity of voice. If medical treatment is advised, the physician's recommendations should be followed and nothing should be done with the vocal exercises until after the pathological condition has been corrected.

Work with the exercises to develop oral, laryngeal, and pharyngeal resonance is helpful in eliminating the other types of throatiness.

THE THIN VOICE. The thin, weak voice is present more often in women than in men and is often due to the use of a pitch range not suited to the structures of the voice-producing mechanisms. With both men and women, it is important to determine the structural pitch level and make suitable adjustments early. Vocal exercises to improve this faulty quality include the coordination of breathing with speech, easy vocalization, and the development of rich, pleasing resonance.

Some general techniques for improving the thin voice. Approaches to the problem of finding the structural pitch are found on pages 103–105. Once this has been found and a good start has been made to produce speech at the correct pitch level, vocal exercises should be practiced. It is suggested that you work in a large room and attempt to produce a voice that can be heard easily anywhere in the room. You will find it helpful to have your instructor or another student serve as a critic as you practice.

EXERCISE 120. Inhale through the mouth, opening the vocal outlet to its fullest extent. Hold the openness, exert a firm pressure below the air column, and produce the [ho] sound. Sustain the sound for several seconds, trying hard to make it full and resonant. Applying the same techniques, speak the sentence, "Ho, ho, ho, and a bottle of rum," using the gusty voice that you think a partially inebriated pirate might use.

EXERCISE 121. Open the throat and apply a firm breath pressure as you produce a sustained [ha] sound. Then, repeat the syllable [ha] several times without sustaining it. Hold the mouth and pharynx open, and produce full tones.

EXERCISE 122. Count from 1 to 8 applying the same principles. Gradually increase the fullness of the tones, and be especially careful that you use your structural pitch.

EXERCISE 123. Speak firmly as you give the following commands:

1. Stop that immediately!
2. We'll have no more of that!
3. Don't let me catch you doing that again!
4. You'll have to slow down or I will drive.
5. Wait for me!
6. You'll have to behave yourself, or you're going home.
7. Hold your tongue!

EXERCISE 124. Assume that you have an audience of 500 people, and make the following announcements using a firm voice:

You are asked to leave the theater in an orderly manner, starting with the last row first. There is a fire in the basement. No one will be hurt if you leave quietly.

There will be a meeting of the program committee immediately following this session of the convention. Members will go promptly to the Blue Room on the second floor as soon as we have adjourned.

Plans for tomorrow night's dance have been changed. It will be held in Reed Gymnasium, rather than at Senior Hall. As you already know, the dance starts at 8:00 and ends at midnight. Some surprises have been planned. We hope all of you will be able to attend.

Some techniques for improving types of thin voice. The *breathy* voice is usually caused by poor approximation of the vocal cords at their mid-line. The quality, as the name implies, is *fuzzy*. Along with the vocal tone produced, there is the sound of escaping air. The fault is difficult to correct and, in most cases, should be handled by an expert. In some, the services of the laryngologist will be required to eliminate organic disorders. In a few cases, this irregularity can be corrected by applying the suggestions which have been offered regarding breathing, easy vocalization, voice production, and projection.

West[1] has presented the *glottal catch* as a means of improving poor vocal quality caused by failure of the vocal cords to approximate properly. In this, the subject learns "to discern the clear tone following the hard attack" on the vowel sounds. The technique should be employed only in the speech clinic, after the larynx has been studied by the physician.

The *metallic* quality in the voice gives the impression of the sharp rustle of sheet metal. A study conducted by the author[2] showed that this quality in male voices is due to a spread of energy in the higher overtones. In female voices, it is due to a preponderance of fundamental energy with little or no energy in the higher overtones. The phenomenon as far as women's voices are concerned seems to be due to the close kinship of the *metallic* to the *thin* voice. To correct the problem in women, the third to fifth overtones need to be developed; in men, frictions and tensions which cause the noisy elements (the extremely high overtones) should be eliminated. In both female and male voices, the best means of correcting the difficulty is through

[1] West, R., L. Kennedy and A. Carr, *The Rehabilitation of Speech*, pp. 287–288. Harper & Brothers, New York, 1937.

[2] Van Dusen, C. R., "A Study of the Metallic Voice," *Journal of Speech Disorders*, vol. 6, pp. 137–140, 1941.

learning throat relaxation and developing oral, laryngeal, and pharyngeal resonance. The most pertinent basic control is throat relaxation.

The person with the *harsh* voice should get improvement in the same manner. In some instances, he and the *whiner* would be wise to approach his difficulty from the standpoint of emotional readjustment and retraining.

THE NASAL VOICE. Ear training is one of the most important phases in the correction of nasality. Throughout the work the student should practice new techniques and then apply them as he records his voice. If equipment is available, he should make a recording every day and study the results carefully after each recording.

The student must learn to guide the air stream through the mouth instead of the nose on oral sounds. One commonly used means of doing this is to obtain control over the soft palate so that it will rise, closing off the nasal passage on all oral sounds, and relax on the nasal sounds.

The yawn has frequently been used to activate the soft palate. The yawn itself is not especially good, because essentially it is a reflex activity and, under ordinary conditions, the individual does not exert voluntary control over it. However, it is useful in that it gives the student the sensation of muscles moving to raise the soft palate. He should become aware of these sensations and observe what happens at the back of the mouth during the yawn. Then he should practice raising and lowering the soft palate as he watches its movement in a mirror. He can further the activity of the soft palate by whistling, blowing up balloons, playing wind instruments, or making bubbles.

Exercises for eliminating nasality. It is helpful to observe the action of the soft palate and the openness at the oral outlet (the space at the back of the tongue where the pharynx opens into the mouth) in a mirror during the practice of the exercises for correcting nasal quality.

EXERCISE 125. Sustain each of the vowel sounds ([a], [e], [i], [o], [u]) for some time, closing and opening the nasal exit with the thumb and forefinger against the side of the nose. Press and release several times during each sound. The change in pressure should not alter the vocal quality. Relax the tongue, and increase, as far as possible, the distance between the back of the tongue and the soft palate during the utterance of the sounds. Follow this with words in which there are no nasal sounds, such as *this*, *that*, *hill*, *hot*, and *happy*.

EXERCISE 126. Work on sentences that contain no [m], [n], or [ng] sounds. Some examples follow:

1. After life's fitful fever he sleeps well.—SHAKESPEARE.
2. Variety is the very spice of life.—COWPER.

> Our hearts, our hopes, are all with thee,
> Our hearts, our hopes, our prayers, our tears,
> Our faith, victorious o'er our fears,
> Are all with thee,—are all with thee.
> —LONGFELLOW.

4. Lift up your hearts, ye people, O be proud.—HAGEDORN.

During the recitation of these lines place the thumb and forefinger over the nose. Exert pressure and release it several times during the utterance to test for nasality. If the pressure causes a change in quality it is probable that some nasality is present.

EXERCISE 127. Sustain an [ah] sound, and after a few seconds, relax the soft palate and add a final [m] to the tone. Diagrammed, it would look like this:

[ah]..............[m]

Next, try:[1]

[ah]..............[n]
[ah]..............[ng]

EXERCISE 128. Now place the nasal sound in the initial position and practice:

[m]..............[ah]
[n]..............[ah]

This time sustain the [m], [n], and [ng] sounds.

EXERCISE 129. Place the nasal sounds between two [ah] sounds, as:

[ah].......[m].......[ah]
[ah].......[n]........[ah]
[ah].......[ng].......[ah]

EXERCISE 130. Place the vowel between two nasal sounds, as

[m].......[ah].......[m]
[n]........[ah].......[n]
[ng].......[ah].......[ng]
[m].......[ah].......[n]
[n]........[ah].......[m]
[m].......[ah].......[ng]
[ng].......[ah].......[n]

[1] The position of the articulators on the [m] [n] and [ng] sounds would be similar to

Practice the above exercises substituting the vowels *a, e, i, o, oo.*

EXERCISE 131. Speak words containing the [m], [n], and [ng] sounds, as, for example, *moment, millstone, many, men, nation, singing, marching,* and *manual,* being careful to avoid carrying nasality into the oral sounds.

EXERCISE 132. Speak sentences containing the nasal sounds. Some that may be used follow:

1. Who knows the thoughts of a child?—NORA PERRY.
2. Every man is the center of a circle, whose fatal circumference he cannot pass.—JOHN J. INGALLS.
3. London is the clearing house of the world.—JOSEPH CHAMBERLAIN.
4. The woman that deliberates is lost.—ADDISON.
5. Now is the time to act.
6. This is a warm day.
7. No, I won't do that.

THE DENASAL VOICE. Some cases of denasality are due to stoppages in the nose or nasal pharynx (the passage behind and above the soft palate). These should be studied by the physician or the speech pathologist, and if the vocal problem is caused by a structural deformity, the case should be referred to a specialist.

The present discussion is of problems that are due to poor habits of vocalization. In many students, denasality is caused by factors which require merely a period of retraining. Hypertension in the soft palate, frequently found in cases of denasality, is one of these. Development of relaxation in this part should be used when this is the cause of the difficulty. In general, relaxation of the tongue, soft palate, and throat, plus the development of nasal and oral resonance, is required to correct the difficulty.

The effect of a voice on the ear of the listener depends largely on its quality. If there are qualities that detract from the effect, great effort should be expended to improve this important factor. There will be little danger of the speaker's losing his vocal individuality in so doing, and the chances are that the voice will come closer to meeting the standards for good voice.

---

the positions they take on the [p] [t] and [g] sounds, respectively, except that, on the nasal sounds, the soft palate is relaxed. The [m] is made with the lips together, as on the [p] and [b] sounds. The [n] is made with the tongue in the same position as it is on the [t] and [d] sounds. The [ng] is made with the tongue in the same position as for the [g] sound.

PRACTICE SELECTIONS

FOR DEVELOPING RESONANCE

CAROLINE, *Thomas Campbell* [*The Poetical Works of Thomas Campbell*, J. Crissy, Philadelphia, 1844.]

Part II

Gem of the crimson coloured even,
Companion of retiring day
Why at the closing gates of heaven,
Beloved star, dost thou delay?

So fair thy pensile beauty burns,
When soft the tear of twilight flows,
So due thy plighted step returns,
To chambers brighter than the rose;

To peace, to pleasure, and to love
So kind a star thou seem'st to be,
Sure some enamoured orb above
Descends and burns to meet with thee.

Thine is the breathing, blushing hour,
When all unheavenly passions fly;
Chased by the soul-subduing power
Of love's delicious witchery.

Oh! sacred to the fall of day,
Queen of propitious stars, appear!
And early rise, and long delay,
When Caroline herself is here.

Shine on her chosen green resort,
Where trees the sunward summit crown;
And wanton flowers, that well may court
An angel's feet to tread them down.

Shine on her sweetly scented road,
Thou star of evening's purple dome!
That lead'st the nightingale abroad,
And guid'st the pilgrim to his home.

Shine, where my charmer's sweeter breath
Embalms thy soft exhaling dew;
Where dying winds a sigh bequeath
To kiss her cheek of rosy hue.

Where, winnowed by the gentle air,
Her silken tresses darkly flow,
And fall upon her brows so fair,
Like shadows on the mountain snow.

Thus, ever thus, at day's decline
In converse sweet to wander far,
Oh! bring with thee my Caroline,
And thou shalt be my ruling star!

HYMN TO SELENE [From *Homeric Hymns*, translated by Percy Bysshe Shelley, in Mark Van Doren, *An Anthology of World Poetry*, Albert & Charles Boni, Inc., New York, 1928.]

Daughters of Jove, whose voice is melody,
Muses, who know and rule all minstrelsy,
Sing the wide-winged Moon! Around the earth,
From her immortal head in Heaven shot forth,
Far light is scattered—boundless glory springs;
Where'er she spreads her many-beaming wings
The lampless air glows round her golden crown.

But when the Moon divine from Heaven is gone
Under the sea, her beams within abide,
Till, bathing her bright limbs in Ocean's tide,
Clothing her form in garments glittering far,
And having yoked to her immortal car
The beam-invested steeds whose necks on high
Curve back, she drives to a remoter sky
A western Crescent, borne impetuously.
Then is made full the circle of her light,
And as she grows, her beams more bright and bright
Are poured from Heaven, where she is hovering then,
A wonder and a sign to mortal men.

The Son of Saturn with this glorious Power
Mingled in love and sleep—to whom she bore
Pandeia, a bright maid of beauty rare
Among the Gods, whose lives eternal are.
Hail Queen, great Moon, white-armed Divinity,
Fair-haired and favorable! thus with thee
My song beginning, by its music sweet
Shall make immortal many a glorious feat
Of demigods, with lovely lips, so well
Which minstrels, servants of the Muses, tell.

TO HELEN, *Edgar Allan Poe* [From *The Poems of Edgar Allan Poe*, edited by Killis Campbell, Ginn & Company, Boston, 1917.]

Helen, thy beauty is to me
  Like those Nicaean barks of yore,
That gently, o'er perfumed sea,
  The weary, wayworn wanderer bore
  To his own native shore.

On desperate seas long wont to roam,
  Thy hyacinth hair, thy classic face,
Thy Naiad airs have brought me home
  To the glory that was Greece
  And the grandeur that was Rome.

Lo! in yon brilliant window-niche
  How statue-like I see thee stand,
The agate lamp within thy hand!
  Ah, Psyche, from the regions which
  Are Holy Land!

THE EVENING STAR, *L. E. L.* [From *The Amulet*, edited by S. C. Hall, published by Frederick Westley, and A. H. Dairs, London, 1833.]

How beautiful the twilight sky,
  Whose starry worlds now spread,
Amid the purple depths of eve,
  Their glory o'er my head!

And there is one—a radiant one—
  Amid the rest shines he,
As if just risen from his sleep,
  Within the mighty sea.

The clouds fall off in glittering flakes
  Before his shining brow;
So moves a ship that flings the waves
  In bright foam from its prow.

I marvel not in former days,
  Ere purer light was given,
That men fell down and worshipped thee
  A spirit-king in heaven.

But now that knowledge great and high
  Is kindled in man's soul,
We know thee but the glorious part
  Of a more glorious whole.

Oh, mysteries of night! that fill
The mind with awe and love!
How visibly the power of God
Is manifest above!

Oh! might and majesty that reign
Upon the midnight sky!—
Creed of my hope! I feel thy truth
Whene'er I gaze on high.

FOR DEVELOPING A CLEAR TONE

FROM THE RAPE OF LUCRECE, *William Shakespeare* [Lines from "The Rape of Lucrece" by William Shakespeare from *Venus and Adonis, Lucrece and Minor Poems*, edited by Albert Feuillerat. Copyright, Yale University Press, New Haven, 1927.]

O shame to knighthood and to shining arms!
O foul dishonour to my household's grave!
O impious act, including all four harms!
A martial man to be soft fancy's slave!
True valour still a true respect should have;
Then my digression is so vile, so base,
That it will live engraven in my face.

HOW DO I LOVE THEE? *Elizabeth Barrett Browning* [From "Sonnets from the Portuguese," in Franklin Bliss Snyder and Robert Grant Martin, *A Book of English Literature*, Vol. II, 4th ed., The Macmillan Company, New York, 1943.]

How do I love thee? Let me count the ways.
I love thee to the depth and breadth and height
My soul can reach, when feeling out of sight
For the ends of Being and ideal Grace.
I love thee to the level of every day's
Most quiet need, by sun and candle-light.
I love thee freely, as men strive for right;
I love thee purely, as they turn from praise.
I love thee with the passion put to use
In my old griefs, and with my childhood's faith.
I love thee with a love I seemed to lose
With my lost saints—I love thee with the breath,
Smiles, tears, of all my life!—and, if God choose,
I shall but love thee better after death.

ON THE BEACH AT CALAIS, *William Wordsworth* [From *Prose, Poetry and Drama for Oral Interpretation*, selected and arranged by William J. Farma, Harper & Brothers, New York, 1930.]

It is a beauteous evening, calm and free;
The holy time is quiet as a nun
Breathless with adoration; the broad sun
Is sinking down in its tranquillity;
The gentleness of heaven is on the sea:
Listen! the mighty Being is awake,
And doth with his eternal motion make
A sound like thunder—everlastingly.
Dear child! dear girl! that walkest with me here,
If thou appear untouch'd by solemn thought,
Thy nature is not therefore less divine:
Thou liest in Abraham's bosom all the year,
And worship'st at the Temple's inner shrine,
God being with thee when we know it not.

THE BOOK OF PSALMS [From *The Holy Bible*, edited by C. I. Scofield, Oxford University Press, New York, 1945. Copyright, 1945, Oxford University Press.]

Psalm 8

O Lord our Lord, how excellent is thy name in all the earth! who hast set thy glory above the heavens.

Out of the mouth of babes and sucklings hast thou ordained strength, because of thine enemies, that thou mightest still the enemy and the avenger.

When I consider thy heavens, the work of thy fingers, the moon and the stars, which thou hast ordained;

What is man, that thou art mindful of him? and the son of man, that thou visitest him?

For thou hast made him a little lower than the angels, and hast crowned him with glory and honour.

Thou madest him to have dominion over the works of thy hands; thou hast put all things under his feet:

All sheep and oxen, yea, and the beasts of the field;

The fowl of the air, and the fish of the sea, and whatsoever passeth through the paths of the seas.

O Lord our Lord, how excellent is thy name in all the earth!

Psalm 29

Give unto the Lord, O ye mighty, give unto the Lord glory and strength.

Give unto the Lord the glory due unto his name; worship the Lord in the beauty of holiness.

The voice of the Lord is upon the waters: the God of glory thundereth: the Lord is upon many waters.

The voice of the Lord is powerful; the voice of the Lord is full of majesty.
The voice of the Lord breaketh the cedars; yea, the Lord breaketh the cedars of Lebanon.
He maketh them also to skip like a calf; Lebanon and Sirion like a young unicorn.
The voice of the Lord divideth the flames of fire.
The voice of the Lord shaketh the wilderness; the Lord shaketh the wilderness of Kadesh.
The voice of the Lord maketh the hinds to calve, and discovereth the forest: and in his temple doth every one speak of his glory.
The Lord sitteth upon the flood; yea, the Lord sitteth King for ever.
The Lord will give strength unto his people; the Lord will bless his people with peace.

FOR IMPROVING THE THIN VOICE

FROM "THE BASTILLE," *Thomas Paine* [From *The Complete Writings of Thomas Paine*, edited by Philip S. Foner, The Cathedral Press, New York, 1945. Copyright, 1945, The Cathedral Press.]

As to the tragic paintings by which Mr. Burke has outraged his own imagination, and seeks to work upon that of his readers, they are very well calculated for theatrical representation, where facts are manufactured for the sake of show and accommodated to produce, through the weakness of sympathy, a weeping effect. But Mr. Burke should recollect that he is writing history, and not *plays*, and that his readers will expect truth, and not the spouting rant of high-toned exclamation.

When we see a man dramatically lamenting in a publication intended to be believed that *The age of chivalry is gone!* that *The glory of Europe is extinguished for ever!* that *The unbought grace of life* (if anyone knows what it is), *the chief defence of nations, the nurse of manly sentiment and heroic enterprise is gone!* and all this because the Quixote age of chivalry nonsense is gone, what opinion can we form of his judgment, or what regard can we pay to his facts? In the rhapsody of his imagination he has discovered a world of windmills, and his sorrows are that there are no Quixotes to attack them. But if the age of aristocracy, like that of chivalry, should fall (and they had originally some connection) Mr. Burke, the trumpeter of the order, may continue his parody to the end, and finish with exclaiming: "*Othello's occupation's gone!*"

DECLARATION OF INDEPENDENCE [From "A Declaration by the Representatives of the United States of America, in General Congress, Assembled, July 4, 1776," in Edward Dumbauld, *The Declaration of Independence and What It Means Today*, University of Oklahoma Press, Norman, 1950. Copyright, 1950, University of Oklahoma Press.]

We hold these truths to be self-evident, that all Men are created equal, that they are endowed by their Creator with certain inalienable Rights, that among these are Life, Liberty and the pursuit of Happiness, That to secure these rights, Governments are instituted among Men, deriving their just Powers from the Consent of the Governed, That whenever any Form of Government becomes destructive of these Ends, it is the Right of the People to alter or to abolish it.

SONG TO THE MEN OF ENGLAND, *Percy Bysshe Shelley* [From *The Poetical Works of Percy Bysshe Shelley*, edited by Edward Dowden, Macmillan and Company, Ltd., London, 1926. Copyright, 1890, The Macmillan Company.]

Men of England, wherefore plough
For the lords who lay ye low?
Wherefore weave with toil and care
The rich robes your tyrants wear?

Wherefore feed, and clothe, and save,
From the cradle to the grave,
Those ungrateful drones who would
Drain your sweat—nay, drink your blood?

Wherefore, bees of England, forge
Many a weapon, chain, and scourge,
That these stingless drones may spoil
The forced produce of your toil?

Have ye leisure, comfort, calm,
Shelter, food, love's gentle balm?
Or what is it ye buy so dear
With your pain and with your fear?

The seed ye sow, another reaps;
The wealth ye find, another keeps;
The robes ye weave, another wears;
The arms ye forge, another bears.

Sow seed,—but let no tyrant reap;
Find wealth,—let no impostor heap;
Weave robes,—let not the idle wear;
Forge arms,—in your defence to bear.

Shrink to your cellars, holes, and cells;
In halls ye deck, another dwells.
Why shake the chains ye wrought? Ye see
The steel ye tempered glance on ye.

With plough and spade, and hoe and loom,
Trace your grave, and build your tomb,
And weave your winding-sheet, till fair
England be your sepulchre.

FOR INCREASING ORAL RESONANCE TO IMPROVE THE NASAL VOICE

The following sentences contain no nasal sounds. Move the back wall of the pharynx toward the soft palate to avoid nasal resonance as you read the sentences aloud.

He lives at the big house.
She looks like a girl who used to live here.
It is hot today.
Dig a deep hole here.
Does the cat like to play with the ball?
Have you ever walked over that bridge?
Were you at Kiska or Carthage?
If you wish, we will walk to the village.
The sisters were very beautiful.
Hazards are everywhere, so be careful.
Sleep lightly, a burglar walks the city streets.
Give your all.
There is a load of hay back of the shed.
Did you go to the Railway Fair?

FOR INCREASING NASAL RESONANCE TO IMPROVE THE DENASAL VOICE

Chant all the underlined words in the selection that follows for full nasal resonance:

Blow, west *wind* by the *lonely mound*
And *murmur*, summer *streams;*
There is no *need* of further *sound*
To soothe my lady's *dreams*.
—EMILY BRONTË

Chant the following lines:

There is a lonely moorland stream.

Blow, west wind, by the lonely stream.

My Mary's asleep by the murmuring stream.

Cities drowned in olden time.

We are the music makers and we are the dreamers.

Once upon a midnight dreary, while I pondered, weak and weary,
Over many a quaint and curious volume of forgotten lore—
While I nodded, nearly napping, suddenly there came a tapping,
As of someone gently rapping—rapping at my chamber door.
"'Tis some visitor," I muttered, "tapping at my chamber door—
Only this and nothing more."

—EDGAR ALLAN POE

FOR MIXING ORAL AND NASAL RESONANCE

It is not good that the man should be alone.—*Genesis.*

Lift up your head, O ye gates; and be ye lifted up, ye everlasting doors.—*Psalms.*

He clasps the crag with crooked hands.—TENNYSON.

They kept the noiseless tenor of their way.—GRAY.

Be there a will, then wisdom finds a way.—CRABBE.

The fair breeze blew, the white foam flew,
The furrow followed free.

—COLERIDGE.

The splendor falls on castle walls
And snowy summits old in story:
The long light shakes across the lakes,
And the wild cataract leaps in glory.
Blow, bugle, blow, set the wild echoes flying,
Blow, bugle; answer, echoes, dying, dying, dying.

O hark, O hear! how thin and clear,
And thinner, clearer, farther going!
O sweet and far from cliff and scar
The horns of Elfland faintly blowing!
Blow, let us hear the purple glens replying:
Blow, bugle; answer, echoes, dying, dying, dying.

O love, they die in yon rich sky,
They faint on hill or field or river:
Our echoes roll from soul to soul,
And grow for ever and for ever.
Blow, bugle, blow, set the wild echoes flying,
And answer, echoes, answer, dying, dying, dying.

—ALFRED, LORD TENNYSON.

14

IMPROVING FLEXIBILITY OF THE VOICE

The voice is no exception to the old saw which states "Variety is the spice," etc. As well as being pleasant in quality, the voice should be dynamic and flexible. The tones should vary in degrees of force, and the pitch should change easily with the ideas and emotions expressed by the speaker. As Lew Sarett[1] has put it: "A voice that has resonance, mellowness, flexibility and control expresses nuances of thought and feeling that a bad voice, uttering the same words, fails to express. . . . "

A flat, monotonous voice not only fails as a medium for the speaker's mental and physical inner workings but also detracts from his general effect on the listener; it may level him to the category of the drab, uninteresting bore. A voice that varies in quality, pitch, rate, and intensity adds life and color to his personality; it makes others sit up and take notice when he begins to speak, and it helps him to hold the attention of his audience until he has finished what he has to say. A voice that lacks variety in one or another of these attributes falls flat at the very outset, and the listener's attention wanes.

The causes for vocal monotony are numerous; among them are mental and physical apathy, defective hearing, and poor habits of vocalization.

Each of these faults requires a special correction program. This chapter considers only poor habits of vocalization, that is, vocal variety from the standpoint of voice production. Vocal variations for interpreting the printed word will not be considered here, since this subject is outside the bounds of a program in voice training. The work in improv-

[1] Sarett, L., and W. T. Foster, *Basic Principles of Speech*, p. 202, Houghton Mifflin Company, Boston, 1946.

ing vocal flexibility will merely lay the foundation for training in oral interpretation.

Techniques that help to vary pitch, loudness, and rate of speaking have been presented in pertinent chapters.[1] The purpose of this portion of the book is to give the student practice in varying all elements simultaneously.

The variations of vocal quality will not be discussed, even though it is possible to learn to effect changes in quality. The quality of most persons' voices changes automatically with changes in the emotional state. If an individual does not have a vocal disorder or if he is not apathetic, the qualities of the voice will be many, depending upon the state of his mind and emotions. The teacher of dramatics and oral interpretation may want to deal with the affected qualities. Fundamentally, these are not problems to be considered in this course.

VARYING THE PITCH AND INTENSITY SIMULTANEOUSLY

EXERCISE 133. Vary the pitch and intensity as you count from 1 to 8, using the following patterns. Raise and lower the pitch as you did in the exercise on page 107 and let the size of the print indicate the degree of loudness.

1 2 3 4 5 6 7 8
(average)

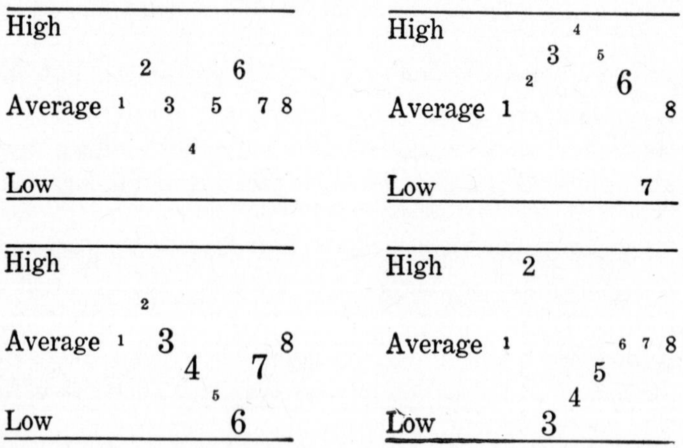

```
High                         High            4
                                           3   5
       2       6                         2       6
Average 1  3   5   7 8       Average 1             8
           4
Low                          Low                 7

High                         High      2

       2
Average 1  3          8      Average 1         6 7 8
            4      7                          5
              5                             4
Low                6         Low          3
```

[1] Chapters 10, 11, 12, 18, and 19.

VARYING THE INTENSITY AND RATE SIMULTANEOUSLY

EXERCISE 134. Vary the intensity and rate as you count from 1 to 8, using the following patterns. Let the size of the number indicate the degree of intensity and the dots between numbers, the length of pause.

1 . 2 . 3 . 4 . 5 . 6 . 7 . 8

1 . 2 3 . 4 . 5 . . 7 . 6 . . 8

1 . 2 . . . 4 . 5 . 7 . 8

1 . . 2 . . 3 . . . . . 4 . 5 . 6 . . . 7 . 8

1 2 . . 3 . 4 5 . 6 . 7 8

1 2 . 3 4 . 5 . . . . . 6 . . . . . . 7 . 8

1 . 2 . . . 3 4 . 5 . 6 . 7 8

1 . . . . 2 . 3 . . . . 4 . . . 5 . 6 . 7 8

VARYING PITCH AND RATE SIMULTANEOUSLY

EXERCISE 135. Vary the pitch and rate as you count from 1 to 8, using the following patterns:

```
PITCH

High
             2 .             6 .
Average  1 .     3 .     5 .     7 . 8
                     4 .
Low

High
                                 6 .
Average  1 . .         4 . . 5 .     7 . 8
               2 .
Low                3 .

High           2
                 3 . . .
Average  1 . .           4 .               8
                             5 .     7 . .
Low                              6 .

High                                   6 . . .
                                   5 .         7 .
Average  1 . . .           4 . . .                 8
                     3 . .
Low              2 .

High     1 .                 5 . . .
             2 .     4 . . .         6 .
Average          3 .                     7 . 8
Low

High
Average  1 . .                     5 .             8
               2 .         4 . . .     6
Low                3 . . .               7 . . . .

High         2                     6 .
                           5 . . .
Average  1         4 . . .                 8
Low              3                     7
```

VARYING ALL ELEMENTS SIMULTANEOUSLY

EXERCISE 136. Vary the pitch, intensity, and rate as you count from 1 to 8, using the following patterns. Let the place of the number on the scale indicate the pitch; the size of the number, the degree of intensity; and the distance between numbers, the length of the pause.

PITCH

High

2 . .

Average 1 . 3 . 7 . . 8

4 . . 6 .

Low 5

High 2 . . .

Average 1 3 8

7 .

4 . . 6 .

Low 5 .

High 6

7

Average 1 . . . 5 . . 8

2 .

3 .

Low 4 . .

PITCH

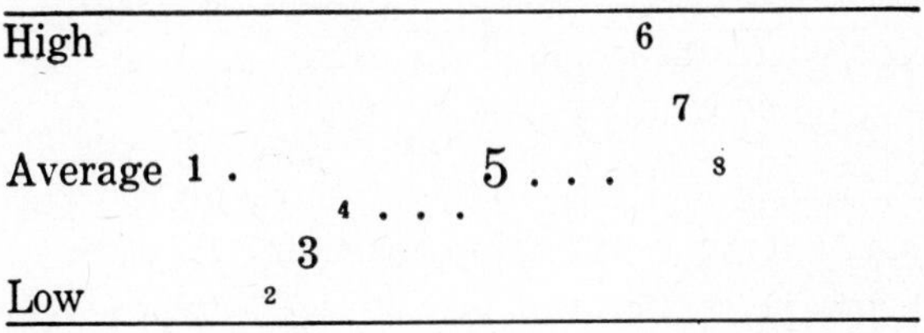

High 6
7
Average 1 . 5 . . . 8
4 . . . .
3
Low 2

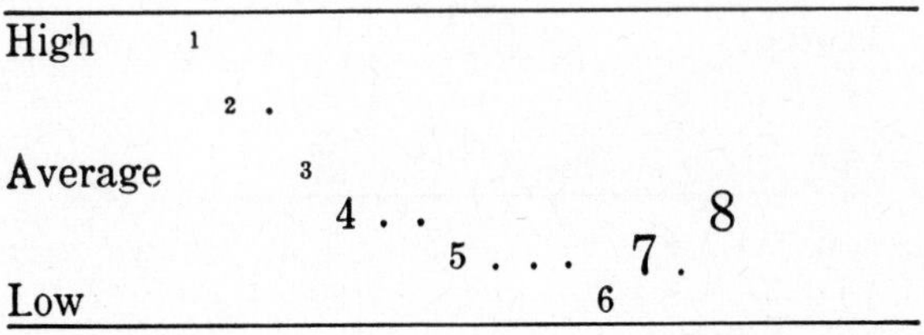

High 1
2 .
Average 3
4 . . 8
5 . . . 7 .
Low 6

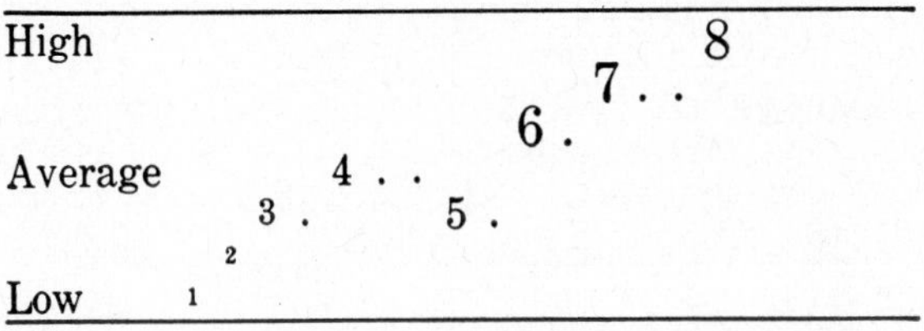

High 8
7 . .
6 .
Average 4 . .
3 . 5 .
2
Low 1

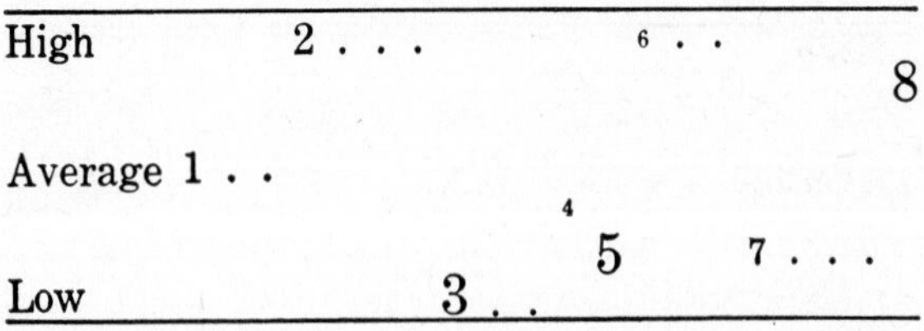

High 2 . . . 6 . .
8
Average 1 . .
4
5 7 . . .
Low 3 . .

Use the metronome as you practice these patterns. Set the tempo at 85 beats per minute, and then, as you develop the ability to vary all elements simultaneously at this tempo, increase the rate in steps of 5 beats per minute.

Develop vocal flexibility through reading the newspaper aloud. Try to emulate the news commentator on the radio as you do so. You might gain by setting up an imitation microphone and imagining that you are actually broadcasting. If you have a public-address system in your radio, use that for your faked broadcast.

Vary the pitch, intensity, and rate as you read passages from well-written books and magazines. Apply the principles of tone production outlined in Chap. 10 as you practice the exercises and do the reading. Use your ability to vary the voice every time you speak.

PRACTICE SELECTIONS

FOR VARYING ALL FACTORS SIMULTANEOUSLY

La Mexicana, *Charles Swain* [From *The Amulet*, edited by S. C. Hall, published by Frederick Westley, and A. H. Davis, London, 1833.]

A vision from the world of thought—
  A dream of golden bowers;
When Youth and Time, like happy friends,
  Were wandering 'mid the flowers:
When Love came like an angel down,
  His radiant spells to weave;
And Hope sang like the lark at morn—
  The nightingale at eve.

Within the mirror of the past,
  How beautiful arise
The long-lost hues of early life—
  The stars of Memory's skies!
When *one* bright beam of maiden's eye
  Was sunlight to the mind;
One voice, a melody more sweet
  Than Poesy may find!

Our painter's hand hath caught the power
  And spirit of romance;
How graceful that declining head!
  How soft the downcast glance!
She lists!—'tis not the vesper-hymn

Along the valley borne,
Nor distant voice of forest-streams—
'Tis for her hunter's horn!

Her hunter's horn!—at break of day,
She heard his signal sound;
She saw across the misty hills
His own proud courser bound:
With rifle, lance, and bended bow,
To hunt the llama there;
Or chase, perchance, a nobler foe—
The panther from his lair.

Why stays he yet?—the lonely moon
Looks o'er the mountains blue;
The wild swan seeks her reedy nest;
The stars gleam faint and few;
The deer lie slumbering by the stream,
Half hid their crested brow;
And dreary chime the midnight bells:—
Where stays her hunter now?

Why spring the startled deer afoot?
Why wake the wild birds near?
She lists!—but, save the midnight chime,
No whisper meets her ear.
Hark!—hark! they *are* his bugle-notes
That up the river glide!
And, swift as echo to the sound,
Her hunter's at her side!

FROM "THE TRAVELLER," *Oliver Goldsmith* [From *The Works of Oliver Goldsmith*, edited by Peter Cunningham, F.S.A., G. P. Putnam's Sons, New York, 1908.]

When thus Creation's charms around combine,
Amidst the store, should thankless pride repine?
Say, should the philosophic mind disdain
That good which makes each humbler bosom vain?
Let school-taught pride dissemble all it can,
These little things are great to little man;
And wiser he, whose sympathetic mind
Exults in all the good of all mankind.
Ye glittering towns, with wealth and splendour crown'd;
Ye fields, where summer spreads profusion round;
Ye lakes, whose vessels catch the busy gale;
Ye bending swains, that dress the flowery vale;
For me your tributary stores combine:
Creation's heir, the world, the world is mine!

THE TABLES TURNED, *William Wordsworth* [From *Prose, Poetry and Drama for Oral Interpretation*, selected and arranged by William J. Farma, Harper & Brothers, New York, 1930.]

Up! Up! my friend, and quit your books;
Or surely you'll grow double:
Up! Up! my friend, and clear your looks;
Why all this toil and trouble?

The sun, above the mountain's head,
A freshening lustre mellow
Through all the long green fields has spread
His first sweet evening yellow.

Books! 'tis a dull and endless strife:
Come, hear the woodland linnet,
How sweet his music! on my life
There's more of wisdom in it.

And hark! how blithe the throstle sings!
He, too, is no mean preacher:
Come forth into the light of things,
Let Nature be your teacher.

She has a world of ready wealth,
Our minds and hearts to bless—
Spontaneous wisdom breathed by health,
Truth breathed by cheerfulness.

One impulse from a vernal wood
May teach you more of man,
Of moral evil and of good,
Than all the sages can.

Sweet is the lore which Nature brings;
Our meddling intellect
Misshapes the beauteous forms of things:—
We murder to dissect.

Enough to Science and of Art;
Close up those barren leaves;
Come forth, and bring with you a heart
That watches and receives.

TRANSLATION FROM "MEDEA," *Thomas Campbell* [From *The Poetical Works of Thomas Campbell*, J. Crissy, Philadelphia, 1844.]

Tell me, ye bards, whose skill sublime
First charmed the ear of youthful Time,
With numbers wrapt in heav'nly fire;
Who bade delighted Echo swell
The trembling transport of the lyre,
The murmur of the shell,—
Why to the burst of Joy alone
Accords sweet Music's soothing tone?
Why can no bard, with magic strain
In slumbers steep the heart of pain?
While varied tones obey your sweep
The mild, the plaintive, and the deep,
Bends not despairing Grief to hear
Your golden lute, with ravished ear?
Oh! has your sweetest shell no power to bind
The fiercer pangs that shake the mind,
And lull the wrath, at whose command
Murder bares her gory hand?
When flushed with joy, the rosy throng
Weave the light dance, ye swell the song!
Cease, ye vain warblers! cease to charm
The breast with other raptures warm!
Cease! till your hand with magic strain
In slumbers steep the heart of pain!

TO NIGHT, *Percy Bysshe Shelley* [From *The Poetical Works of Percy Bysshe Shelley*, edited by Edward Dowden, Macmillan & Co., Ltd., London, 1926. Copyright, 1890, Macmillan & Co., Ltd.]

Swiftly walk o'er the western wave,
    Spirit of Night!
Out of the misty eastern cave,
Where all the long and lone daylight
Thou wovest dreams of joy and fear,
Which make thee terrible and dear—
    Swift be thy flight!

Wrap thy form in a mantle gray,
    Star-inwrought!
Blind with thine hair the eyes of Day;
Kiss her until she be wearied out;
Then wander o'er city, and sea, and land,
Touching all with thine opiate wand—
    Come, long-sought!

When I arose and saw the dawn,
  I sighed for thee;
When light rode high, and the dew was gone,
And moon lay heavy on flower and tree,
And the weary Day turned to his rest,
Lingering like an unloved guest,
  I sighed for thee.

Thy brother Death came, and cried,
  Wouldst thou me?
Thy sweet child Sleep, the filmy-eyed,
Murmured like a noontide bee,
Shall I nestle near thy side?
Wouldst thou me?—And I replied,
  No, not thee!

Death will come when thou art dead,
  Soon, too soon—
Sleep will come when thou art fled;
Of neither would I ask the boon
I ask of thee, belovèd Night—
Swift be thine approaching flight,
  Come soon, soon!

Come Back, *Arthur Hugh Clough* [From *Prose, Poetry and Drama for Oral Interpretation*, selected and arranged by William J. Farma, Harper & Brothers, New York, 1930. Copyright, 1930, William J. Farma.]

Come back, come back, across the flying foam,
We hear faint far-off voices call us home.

Come back, come back! And whither back and why?
To fan quenched hopes, forsaken schemes to try;
Walk the old fields; pace the familiar street;
Dream with the idlers, with the bards compete.
  Come back, come back?

Come back, come back; and whither and for what?
To finger idly some old Gordian knot,
Unskilled to sunder, and too weak to cleave,
And with much toil attain to half-believe.
  Come back, come back?

Come back, come back!
Back flies the foam; the hoisted flag streams back;
The long smoke wavers on the homeward track.
Back fly with winds things which the winds obey,
The strong ship follows its appointed way.

PART SIX

IMPROVING ARTICULATION

15

MOVING THE MECHANISM

Most of us wobble the tongue and the lips as we speak. We move them with the bulkiness of a bag of rags on a junk dealer's pushcart, and as a result, our speech is muffled and indistinct. Our listeners either must stand their ears at attention to hear what we are talking about or must apologetically say, "Sorry, I didn't get it."

Several such remarks daily from various persons should make us realize that we should speak more clearly and distinctly. Very frequently, however, we continue to munch over our words as though they were ice cream, and they melt in our mouths. Recently, a friend of the author received a genuine compliment. A hard-of-hearing friend told him that she had no difficulty understanding him as long as she could watch his lips. He was moving these articulatory mechanisms with precision and as a result improving upon his communicative abilities.

Every syllable of our speech will carry if we move the lips, tongue, and jaw with vigor and precision. Many of us in America need more vitality in these mechanisms. We can improve the clarity of our speaking if we become more energetic as we move these parts during speech. Unless we do this, we shall continue to embarrass others, as well as ourselves, because we shall be forced to repeat what we have said. We should be ever on the alert for failure on the part of the listener to understand what we have said. Probably the failure is not his. It is ours. We have not spoken the words clearly.

PRINCIPLES TO APPLY FOR ADEQUATE PROJECTION

Clear, distinct articulation plays a vital part in projecting the voice to the ears of the listener. This basic consideration plus a forceful air column, open resonators, and a clear, resonant tone combine to make the voice pleasing and understandable to the person "out there."

You have observed this many times when listening to plays and speeches presented in buildings with large auditoriums. When the author was in his teens, he attended frequently the Chicago Civic Theatre. Of financial necessity, he took his seat in the very last row of the balcony and marveled at the ease with which the actors were able to make him hear the lines of *The Taming of the Shrew*, *Romeo and Juliet*, and other classics. He knows now that they accomplished this, not by straining their throats and yelling, but by applying principles of good vocalization and carefully carving each of their words so that there would be no doubt as to what they had said. They did not slur over their words, omitting some sounds and swallowing others. They made every word ring clear so that there was no doubt in any listener's mind as to what had been said. They were successful in projecting their voices from the stage to the very last row.

From study of Chap. 16 you will learn some of the fundamental principles regarding the formation of specific speech sounds. If you are successful in applying this information, you will accomplish much toward projecting your voice when you begin to speak.

MAKE THE MUSCLES MOVE

As a first step in correcting mumbled, indistinct speech, you should work toward making the muscles of the lips, tongue, and jaw move with precision. You can do this if you make the effort. In fact, the tongue can be taught all sorts of tricks. At a meeting of the Speech Association of America, some pictures were presented showing a man who, through persistent practice, had learned to make his tongue turn somersaults. He had become so adept at rolling the tongue back that he could place it behind the soft palate with the greatest of ease. He could flip the tongue over so that the bottom was on top, an ability he had gained through exercising the muscles.

You would be wise to get some of the same sort of practice. Of course you do not need to go to the extreme that this man did, but you should develop your ability to move the mechanisms involved in speech and do what you can to put action into your enunciation.

If you decide to make a self-inventory, you may find that one of two conditions exist. Either the muscles of these parts are inert and flaccid, or they are tense. In either case, you need to get them ready for the highly specific movement required for speech.

EXERCISES TO ACTIVATE THE MECHANISM

If the muscles are limp you should learn to develop conscious control over them, that is, to exert mind over body and make the muscles move:

LIPS. Some exercises you can use to activate the lips are:

EXERCISE 137. Pull the lips back, making a narrow slit of the mouth, and then push them forward into a pucker.

EXERCISE 138. Push the upper lip down so that it covers the upper teeth, then relax it.

EXERCISE 139. Interchange a simple, hung-jaw look for the facial expression of Stan Laurel.

EXERCISE 140. After you have repeated each of these exercises several times and can successfully mimic a Cheshire cat, George Arliss, and Stan, you are ready to combine lip movement with sound.

Start by speaking:

1. pa . . pa . . pa . . pa (at slow speed).
2. papa . . papa . . papa (a little faster).
3. papapapapapapapapa (running one sound after the other at rapid rate).

After you have practiced the [p] sound, substitute [b] and later [m], using the same patterns.

TONGUE. When you are sure that you have the lips moving freely, start putting the tongue through its paces.

EXERCISE 141. Protrude it and move it from right to left, in these cadences:

1. Right, left . . . right, left.
2. Right, left, right . . . left, right, left . . . right, left, right.
3. Right, left . . . right, left, right . . . right, left . . . right, left, right.

EXERCISE 142. Repeat the above exercise, this time moving the tongue upward and downward.

EXERCISE 143. Open the mouth and make circular movements with the protruded tongue.

Now find yourself a piece of wood about as big around as a lead pencil. Cut it down so that it is half an inch in length. Whittle a groove in each end, making the grooves parallel. Tie a piece of string (about 3 feet in length) to the prop. Now place the prop in your mouth so that the upper front teeth sink into one groove and the lower teeth into the other groove. Hang on to the string (to avoid sucking the piece of wood into the windpipe) and give the tongue another workout. Avoid biting down on the piece of wood and thus increasing tension in the mechanism.

EXERCISE 144. Say:

to . . to . . to . . to.
do . . do . . do . . do.
todo . . todo . . todo.
todotodotodotodotodotodotodo.
goo . . goo . . goo.
dogoo . . dogoo . . dogoo.
dogooto . . dogooto.
dogootodogootodogooto.

JAW AND LIPS. EXERCISE 145. Take the tooth prop out and speak the words "sea hag," emphasizing the movement of the jaw and lips. Then try your articulators on such difficult words as "conversationalist," "anthropologist," "aluminum," "statistical." When you are really good, try the sentence "He was inebriated by the exuberance of his own verbosity," or "The monstrosity of the offense extinguished the absurdity of the man's costume."

FREEING THE MUSCLES FOR MOVEMENT

If you have checked and found that the seat of your enunciation problem is tense muscles, rather than flaccid, you should approach your problem through relaxation.

EXERCISE 146. Begin by grasping the chin with the thumb and forefinger of both hands. Hold it firmly, and allow the head to tilt backward and forward. Make the back of the neck do the work. Be careful that you do not allow the muscles of the jaw to assist in the movement.

EXERCISE 147. Move the lips into a stiff pucker and then relax them.

EXERCISE 148. Tense the tongue, and then release the tension.

Repeat each exercise[1] until you have developed considerable ability in relaxing the speech mechanisms. Carry over this ability as you talk to yourself—in practice, of course—or to another person. Pay no attention to the distinctness of the articulation.

[1] Some other exercises for developing relaxation in the muscles involved in articulation were presented by the author in his article "Cup Your Ears and Speak," *Coronet*, November, 1939, pp. 123–126.

GETTING THE RIGHT AMOUNT OF MUSCLE TONUS

After you have activated or relaxed your tongue, lips, and jaw according to your specific needs, find the middle of the road as far as muscle tonus in these parts is concerned and speak with quick precision. Put just enough energy into your speech to get easy, vigorous articulation. Then apply your principles every time you speak. At first, you will find this difficult when you talk because you will be thinking about what you are saying and you will forget to apply the principles. Read poetry and prose at first. Later, have some brief conversations during which you make a conscious effort to put your principles into use. Eventually, you will want the new patterns to *be there*, automatically going into action each time you speak. When conditions are right, your speech will be more distinct and your listeners will have no difficulty understanding what you have to say.

SOME EXERCISES FOR IMPROVING PROJECTION

Along with your efforts to improve your enunciation you should practice the following exercises:

EXERCISE 149. Stand in one corner of a large room, and whisper sentences to an imaginary person in the opposite corner. You will have to form the words very carefully and whisper loudly in order to make him hear you. Keep your throat relaxed, and speak such sentences as "It is warm today, isn't it?" and "We are having pleasant weather these days, aren't we?"

EXERCISE 150. After you have whispered the sentences across the room several times, speak them aloud. Do not tense the muscles of the jaw, throat, and larynx or attempt to speak loudly. Your voice will carry very well if you enunciate the words clearly and distinctly and apply all the principles of vocalization.

EXERCISE 151. Find an auditorium or a band shell where you can practice projecting the voice and proceed with Exercises 149 and 150. Station another person near the platform at first, then have him gradually move away. Do not increase the loudness of the voice as he moves back, but make him hear you easily.

After the mechanism has been activated sufficiently and ability to project has been improved, practice the selections on pages 174 to 175 in a large room or out of doors. Post another student at a considerable distance, and have him warn you if he fails to hear or understand what you are saying.

PRACTICE SELECTIONS

FOR MOVING THE MECHANISM

THE FIREFLIES WINK AND GLOW, *Robert Hillyer* [Reprinted from *The Seventh Hill* by Robert Hillyer, by permission of and special arrangement with Alfred A. Knopf, Inc., authorized publishers. Copyright, 1928, by the Viking Press, New York.]

The fireflies wink and glow,
The night is on the march,
The cricket clacks his castanets
And the moon hangs in the larch.
I will take my violin
And a few themes I will play:
Pizzicati for the fireflies,
Harmonies for the moonlight,
And a chord for the smell of hay.

I will play but a few bars
And when the moon has set
I will listen to the stars.

SWISS AIR, *Bret Harte* [From the works of Bret Harte, Houghton Mifflin Company, authorized publishers.]

I'm a gay tra, la, la,
With my fal, lal, la, la,
And my bright—
And my light—
Tra, la, le.
(Repeat)

Then laugh, ha, ha, ha,
And ring, ting, ling, ling,
And sing, fal, la, la,
La, la, le.
(Repeat)

LAUGHTER HOLDING BOTH HIS SIDES, *James Whitcomb Riley* [From *Afterwhiles*, by James Whitcomb Riley. Copyright, 1887, 1915, used by special permission of the publishers, Bobbs-Merrill Company.]

Ay, thou varlet! Laugh away!
All the world's a holiday!
Laugh away, and roar and shout
Till thy hoarse tongue lolleth out!
Bloat thy cheeks, and bulge thine eyes

Unto bursting; pelt thy thighs
With thy swollen palms, and roar
As thou never hast before!
Lustier! wilt thou! peal on peal!
Stiflest? Squat and grind thy heel—
Wrestle with thy loins, and then
Wheeze thee whiles, and whoop again!

THE NYMPHOLEPT, *Alan Seeger* [From *Poems* by Alan Seeger, Charles Scribner's Sons, New York, 1918. Copyright, 1916, Charles Scribner's Sons.]

There was a boy—not above childish fears—
With steps that faltered now and straining ears,
Timid, irresolute, yet dauntless still,
Who one bright dawn, when each remotest hill
Stood sharp and clear in Heaven's unclouded blue
And all Earth shimmered with fresh-beaded dew,
Risen in the first beams of the gladdening sun,
Walked up into the mountains. One by one
Each towering trunk beneath his sturdy stride
Fell back, and ever wider and more wide
The boundless prospect opened. Long he strayed,
From dawn till the last trace of slanting shade
Had vanished from the canyons, and, dismayed
At that far length to which his path had led,
He paused—at such a height where overhead
The clouds hung close, the air came thin and chill,
And all was hushed and calm and very still,
Save, from abysmal gorges, where the sound
Of tumbling waters rose, and all around
The pines, by those keen upper currents blown,
Muttered in multitudinous monotone.
Here, with the wind in lovely locks laid bare,
With arms oft raised in dedicative prayer,
Lost in mute rapture and adoring wonder,
He stood, till the far noise of noontide thunder,
Rolled down upon the muffled harmonies
Of wind and waterfall and whispering trees,
Made loneliness more lone. Some Panic fear
Would seize him then, as they who seemed to hear
In Thracian valleys or Thessalian woods
The god's hallooing wake the leafy solitudes;
I think it was the same: some piercing sense
Of Deity's pervasive immanence,
The Life that visible Nature doth indwell

Grown great and near and all but palpable . . .
He might not linger, but with winged strides
Like one pursued, fled down the mountain-sides—
Down the long ridge that edged the steep ravine,
By glade and flowery lawn and upland green,
And never paused nor felt assured again
But where the grassy foothills opened. Then,
While shadows lengthened on the plain below
And the sun vanished and the sunset-glow
Looked back upon the world with fervid eye
Through the barred windows of the western sky,
Homeward he fared, while many a look behind
Showed the receding ranges dim-outlined,
Highland and hollow where his path had lain,
Veiled in deep purple of the mountain rain.

IMPROVING PROJECTION

RULES FOR THE ROAD, *Edwin Markham* [From *Gates of Paradise* by Edwin Markham, Doubleday & Company, Inc., New York, 1924. Copyright, 1920, Edwin Markham, reprinted by permission.]

Stand straight:
Step firmly, throw your weight:
The heaven is high above your head,
The good gray road is faithful to your tread.

Be strong:
Sing to your heart a battle song:
Though hidden foemen lie in wait,
Something is in you that can smile at Fate.

Press through:
Nothing can harm if you are true.
And when the night comes, rest:
The earth is friendly as a mother's breast.

FROM "THE RAPE OF LUCRECE," *William Shakespeare* [Lines from "The Rape of Lucrece" by William Shakespeare from *Venus and Adonis, Lucrece and the Minor Poems*, edited by Albert Feuillerat. Copyright, Yale University Press, New Haven, 1927.]

O' comfort-killing Night, image of hell!
Dim register and notary of shame!
Black stage for tragedies and murders fell!

Vast sin-concealing chaos! nurse of blame!
    Grim cave of death! whispering conspirator
    With close-tongu'd treason and the ravisher!

O' hateful, vaporous, and foggy Night!
Since thou art guilty of my cureless crime,
Muster thy mists to meet the eastern light,
Make war against proportion'd course of time;
Or if thou wilt permit the sun to climb
    His wonted height, yet ere he go to bed,
    Knit poisonous clouds about his golden head.

FROM "OF TRUTH," *Francis Bacon, Lord Verulam* [From *Bacon's Essays*, introduced by Sir Henry Newbolt, Thomas Nelson & Sons, Ltd., London.]

The poet that beautified the sect that was otherwise inferior to the rest, saith yet excellently well: *It is a pleasure to stand upon the shore, and to see ships tost upon the sea: a pleasure to stand in the window of a castle, and to see a battle and the adventures thereof below: but no pleasure is comparable to the standing upon the vantage ground of truth* (a hill not to be commanded, and where the air is always clear and serene), *and to see the errors, and wanderings, and mists, and tempests, in the vale below:* so always that this prospect be with pity, and not with swelling or pride. Certainly, it is heaven upon earth, to have a man's mind move in charity, rest in providence, and turn upon the poles of truth.

16

ARTICULATING THE CONSONANTS AND VOWELS

The college student or graduate is expected to have cultured speech because of the influences of his academic environment and his opportunity to correct defects. His teachers and other students may call his attention to irregularities that they observe, and if he is alert, he will not let such criticisms pass without doing something about them. His pride in his speech and his desire to excel in communicating his ideas to his listeners should cause him to seek improvement immediately.

Man was given several means of informing others of his ideas and emotions. He lets people know what he thinks, feels, and wants through gestures, facial expressions, and speech. The last capability is his greatest gift of communication because it can be the most efficient of all in expressing complex thoughts and feelings. Untrained and unpolished, however, it operates at only a fraction of its peak efficiency and often implies carelessness on the part of the student. In some instances, his failure to use clear, distinct articulation results from an undoing of earlier good work and high standards in the home.

Educated society demands that members of their own cultural level speak well. A teen-age girl was brought to the clinic recently by her wealthy foster parents. The girl's articulation was faulty as a result of the influences of her early years in a poverty-stricken home in New York City. Her new parents had been quick to recognize her deficiency. They realized that she would need superior speech in her new home, and they wanted her to have the training that would prepare her to meet the high standards set by their associates.

The kind of training a child receives in the home and at school plays a vital role in the kind of speech he will have in later years. A case in point is that of a woman whom the author met casually at a filling station where her husband works. Although she was apparently quite poor, her articulation had all the marks of culture and refinement. A compliment from the author on her excellent speech prompted her to tell him that her father had stimulated the very best of diction in his family and would allow no slang or careless articulation. "If my speech is good, I owe the debt to my father," she confided. "His lessons were so well taught I seldom become careless."

Although good habits may be firmly fixed, the student sometimes allows his articulation to become slovenly. At home, in the student club, and even in classes during recitations he may slump in his speech, and the listener finds it difficult to understand what he is saying. The student who continues to speak in this manner over a long period may find that his poor speech patterns become habitual and that abilities he may have had disappear. The student needs to make an effort to speak clearly in every speaking situation. Lazy articulation can result only in distorted speech sounds, mumbling, and poor communication.

The physiological mechanisms involved in articulation perform other functions than speech. Basically, they serve the purposes of chewing, sucking, and swallowing. Speech is a superimposed (or *overlaid*) function and tends to be less stable than the more basic functions. Were it not for our hearing, which has already been shown as an important guide for speech, the instability of the superimposed function would be even greater. Therefore, care in articulation of the vowels and consonants, as well as ear training, becomes increasingly important for good speech.

CONSONANT ARTICULATION

The consonant sounds are defined as speech sounds that result from hindering, diverting, or stopping the breath stream. There is no flowing from one sound into another. For example, in the word *see*, the consonant *s* is formed because the breath coming through the oral cavity is restricted by the tongue and there is a minute period of silence between the consonant and vowel. In the word *am*, the vowel and consonant are separated because the breath stream is diverted from the oral to the nasal cavity. In the word *bar*, the outflowing air is completely stopped as pressure is built up behind closed lips until the open vowel gives it release.

We were taught in school that there are twenty-one consonants and that all letters in our alphabet which are not vowels are consonants.

Through continuous speech association, however, the ear actually isolates approximately twenty-five separate nonvowel sounds (see list below).

The International Phonetic Alphabet, which is the accepted scientific codification of sounds, gives us a symbol for each of the consonants. For instance, instead of calling the letter *t*, "tee," it is shown as an isolated sound—a voiceless explosion. In the word *ate*, the final sound can be articulated distinctly. First, there is the vocalization of the vowel *a* (or phonetically [e]), then the tongue tip is placed behind the upper gum ridge. Air pressure in the mouth behind the tongue is built up, and with the release of the tongue, the desired sound is exploded.

To clarify this explanation further, the following list of consonant sounds, their phonetic symbols, word examples, and sonancy are provided. The word "sonant" means *voiced*, that is, sounds resulting from vocal-fold vibration. Sonants identify fifteen of the twenty-five consonant sounds. The remaining ten are called *surds*, or unvoiced sounds.

[m] as in *M*ary, ha*mm*er, hi*m* (voiced).
[n] as in *n*ot, a*nn*oy, wi*n* (voiced).
[ŋ] as in si*ng*, fra*n*k, ga*ng* (voiced).
[p] as in *p*ay, a*pp*le, u*p* (unvoiced).
[b] as in *b*oy, a*b*le, ca*b* (voiced).
[t] as in *t*able, bu*tt*er, a*t* (unvoiced).
[d] as in *d*o, sa*dd*le, a*dd* (voiced).
[k] as in *k*ing, a*c*cept, bac*k* (unvoiced).
[g] as in *g*et, a*g*o, e*gg* (voiced).
[f] as in *f*in, o*f*ten, lau*gh* (unvoiced).
[v] as in *v*ery, a*v*ow, o*f* (voiced).
[θ] as in *th*ing, e*th*er, ba*th* (unvoiced).
[ð] as in *th*e, mo*th*er, ba*th*e (voiced).
[s] as in *s*ee, li*st*en, a*ce* (unvoiced).
[z] as in *z*oo, scis*s*ors, ha*z*e (voiced).
[ʃ] as in *sh*ip, ba*sh*ful, la*sh* (unvoiced).
[ʒ] as in *a*zure, beig*e*, trea*s*ure (voiced).
[tʃ] as in *ch*in, ques*t*ion, hat*ch* (unvoiced).
[dʒ] as in *g*em, a*g*ed, bri*dg*e (voiced).
[h] as in *h*ow, a*h*oy, *wh*o (unvoiced).
[hw] as in *wh*en, a*wh*ile, *wh*at (unvoiced).
[w] as in *w*on, *qu*ip, a*w*ay (voiced).
[j] as in *y*ou, *y*ellow, on*i*on (voiced).
[r] as in *r*ed, *wr*ight, ca*r* (voiced).
[l] as in *l*imb, a*ll*ow, pa*l* (voiced).

Some of these symbols may appear to be quite foreign. Yet through the medium of phonetics it is possible to assign each code letter a sound which, when articulated, will achieve a consistent acoustical result. Unlike the inconsistencies of sound-letter alliances that frequently exist in our English alphabet ([v], of; [ng], fra*n*k; [z], sci*s*sor*s*; [f], lau*gh*) the phonetic system assures the speaker of accurate articulation and pronunciation.

EXERCISES IN CONSONANT ARTICULATION

EXERCISE 152. Practice the consonant sounds in the phonetic alphabet while watching the oral formation in a mirror. In all the articulation work, it is advisable to have someone with excellent speech and a sensitive ear guide you in your work.

EXERCISE 153. The *nasal sounds*—[m], [n], [ng]—are produced by relaxing the soft palate and allowing the tones to pass into the nasal passageways. Prolong the specified sound in the sentences which follow. Listen to the nasal resonance; feel the vibration in the nose.

[m] The man came home from the mill in the morning.
Our plum tree bore a diadem of blossoms.
Matt climbed out on the small limb.
[n] No one will ever find the girl named Anne.
Out in the garden, Jane played with the kitten.
Neither man nor woman wants to be unhappy.
[ŋ] Frank sang a song in a foreign language.
This morning, I will bring the donkey.
The angle worm hung on the hook.

EXERCISE 154. The *plosives*—[p], [b], [t], [d], [k], [g], [tʃ], [dʒ]—are exploded on the outflowing breath stream. The [b], [d], [g], and [dʒ] are voiced, while the [p], [t], [d], [k], and [tʃ] are unvoiced. Since these sounds cannot be prolonged, accent the explosion. Give them force so that they become audible not only to yourself but to your listeners.

[p] Some people borrow from Peter to pay Paul.
The man was very surprised to see his picture in the paper.
Papa put the potatoes in the pail.
[b] Bill threw the ball into the old tub.
I asked Bob to set the table while I attended the baby.
Nobody missed the boy's birthday party.
[t] I slept all night on the terribly dirty train.
The teacher taught us to say "little" and "butter."
What time does Tilly leave the store?
[d] I saw the children run through the garden.
Doris sat by the window and listened to the pounding rain.

[k] Because of the accident, Dick never walked again.
Could you keep a secret about the cake?
I cannot visit your cottage on my vacation.
[g] I stood aghast as he released the trigger on the gun.
From the green bag she extracted two gorgeous rubies.
Please go with me to the garage.
[tʃ] The child could not reach the latch.
From the church tower, chimes beckoned the worshipers.
The old bachelor would always cheat at chequers.
[dʒ] Jim walked out on the bridge, then jumped.
They will never serve orange juice in jail.
The judge asked the jury for their decision.

EXERCISE 155. The *fricatives*—[f], [v], [θ], [ð], [s], [z], [ʃ], [ʒ], [h], [hw]—are articulated as a result of friction of the outflowing air as it is forced through the front teeth and the lips. The [v], [ð], [z], and [ʒ] are voiced.

[f] The coffee, by breakfast, had lost its flavor.
If you won't laugh, I'll prophesy your future.
Five of the fire fighters were overcome by smoke.
[v] Vera went to Vermont on her vacation.
Of all the gloves, I am most fond of the violet pair.
Vinegar will quickly dissolve a natural pearl.
[θ] I was thankful I had left the theater before the earthquake struck.
I lived through a thousand deaths these three days.
Nothing could soothe Cathy when she had a toothache.
[ð] Mother and father gave me some new clothes.
We almost smothered during the hot weather.
The other evening I bathed in the lake.
[s] If there is a mistake in your [s] sound, you may have a lisp.
Susie hates school almost as much as her sister Grace.
Last year I spent Christmas in France.
[z] The zebra at the zoo was very lazy.
My cousin does not like his brothers and sisters.
We spent a pleasant evening listening to music.
[ʃ] Shall I finish the washing after lunch?
Fresh fish fried in butter makes a delicious dish.
Ocean City is a popular seashore resort.
[ʒ] It was a pleasure to see a television show.
The explosion rocked the garage.
The girl applied the rouge very casually.

EXERCISE 156. The *semivowel sounds*—[r], [l], [w], [j]—are voiced and can be prolonged. They possess such vowel properties as vocalization, oral resonance, and a minor degree of restriction.

[r] Every evening the rabbits run through the grass.
I will be ready to write that rush material.
"Ring down the curtain," cried the stage manager.

[l] The film played to the lower class movie lover.
The children all waved "Hello" on their way to school.
Last night, about eleven o'clock, all the lights went out.

[w] Will you walk with me on my way home?
I wish that women would stop wearing silly hats.
This liverwurst sandwich tastes like seaweed.

[j] Yesterday I amused myself on my yacht.
The young boy yawned at the familiar story.
If you like onions, I have a million out in the yard.

VOWEL ARTICULATION

A vowel sound demands first vocalization at the laryngeal level of the speech mechanism, then modification in the pharyngeal and oral cavities. Each vowel is open, sonorous and can be prolonged or continued. It is impossible to blend consonants, but vowels will connect smoothly because there is little restriction at the lips or inside the mouth. Each vowel is formed by specific alterations of the pharyngeal muscles, soft palate, tongue, jaw openings, and lips.

The following thirteen phonetic vowel sounds and four vowel blends (the diphthongs) represent distinct sounds used in standard American speech.

[i] as in *e*asy, s*ee*d, b*e*.
[ɪ] as in *i*t, d*i*d, cand*y*.
[e] as in *a*te, s*a*ble, del*ay*.
[ɛ] as in *e*very, d*ea*d, b*e*t.
[æ] as in *a*tom, d*a*d, att*a*ck.
[ɑ] as in *ah*, f*a*ther, t*au*ght.
[ɔ] as in *aw*e, t*a*ll, j*aw*.
[o] as in *o*bey, al*o*ne, n*o*.
[ʊ] as in b*oo*k, p*u*ll, b*u*sh.
[u] as in *oo*ze, m*oo*n, t*o*.
[ɝ] as in *ur*n, w*or*k, moth*er*.
[ʌ] as in *u*p, m*u*ch, j*u*st (occurs in accented syllables).
[ə] as in *a*bove, b*a*nan*a*, sof*a* (occurs in unaccented syllables).
[aɪ] as in *i*ce, t*i*de, b*uy*.
[aʊ] as in *ou*r, br*ow*n, th*ou*.
[ɔɪ] as in *oi*l, l*oy*al, b*oy*.
[ju] as in *u*se, T*ue*sday, n*ew*.

Whereas the consonants give intelligibility to speech, the vowels give body or carrying power to words. For example, if the word "pet" is spoken, minus the vowel, a person standing a few feet away will have a difficult time hearing the weak, plosive consonants *p* and *t*. But with the addition of the vowel sound, the word can be projected easily. Therefore, the amount of energy the vowels receive correspondingly reflect the intensity of the voice.

To a great degree, the vowel sounds are responsible for regional accents. Not only the rhythm of words but the articulation of the vowels identify a person's speech background. How he says the following words gives the listener an objective insight into his past or present environment:

[nɑt] or [nɔt]; [əbaut] or [əbut]; [kɑr] or [kær]; [wɑtʒ] or [wɔtʒ]; [ɑnt] or [ænt]; [krik] or [krɪk]; [baɪ] or [bɑ:ɪ]; [gɝl] or [gɔɪl]; [dɪr] or [dɪə]

Except for the words [gɔɪl] and [əbut], which are not accepted pronunciations, there is little reason for a person to alter his manner of speaking these words provided he uses the pronunciation of the majority of educated speakers in his given speech area.

The person who has acquired bad habits of vowel articulation or who is striving to change his accent should work on an extensive program of consonant and vowel articulation as well as training the ear to control the new tone patterns which he wishes to adopt.

There are five vowel letters in our English alphabet that do the work of seventeen phonetic speech sounds. An [a] sound can be articulated differently in each of these words: *a*bout, *a*ble, b*a*d, *a*ll, c*a*r, and c*a*re. There are as many variations for the [o] sound, and the remaining vowels *e*, *i*, and *u* change their sound values according to standard pronunciations.

EXERCISES IN VOWEL ARTICULATION

EXERCISE 157. Practice the vowel sounds in the phonetic alphabet, watching the oral function in a mirror.

EXERCISE 158. The following practice groups contain the vowel in isolation, in words, and in sentences. It is suggested that the isolated sound first be vocalized so that an awareness of its acoustical properties is developed. Then prolong the sound in each of the words.

[i] need, beast, sleep, me, disagree, we, please, employed, Tennessee, three, east, meat, decree, ego, eaten, leak, freak, nicotine, beam, dungaree.

A decree from the king prohibited the eating of meat on Mondays.
Each of us needs a certain amount of sleep every day.
I will not disagree that Tennessee has beautiful green hills.

[ɪ] big, India, scenario, dizzy, mix, its, into, wig, little, distant, pits, bid, hill, six, pig, thing, middle, zip, brisk, idiot, issue, pick, gig, did.

In this week's issue of *Report*, India is given a pictorial review.
The ship tossed dizzily on the big waves.
Jim became very irritated when I criticized his scenario.

[e] ate, able, hay, make, Fay, eight, ape, eighty-eight, chaos, slay, acre, sail, radio, Yale, fail, Asia, today, consommé, apron, locate, daily, résumé, hate.

I am afraid that I will be late for the play.
Every day, the amiable old man wheeled the baby in the sun.
When you play this game, turn the aces face up.

[ɛ] met, edible, elephant, deck, beg, Kent, men, pen, rents, head, then, edge, devil, friend, sell, test, pencil, shell, felony, pep, hell, never, guess, red.

The men, with their elephant, lead the parade.
You could never guess the number of eggs in the omelet.
Greg would not sell his red boat to Mr. Kent.

[æ] add, map, animal, vance, fan, after, catch, ran, Astor, pack, lag, mat, agony, candy, avenue, sad, atom, lamp, basket, family, absent, addict, apple, rat.

In Manhattan, the Astor Hotel is a familiar landmark.
Animals were stampeding in front of flames.
The rat climbed into the basket and ate the candy.

[ɑ] art, car, father, army, author, psalm, not, calm, dock, fawn, card, Tom, don, honest, yon, bomb, bazaar, hot, mop, farmer, bar, doctor, flog, cosmic.

Father gave me a car when I returned from the army.
The author of the popular novel used to be a doctor.
Honestly, I am not familiar with card games.

[ɔ] walk, taught, Paul, saw, on, taught, haughty, gauze, autumn, awful, salt, auto, often, wrought, awl, dawn, corpse, auction, haul, audible, form, haunt, law, all.

In the autumn we always drove into the mountains to see deer and faun.
Paul and I would walk to the lake to see the sun at dawn.
The call for help, from under the straw, was hardly audible.

[o] row, only, dow, obey, over, coat, soap, window, solo, odor, hello, ocean, open, though, soul, pope, goal, phone, wholly, stone, omen, yellow, known, polo, hoe.

His coat was hanging by the open window.
Joan would ride her pony along the shore of the ocean.
The cold snow came tiptoeing across the roof.

[ʊ] book, hood, could, cook, hoof, put, look, should, good, wood, bush, took, hook, wool, pull, good, brook, full, rook, shook, cushion, push, crooks, poor, foot, cuckoo.

I took the cushion and sat at the foot of the tree.
I could not put any more wood into the shed.
There are no good crooks, and they usually die poor.

[u] blue, do, Sioux, school, moon, shoes, tattoo, June, spoon, who, grew, to, root, undo, through, blew, ooze, igloo, boot, noon, glue, group, brew, soothe.

These boots were made by Sioux Indians.
Children always hurry to the last day of school in June.
It is true that the root grew into the living room.

[ɝ] were, bird, work, Herman, absurd, herd, curl, sir, purr, earn, hurt, myrrh, burn, burst, fern, further, pearl, world, curb, hurl, inert, irk, girl, leather.

"How much further is the circus?" asked Herman.
The burn did not hurt, but his leather jacket was ruined.
On his way from work, a car hurled him to the curb.

[ʌ] dove, but, ugly, rub, flood, upper, drum, come, up, us, young, duck, oven, utter, cup, dumb, bum, umpire, mother, gun, huckster, mumps, won, summer, southern.

The flood left mud an inch thick in our oven.
Last Sunday we had duck for supper.
The usher escorted us to the upper balcony.

[ə] above, camera, balloon, government, soda, alive, possible, opened, given, enemies, ago, China, conclude, quota, relative, papa, asleep, pilot, Dana, away, sofa, avow.

We concluded it was not possible to stay alive in a vacuum.
The enemies of the government were massacred.
The camera, when opened, contained jade from China.

[aɪ] dye, idle, buy, sigh, tight, ire, find, light, I, cry, wine, ice, lime, type, ivory, idea, shine, mile, sky, iodine, pie, died, miter, iota, jai alai, tie.

I had to dry my clothes in the sunshine.
In the fading light, we saw an iceberg about a mile from shore.
She began to cry when we could not find the ivory.

[aʊ] house, now, Faust, brow, outside, our, town, brown, about, mouth, found, drought, gout, cowl, plough, count, devour, endow, loud, how, allow, crowded, owl.

In back of the brown house was a garden of flowers.
The mouse ran outdoors and down the cellar wall.
We found the old owl on a bough in the tree.

[ɔɪ] oil, Savoy, toiler, loin, ointment, point, voice, noise, poison, boy, coil, oyster, Roy, poise, voile, soy, employ, enjoyable, hoi polloi, joist, deploy, foil.

Roy always enjoyed eating fried oysters.
He pointed to the coiling, poisonous snake.
The boy in the corduroy suit caught the coin.

[ju] Tuesday, tune, Sue, new, use, music, view, neutrality, steward, duty, union, review, ewe, huge, feud, few, use, Buick, museum, fugue, utility, universe, beauty.

Next Tuesday, Sue gives her music recital.
The new Buick was really a beauty.
A few people think that neutrality is universal stagnation.

PRACTICE SELECTIONS

THE CATARACT OF LODORE, *Robert Southey* [From *The Poetical Works of Robert Southey,* The Thomas Y. Crowell Company, New York, 1909.]

"How does the Water
Come down at Lodore?"
My little boy ask'd me
Thus, once on a time;
And moreover he tasked me
To tell him in rhyme.
Anon at the word,
There first came one daughter
And then came another,
To second and third
The request of their brother,
And to hear how the water
Comes down at Lodore,
With its rush and its roar,
As many a time
They had seen it before.
So I told them in rhyme,
For of rhymes I had store:
And 'twas in my vocation
For their recreation
That so I should sing;
Because I was Laureate
To them and the King.
From its sources which well
In the Tarn on the fell;
From its fountains
In the mountains,
Its rills and its gills;
Through moss and through brake,
It runs and it creeps
For awhile, till it sleeps
In its own little Lake.
And thence at departing,
Awakening and starting,
It runs through the reeds
And away it proceeds,
Through meadow and glade,
In sun and in shade,
And through the wood-shelter,
Among crags in its flurry,

Helter-skelter,
Hurry-scurry.
Here it comes sparkling,
And there it lies darkling;
Now smoking and frothing
Its tumult and wrath in,
Till in this rapid race
On which it is bent,
It reaches the place
Of its steep descent.
The Cataract strong
Then plunges along,
Striking and raging
As if a war waging
Its caverns and rocks among:
Rising and leaping,
Sinking and creeping,
Swelling and sweeping,
Showering and springing,
Flying and flinging,
Writhing and ringing,
Eddying and whisking,
Spouting and frisking,
Turning and twisting,
Around and around
With endless rebound!
Smiting and fighting,
A sight to delight in;
Confounding, astounding,
Dizzying and deafening the ear with its
sound.

Collecting, projecting,
Receding and speeding,
And shocking and rocking,
And darting and parting,
And threading and spreading,
And whizzing and hissing,
And dripping and skipping,
And hitting and splitting,
And shining and twining,
And rattling and battling,
And shaking and quaking,
And pouring and roaring,
And waving and raving,
And tossing and crossing,

And flowing and going,
And running and stunning,
And foaming and roaming,
And dinning and spinning,
And dropping and hopping,
And working and jerking,
And guggling and struggling,
And heaving and cleaving,
And moaning and groaning;
And glittering and frittering,
And gathering and feathering,
And whitening and brightening,
And quivering and shivering,
And hurrying and skurrying,
And thundering and floundering;

Dividing and gliding and sliding,
And falling and brawling and sprawling,
And driving and riving and striving,
And sprinkling and twinkling and wrinkling,
And sounding and bounding and rounding,
And bubbling and troubling and doubling,
And grumbling and rumbling and tumbling,
And clattering and battering and shattering;

Retreating and beating and meeting and sheeting,
Delaying and straying and playing and spraying,
Advancing and prancing and glancing and dancing,
Recoiling, turmoiling and toiling and boiling,
And gleaming and streaming and steaming and beaming,
And rushing and flushing and brushing and gushing,
And flapping and rapping and clapping and slapping,
And curling and whirling and purling and twirling,
And thumping and plumping and bumping and jumping,
And dashing and flashing and splashing and clashing;
And so never ending, but always descending,
Sounds and motions for ever and ever are blending,
All at once and all o'er, with a mighty uproar,
And this way the Water comes down at Lodore.

17

PRONOUNCING THE WORDS

In this radio and television age, we are more concerned with audible speech than we are with the printed symbol.

Changes in the writing of words and sentences—which is a secondary attempt to symbolize language—has lagged far behind alterations in the spoken sounds. A tremendous problem in pronunciation has been created by our tendency to hang onto the traditional representations of sound in spelling while on the other hand we have been very flexible in our tendency to change the audible factors. As a result, spoken and written English are markedly inconsistent. We have progressed to the point where forty-four English sounds are now represented by at least two hundred and fifty spellings. It seems that eventually the differences existing between spelling and pronunciation will become so chaotic that a revolution in the written symbol must occur. The obvious solution to the problem is to reduce the number of visual symbols representing each phoneme (or sound family) and thereby make our spelling actually phonetic. Thus far, attempts to simplify the spelling have met with only a small measure of acceptance.

PROBLEMS OF PRONUNCIATION

INCONSISTENCY IN VOWELS. Although there is little hope for immediate adoption of phonetic spelling, such a change would correct the present system of spelling, which allows the letter *o* to represent different sounds in woman, women, does, shoes, hoes, dog, and not. Under such a system the sound called "short i" could not be represented as it is now by more than twenty different spellings. Since such vagaries and inconsistencies do exist in present spelling, we are forced to use a system of diacritical marks (never completely accurate) to give the various values to the vowels in specific spellings.

UNSTRESSING THE VOWELS. Even with the use of these markings we do not have a valuable concept of vowel sounds unless the words are marked as they sound in connected discourse. The pronunciation of *the* and *a* as articles are usually thought of in connection with this problem of reducing or unstressing the vowels; they characterize the problem rather than represent it. All the vowels—*a*, *e*, *i*, *o*, and *u*—occur in the unstressed form and appear in audible speech as the phoneme [ə], pronounced [uh]. This same principle of reducing the value of certain sounds leads in discourse to the complete elimination of some vowel and consonant sounds. When we say "bread and butter" the *n* is all that is heard from the spelling *and*. It would appear ridiculous to pronounce words in discourse as they are pronounced in isolation.

SILENT AND VARIANT CONSONANTS. Difficulty in pronunciation of the consonant sounds as they appear in spelling is also obvious. Many letters in words are completely silent and in other words have very small audible value given them. Instances such as su*b*tle, *k*new, *g*nat, and thou*gh* are all too numerous. Moreover, in many cases the consonant sound is produced as though it were another sound; for example, the *s* in plurals is commonly [z], the suffix *ed* is frequently [t], and the initial *s* is often [sh].

ACCENT. When words are so constructed that the combinations of sounds are grouped together in syllables, the problem of accent arises. There are no good rules for knowledge of accent, and the only practical solution is either to hear the accent placed correctly or to refer to the dictionary. Fortunately, the reading of the dictionary in reference to accent is an easy matter.

REGIONAL DIFFERENCES. In *The Grapes of Wrath* John Steinbeck called attention to differences in pronunciation. "'Everybody says words different,' said Ivy. 'Arkansas folks says 'em different, and Oklahomy folks says 'em different. And we seen a lady from Massachusetts, an' she said 'em differentest of all. Couldn' hardly make out what she was saying.'"

There is no standard pronunciation for the entire United States, for there are at least three general areas within our country which present distinctive characteristics. These regions are known as Eastern, Southern, and General American. Roughly, about 70 per cent of our population speak General American dialect, about 20 per cent speak the Southern dialect, and about 10 per cent the Eastern dialect. Because of the mobility of the population, these regional differences are not so marked as formerly, and it is not uncommon to find whole islands of Eastern or General American in areas once almost entirely Southern. Similarly, much Southern dialect may be found in Eastern and General American regions.

The chief difference between the regional dialects is one of vowel quality, although the dropping of or the addition of the [r] sound is probably more spectacular. Dialectical differences within each region are also quite marked and complicate the attempt to set up a standard of pronunciation. Common sense would seem to dictate that there should be no attempt to install any one of the American dialects as a favorite but that substandard pronunciations (as judged by the usage of the majority of the educated speakers within any area) should be eliminated. With no attempt to cultivate a standard even within a region, it is conceivable that pronunciation might become so chaotic that communication of thought would become difficult.

LEVELS OF USAGE. It would be well to recognize that pronunciation is more careful on some occasions than on others. On informal occasions a use of colloquial pronunciation might be perfectly acceptable, whereas the same usage might not fit the needs of the formal occasion. Let us remember that there is no "right way" to pronounce words but that there may be an *acceptable way* to pronounce words depending upon the region, the audience, and the formality of the occasion. Already too many individuals with arbitrary standards have set themselves up as authorities on pronunciation and have added to the confusion. Clarity in communication and social acceptability are the best and probably the only standards that can be maintained. The job is to cultivate such standards throughout our educational system.

STUDY OF PRONUNCIATION

Good advice for students interested in pronunciation would be (1) to acquire a working knowledge of the phonetic alphabet and (2) through this study, to achieve a sensitivity to speech sounds.

The use of the alphabet is an efficient training device because it more accurately describes in visual symbols what happens in speech. Consult the dictionary often, and develop an acute awareness of spoken language. To prevent errors, check the pronunciation of strange words before using them. Spelling alone is not sufficiently accurate, and the pronunciation of words heard only once fades in exactness before the occasion to use them arises.

PRONUNCIATION ERRORS. Pronunciation errors consist of the following types:

1. Incorrect production of an individual sound or sounds in a word. This error usually occurs because the wrong phonemic value is given to the vowel in the spelling or because silent letters are given values.

   git for *get*.
   subtle for *su(b)tle*.
   jest for *just*.
   sich for *such*.
   aig for *egg*.
   ketch for *catch*.
   sody for *soda*.
   deef for *deaf*.
   pore for *poor*.
   hern for *hers*.

2. Addition of sound elements not actually present in the word.

   athalete for *athlete*.
   filum for *film*.
   hisn for *his*.
   idear for *idea*.
   stastistics for *statistics*.
   colyum for *column*.

3. Omission of a sound or sounds which should be present in the word.

   reco(n)*nize* for *recognize*.
   su( )*prise* for *surprise*.
   hep for *help*.
   yestiddy for *yesterday*.
   sommer for *somewhere*.
   allus for *always*.

4. Reversing the positions of sounds in the word.

   preform for *perform*.
   prespiration for *perspiration*.
   modren for *modern*.
   calvary for *cavalry*.
   hunderd for *hundred*.
   interduce for *introduce*.

5. Faulty contractions in rapidly spoken phrases or sentences. This error might be classed as omissions, although the problem is not completely identical.

   Wha-cha-doin?
   When-ya-goin?
   smatter? for *what's the matter?*
   zatso? for *is that so?*

6. Incorrect placing of syllabic accent. This error is due often to lack of knowledge concerning syllabication.

   pre fer' a ble for *pref' er a ble*.
   pre' late for *prel' ate*.
   mu ni cip' al for *mu nic' i pal*.
   sup pli' ant for *sup' pli ant*.
   hos pi tal' for *hos' pit al*.
   sec' re tive for *se cre' tive*.

RULES OF PRONUNCIATION. Adequate rules for pronunciation are not possible, but the following list may be of some help:

1. The *e* of the suffix *ed* is silent except for infinitive forms ending in *d* or *t*. The suffix is then pronounced [ɪd] or [əd] (pad, [pæd]; padded, [pædɪd]).
2. The suffix *ed* is pronounced [t] when the infinitive ends in a voiceless consonant (stop, [stɑp]; stopped, [stɑpt]).
3. The suffix *ed* is pronounced [d] when the infinitive ends in a vowel or voiced consonant (call, [kɔl]; called, [kɔld]) (drag, [dræg]; dragged, [drægd]).
4. The *s* or *es* of the third person singular is pronounced [ɪz] or [əz] if the infinitive ends in [s], [z], [ʃ], [ʒ], [tʃ], or [dʒ] (lose, [luz]; loses, [luzəz]).
5. The *s* of the third person singular following any voiced sound except [dʒ], [z], or [ʒ] is pronounced [z] (run, [rʌn]; runs, [rʌnz]).
6. The *s* of the third person singular of any voiceless consonant except [s], [tʃ], [ʃ] is pronounced [s] (walk, [wɔk]; walks, [wɔks]).
7. The *s* of the plural noun is pronounced [s] if the singular form of the noun ends in [p], [*t*], [k], [f], or [*θ*] (rock, [rɑk]; rocks, [rɑks]) (walk, [wɔk]; walks, [wɔks]).
8. Most of the other nouns will form the plural by adding the [z] sound (head, [hɛd]; heads, [hɛdz]).
9. The *es* of the plural noun is pronounced [ɪz] or [əz] if the singular form ends in [s], [z], [ʃ], [ʒ], [tʃ], [dʒ] (bus, [bʌs]; buses, [bʌsɪz]) (horse, [hɔrs]; [hɔrzəz]).
10. When nouns and verbs have the same spelling, the noun is usually accented on the first syllable and the verb on the second (noun, ′contract, [′kantrækt]; verb, con′tract, [kən′trækt]). Not only does the accent differ from verb to noun, but the first vowel undergoes change also.
11. Most *ile* endings are pronounced [əl] (virile, [vɪrəl]). Some *ile* endings become [ɑɪl] (quartile, [kwɔrtɑɪl]).
12. The letter *t* preceded by *s* or *f* in the endings *tle* and *ten* is silent (bustle, hasten).
13. The letter *n* when preceded by *m* or *l* in the same syllable is usually silent (hymn, kiln).
14. When the letter *l* is followed by *m* in the same syllable, it is silent (palm, calm).
15. Many other rules on silent letters need not be considered here, since they cause little or no trouble.

EXERCISES IN PRONUNCIATION

EXERCISE 159. Listen for pronunciations as heard on the radio. Check those pronunciations which seem impossible variants to you. Notice the difference in the vowel quality of the same words used by speakers of various areas.

EXERCISE 160. Keep a list of words that bother you from the standpoint of pronunciation. Look up these words, and make a point of using them in conversations with fellow students.

EXERCISE 161. Make a list of difficult proper names of artists and composers and place names. Check these in the biographical section of Webster's dictionary or in the Kenyon and Knott Pronouncing Dictionary.

PART SEVEN

IMPROVING RATE OF UTTERANCE AND SPEECH RHYTHM

18

IMPROVING RATE OF UTTERANCE

The rate of utterance may be considered defective if it is very rapid, exceedingly slow, or monotonous. Staccato speech brings forth more comments from listeners than either of the others because, with this irregularity, the listener has great difficulty understanding what has been said. Labored and monotonous rates have equally bad effects because they fail to hold the auditor's attention; frequently his mind will wander before the speaker has made his point. When the rate is slow or monotonous, the voice fails to express thoughts and feelings. The person who takes more than two seconds to say, "I'm just bubblin' over with enthusiasm!" appears funny because of the incongruity of the idea expressed and the rate of utterance. Of course, there are times when persons speak at a slower rate than usual—for example, when they are in deep thought—but in general the rate varies around the average used in casual conversation.

TO CORRECT RAPID RATE

Conscious control, general and specific relaxation, and careful articulation should be applied to correct staccato rate when rapidity of utterance results in the failure to communicate ideas. Parents frequently tell their offspring to slow down while they are speaking. They seem to think that this command is all that is required to correct poor articulation, defects of voice, and disorders of fluency. They would get much better results if they would suggest that the child try to relax before and during speech, and they would do much to improve the emotional status of the child by attacking the basic problem.

So few persons operate on the "slow down" or "stop" basis when it comes to changing habits or altering forms of conduct that they need to be told what *to do* and not what *not to do.* If what you are doing is wrong, you can correct it only by doing the same thing in a different manner or by doing something else. If you talk too rapidly and what you say cannot be understood, you need to be told to try to relax generally, establish the proper tonicity in the vocal and articulatory mechanisms, and speak distinctly. If you do these things, your hearers are able to understand you because you form the sounds more clearly and decrease the speed of utterance.

TO CORRECT LABORED SPEECH

Many persons who slowly drag out sentences need to pay some attention to the condition of their health. Since speech is superimposed upon muscles, nerves, and glands, these structures must be in good condition to support the finely coordinated and integrated activities required for speech. When persons are ill, undernourished, or tired, their speech loses its dynamic quality. The intensity will be less, there will be "breaks," and the entire pattern will suffer in many respects. In most cases, the rate will be markedly slower than usual. As health improves, the voice and articulation will more closely approximate normal. The rate of utterance will increase, and there will be greater variety in the speaking voice.

It seems strange to suggest deliberation (thought during logical pauses) as a means of improving labored speech, but the author believes that, if the speaker takes time out to collect his thoughts at the periods, commas, and semicolons, he will speak with great fluency in between these brief stops. Naturally, too much time should not be allowed for this, because the rate of utterance may be slowed down seriously. Just enough time is required to think back on what has been said and then proceed with the next phrase. We would profit, too, by speaking in short sentences and avoiding lengthy dissertations. Instead of taking up a minute and a half at one time in a conversation, the contribution might be divided into three separate half minutes.

EXERCISES

TO CORRECT MONOTONOUS RATE

The monotonous rate has the notorious reputation for dulling the listener's sensibilities and lulling him into a sound slumber.

EXERCISE 162. Use the following patterns as you practice varying the rate of speaking. Be careful to keep the pitch and intensity at your average as you count from 1 to 8. Let the dots between the numbers indicate the length of the pause.

1 2 3 4 5 6 7 8
1 . 2 . 3 . 4 . 5 . 6 . 7 . 8
1 . 2 3 . 4 . 5 6 . 7 . 8
1 2 . 3 4 . 5 6 . 7 8
1 . 2 3 4 . 5 . 6 7 8
1 . . 2 . . 3 . . 4 . . 5 6 7 8
1 2 . . 3 4 5 . 6 . 7 . . 8
1 . . . 2 3 4 . 5 . . 6 . . 7 8

Use a metronome to help you establish the rhythm and to measure the length of time between the counts. Each click of the metronome should indicate a number or a dot. For example, in the pattern:

1 . . 2 . . 3 . . 4 . . 5 6 7 8

there should be 16 clicks of the metronome (the total number of dots and numbers).

EXERCISE 163. Try all the patterns at a speed of 85 clicks per minute. Then increase the speed to 90 clicks per minute and count through each of the patterns. Continue this exercise, increasing the rate in steps of 5 clicks per minute, until you are unable to keep up with the speed of the metronome.

EXERCISE 164. Read the following exclamations, pausing at the / markings as indicated:

My Dear! / You've changed! /
Your hair! / How lovely!

Now read the same words, but vary the pausing in the manner shown:

My Dear! / You've changed
your hair! / How lovely!

Note that the slight alteration in rate changes the entire meaning.

EXERCISE 165. Read the following selections, pausing briefly at the / markings and for a longer period at the / / markings.

Break, / break, / break, /
On thy cold gray stones, / O Sea! / /
And I would that my tongue could utter
The thoughts that arise in me.
—ALFRED, LORD TENNYSON, "Break, Break, Break"

Blow, / high, / blow, / / set the wild echoes flying, / /
and answer, / echoes, / answer, / / dying, /
dying, / dying.
—ALFRED, LORD TENNYSON, "Songs" from THE PRINCESS

Boot, / saddle, / to horse, / and away! / /
Rescue my castle before the hot day
brightens to blue from its silvery gray. / /
Boot, / saddle, / to horse, / and away! /
—ROBERT BROWNING, from "Cavalier Tunes"

It was roses, / roses, / all the way, / /
With myrtle mixed in my path like mad: / /
The house-roofs seemed to heave and sway, /
The church-spires flamed, / such flags they had, /
A year ago on this very day.
—ROBERT BROWNING, "The Patriot"

Good-night? / / ah! / no; / / the hour is ill
Which serves those it should invite: / /
Let us remain together still, /
Then it will be *good* night.
—PERCY BYSSHE SHELLEY, "Good-night"

O world! / O life! / O time! / /
On whose last steps I climb, / /
Trembling at that where I had stood before; / /
When will return / the glory of your prime? / /
No more— / Oh, / never more!
—PERCY BYSSHE SHELLEY, "A Lament"

Yet waft me from the harbor-mouth, /
Wild wind! / / I seek a warmer sky, /
And I will see before I die
The palms and temples of the South.
—ALFRED, LORD TENNYSON, "Ulysses"

Fly, / envious Time, / till thou run out thy race.
—JOHN MILTON, "On Time"

Hence, / vain deluding Joys, / /
The brood of Folly without father bred!
JOHN MILTON, "Il Penseroso"

Yet once more, / O ye laurels, / and once more, /
Ye myrtles brown, / with ivy never sere, / /
I come to pluck your berries harsh and crude, /
And with forced fingers rude
Shatter your leaves before the mellowing year.
JOHN MILTON, "Lycidas"

Verse, / a breeze mid blossoms straying, /
Where Hope clung feeding, / like a bee— / /
Both were mind! / / Life went a-maying
With Nature, / Hope, / and Poesy, /
When I was young!
—SAMUEL TAYLOR COLERIDGE,
"Youth and Age"

PRACTICE SELECTIONS

FOR CORRECTING RAPID RATE

THE INDIA WHARF, *Sara Teasdale* [From *Rivers to the Sea* by Sara Teasdale, by permission of The Macmillan Company, publishers.]

Here in the velvet stillness
The wide sown fields fall to the faint horizon,
Sleeping in starlight. . . .

A year ago we walked in the jangling city
Together . . . forgetful.
One by one we crossed the avenues,
Rivers of light, roaring in tumult,
And came to the narrow, knotted streets.
Thru the tense crowd
We went aloof, ecstatic, walking in wonder,
Unconscious of our motion.
Forever the foreign people with dark, deep-
seeing eyes
Passed us and passed.
Lights and foreign words and foreign faces,
I forgot them all;
I only felt alive, defiant of all death and sorrow,
Sure and elated.
That was the gift you gave me. . . .

The streets grew still more tangled,
And led at last to water black and glossy,
Flecked here and there with lights, faint and
far far off.
There on a shabby building was a sign
"The India Wharf" . . . and we turned back.
I always felt we could have taken ship
And crossed the bright green seas
To dreaming cities set on sacred streams
And palaces
Of ivory and scarlet.

TO THE EARL OF WARWICK, *Joseph Addison* [From *The Miscellaneous Works of Joseph Addison*, edited by A. C. Guthkelch, George Bell & Sons, Ltd., London, 1914.]

Can I forget the dismal night, that gave
My soul's best part forever to the grave!
How silent did his old companions tread,
By mid-night lamps, the mansions of the dead,
Through breathing statues, then unheeded things,
Through rowes of warriors, and through walks of kings!
What awe did the slow solemn knell inspire;
The pealing organ, and the pausing choir;
The duties by the lawn-robe'd prelate pay'd
And the last words, that dust to dust convey'd!
While speechless o'er thy closing grave we bend,
Accept these tears, thou dear departed friend,
Oh gone for-ever, take this long adieu;
And sleep in peace, next thy lov'd Montagu!

GOD'S-ACRE, *Henry Wadsworth Longfellow* [From *The Complete Poetical Works of Henry Wadsworth Longfellow*. Copyright, 1902, Houghton Mifflin Company, Boston, authorized publishers.]

I like that ancient Saxon phrase,
which calls
The burial-ground God's-Acre! It
is just;
It consecrates each grave within its
walls,
And breathes a benison o'er the
sleeping dust.

God's-Acre! Yes, that blessed name
imparts
Comfort to those who in the grave
have sown
The seed that they had garnered in
their hearts,
Their bread of life, alas! no more
their own.

Into its furrows shall we all be cast,
In the sure faith, that we shall rise
again
At the great harvest, when the arch-
angel's blast
Shall winnow, like a fan, the chaff
and grain.

Then shall the good stand in immortal
bloom,
In the fair gardens of that second
birth;
And each bright blossom mingle its
perfume
With that of flowers which never
bloomed on earth.

With thy rude ploughshare, Death,
turn up the sod,
And spread the furrow for the seed
we sow;
This is the field and Acre of our God,
This is the place where human har-
vests grow.

FOR CORRECTING LABORED SPEECH

LETTER TO EUROPE, *Robert Nathan* [Reprinted from *A Winter Tide* by Robert Nathan, by permission of and special arrangement with Alfred A. Knopf, Inc.]

What madness has the world?
It runs like fire through grass;
Patch after patch, field after field—forests,
Yesterday living and green, tossing their branches,
Haven of birds and berries, haven of shadows,
See how they burst into flame, storm into fire,
Flash into ember.
And the clover, sweet with honey and heavy with bees,
Shrivels away to ashes—the very sod
Turns hot with fever, watching the fire coming.

Burn, you people.
Let your dry hearts catch fire.
Let the wild flames blow over you, char out your blood.
Let the green ground of pity wither and perish.
Scorch out the meadows of kindness, the honey and clover.
Be but a stubble. Be ashes, dry and devoured.
Burn, burn, you people.

But remember:
In the black ember, in the waste and desolate morning,
When nothing is left of that sweet world you had—
Those whom the gods would destroy they first make mad.
Take warning. Oh, take warning.

FISHER OF STARS, *Lew Sarett* [From *The Box of God* by Lew Sarett, Henry Holt and Company, Inc., New York, 1922. Copyright, 1922, Henry Holt and Company, reprinted by permission.]

My wild blood leaped as I watched the falling stars
  Flash through the night and gleam,
Like spawning trout that hurtle the riffled bars
  Of a dusky mountain stream.

Like quivering rainbow-trout that run in spring,
  Arching the water-slides,—
Out of the limpid sky, in a wild wet fling,
  They shook their crimson sides.

My sportsman's heart flamed up, as the fishes dashed
  In school on shimmering school,
Through high cascades and waterfalls, and splashed
  In the deep of a cloudy pool.

I fished that pond; I chose my longest line,
  And cast with my supplest rod—
The one was a thing of dreams, oh, gossamer-fine;
  The other a gift from God.

I flicked the Milky Way from edge to edge
  With an iridescent fly;
I whipped the polar rapids, and every ledge
  And cut-bank in the sky.

To the Pleiades I cast with my willowy pole;
  And I let my line run out
To the farthest foamy cove and skyey hole—
  And I raised a dozen trout.

And every time one struck my slender hook,
  He shattered the trembling sea,
With a sweep of his shivering silver fin, and he shook
  A silver rain on me;

My line spun out, my fly-rod bent in twain,
  As over the sky he fought;
My fingers bled, my elbows throbbed with pain—
  But my fishing went for naught.

I landed never a one; my line and hackle
  Were none too subtle and fine;
For angling stars one wants more delicate tackle,—
  A more cunning hand than mine.

TO SPRING, *William Blake* [*Poetry and Prose of William Blake*, edited by Geoffrey Keynes, The Nonesuch Press, Ltd., London, 1939.]

O thou with dewy locks, who lookest down
Thro' the clear windows of the morning, turn
Thine angel eyes upon our western isle,
Which in full choir hails thy approach, O Spring!

The hills tell one another, and the listening
Valleys hear; all our longing eyes are turned
Up to thy bright pavilions: issue forth,
And let thy holy feet visit our clime.

Come o'er the eastern hills, and let our winds
Kiss thy perfumèd garments; let us taste
Thy morn and evening breath; scatter thy pearls
Upon our love-sick land that mourns for thee.

O deck her forth with thy fair fingers; pour
Thy soft kisses on her bosom; and put
Thy golden crown upon her languish'd head,
Whose modest tresses were bound up for thee!

THE GLOVE AND THE LIONS, *Leigh Hunt* [From *Prose, Poetry and Drama for Oral Interpretation* selected and arranged by William J. Farma, Harper & Brothers, New York, 1930.]

King Francis was a hearty king, and loved a royal sport,
And one day, as his lions fought, sat looking on the court.
The nobles filled the benches, and the ladies in their pride,
And 'mongst them sat the Count de Lorge, with one for whom he sighed:
And truly 'twas a gallant thing to see that crowning show,
Valor and love, and a king above, and the royal beasts below.

Ramped and roared the lions, with horrid laughing jaws;
They bit, they glared, gave blows like beams, a wind went with their paws;
With wallowing might and stifled roar they rolled on one another,
Till all the pit with sand and mane was in a thunderous smother;
The bloody foam above the bars came whisking through the air;
Said Francis then, "Faith, gentlemen, we're better here than there."

De Lorge's love o'erheard the King, a beauteous lively dame
With smiling lips and sharp bright eyes, which always seemed the same;
She thought, "The Count my lover is brave as brave can be;
He surely would do wondrous things to show his love of me;

King, ladies, lovers, all look on; the occasion is divine;
I'll drop my glove, to prove his love; great glory will be mine!"

She dropped her glove, to prove his love, then looked at him and smiled;
He bowed, and in a moment leaped among the lions wild;
The leap was quick, return was quick, he has regained his place,
Then threw the glove, but not with love, right in the lady's face.
"By God," said Francis, "rightly done!" and he rose from where he sat;
"No love," quoth he, "but vanity, sets love a task like that."

FOR CORRECTING MONOTONOUS RATE

FROM "THE SNOWBALL," *Leland Schubert* [From an unpublished play, *The Snowball*, by permission of the author.]

"For God so loved the world that He gave His only begotten Son, that whosoever believeth in Him shall not perish, but have everlasting life." That whosoever believeth in Him—whosoever believeth in loving neighbor as self; whosoever believeth in doing unto others as he would have them do unto him; whosoever believeth that the meek are blessed and shall inherit the earth; whosoever believeth that God was kind and God was wise when He gave to Moses the ten laws upon which all good laws are founded.

"For God so loved the world that He gave His only begotten Son"—And the little child was born in a manger—no better place—but He smiled—He understood. As a small boy He worked in the carpenter shop of Joseph. There, among the laborers, the village gossips, the wise and the foolish of the town, He learned to know men and to understand them. He was still a boy when His wisdom amazed the learned doctors of the temple. They wondered at His knowledge. They were helpless at His questions, and startled by His answers. He knew things that they would never know. He understood life and man's way of living.

For nearly thirty years he went about his business of building things for men to use. Years of toil and years of preparation.—Preparation for the building of a greater structure, set upon an eternal foundation—shelter fashioned to stand longer than the oldest man.

He hadn't been about this new business long when one day someone asked the dreaded question, the inevitable, but unfortunate question: "Art Thou the Messiah?"—"Thou sayest that I am," He answered, and it was the beginning of the end—or the end of the beginning.—He had to answer that way, because He knew.—He knew the truth, and He dreaded the question.

A cock crowed, and Peter had denied Him.—He knew that Peter would. He understood.—Thirty pieces of silver changed hands, and Judas had betrayed Him. He knew that Judas would betray Him, and He felt sorry because Judas didn't really want to betray Him. Christ *knew*. *He* understood. They nailed Him up on a cross. Sharp nails! But strong flesh—and a stronger mind—and an understanding compassion. Between two robbers He was crucified; and at the foot of His cross, soldiers gambled for His clothing.—"Father, forgive them, for they know not what they do." He knew. He understood.

He died that God's will might be done, that His Kingdom might come on earth as it is in heaven. He died that men might learn to *live together* happily and peacefully, and according to God's will. He died—"that whosoever believeth in Him shall not perish but have everlasting life."

THE RIVALS: A COMEDY (1775), *Richard Brinsley Sheridan* [From *Types of English Drama* 1660–1780, by David Harrison Stevens, Ginn & Company, Boston, 1923. Copyright, 1923. David Harrison Stevens.]

FAG: What! Thomas! sure 'tis he?—What! Thomas! Thomas!

COACHMAN: Hey!—Odds life! Mr. Fag!—give us your hand, my old fellow-servant.

FAG: Excuse my glove, Thomas.—I'm devilish glad to see you, my lad. Why, my prince of charioteers, you look as hearty!—but who the deuce thought of seeing you in Bath!

COACHMAN: Sure, Master, Madam Julia, Harry, Mrs. Kate, and the postilion be all come.

FAG: Indeed!

COACHMAN: Aye, Master thought another fit of the gout was coming to make him a visit; so he'd a mind to gi't the slip, and whip! we were all off at an hour's warning.

FAG: Aye, aye, hasty in everything or it would not be Sir Anthony Absolute!

SISTER HELEN, *Dante Gabriel Rossetti* [*From Beowulf to Thomas Hardy*, Robert Shafer, Vol. II, New Edition. Copyright, 1940, Odyssey Press Inc. Copyright, 1924, 1931, Doubleday, Doran & Company, Inc., New York.]

"See, see, the wax has dropped from its
place,
Sister Helen,
And the flames are winning up apace!"
"Yet here they burn but for a space,
Little brother!"
(O Mother, Mary Mother,
Here for a space, between Hell and
Heaven!)

"Ah! what white thing at the door has
crossed,
Sister Helen?
Ah! what is this that sighs in the frost?"
"A soul that's lost as mine is lost,
Little brother!"
(O Mother, Mary Mother,
Lost, lost, all lost, between Hell and
Heaven!)

ENGLAND IN 1819, *Percy Bysshe Shelley* [*From Beowulf to Thomas Hardy*, Robert Shafer, Vol. II, New Edition. Copyright, 1940, Odyssey Press Inc. Copyright, 1924, 1931, Doubleday, Doran & Company, Inc., New York.]

An old, mad, blind, despised, and dying
king—
Princes, the dregs of their dull race, who
flow
Through public scorn—mud from a muddy
spring;
Rulers who neither see, nor feel, nor know,
But leech-like to their fainting country cling,
Till they drop, blind in blood, without a
blow;
A people starved and stabbed in the untilled
field—
An army, which liberticide and prey
Makes as a two-edged sword to all who
wield—
Golden and sanguine laws which tempt and
slay;
Religion Christless, Godless—a book sealed;
A Senate—Time's worse statute unrepealed—
Are graves, from which a glorious Phantom
may
Burst, to illumine our tempestuous day.

MY HEART LEAPS UP, *William Wordsworth* [*From Beowulf to Thomas Hardy*, Robert Shafer, Vol. II, New Edition. Copyright, 1940, Odyssey Press Inc. Copyright, 1924, 1931, Doubleday, Doran & Company, Inc., New York.]

My heart leaps up when I behold
A rainbow in the sky:
So was it when my life began;
So is it now I am a man;
So be it when I shall grow old,
Or let me die!
The Child is father of the Man;
And I could wish my days to be
Bound each to each by natural piety.

THE SPIDER AND THE BEE, *Jonathan Swift* [*From Beowulf to Thomas Hardy*, Robert Shafer, Vol. I, New Edition. Copyright, 1939, Odyssey Press, Inc. Copyright 1924, 1931, Doubleday, Doran & Company, Inc., New York.]

"I am glad," answered the bee, "to hear you grant at least that I am come honestly by my wings and my voice; for then, it seems, I am obliged to Heaven alone for my flights and my music; and Providence would never have bestowed on me two such gifts, without designing them for the noblest ends. I visit indeed all the flowers and blossoms of the field and the garden; but whatever I collect from thence, enriches myself, without the least injury to their beauty, their smell, or their taste. Now, for you and your skill in architecture, and other mathematics, I have little to say: in that building of yours there might, for aught I know, have been labor and method enough; but, by woeful experience for us both, 'tis too plain, the materials are naught, and I hope you will henceforth take warning, and consider duration and matter, as well as method and art. You boast, indeed, of being obliged to no other creature, but of drawing and spinning out all from yourself; that is to say, if we may judge of the liquor in the vessel by what issues out, you possess a good plentiful store of dirt and poison in your breast; and, though I would by no means lessen or disparage your genuine stock of either, yet, I doubt you are somewhat obliged, for an increase of both, to a little foreign assistance."

THE VOICE OF HER I LOVE, *Anonymous* [From *Sweet Home*, edited by Frances E. Percival, L. P. Crown and Company, Boston, 1856.]

How sweet at the hour of silent eve
  The harp's responsive sound!
How sweet the vows that ne'er deceive,
  And deeds by virtue crowned!
How sweet to sit beneath a tree
  In some delightful grove!
But O, more soft, more sweet, to me
  The voice of her I love.

AIR, *Oliver Goldsmith* [From *The Works of Oliver Goldsmith*, edited by Peter Cunningham, F.S.A., G. P. Putnam's Sons, New York, 1908.]

O Memory, thou fond deceiver!
  Still importunate and vain;
To former joys recurring ever,
  And turning all the past to pain.

Hence, deceiver, most distressing,
  Seek the happy and the free;
They who want each other blessing,
  Ever want a friend in thee.

THE OLD CLOCK ON THE STAIRS, *Henry Wadsworth Longfellow* [From *The Complete Poetical Works of Henry Wadsworth Longfellow*. Copyright, 1902, Houghton Mifflin Company, Boston.]

Somewhat back from the village street
Stands the old-fashioned country-seat.
Across its antique portico
Tall poplar-trees their shadows throw
And from its station in the hall
An ancient timepiece says to all,—
"Forever—never!
Never—forever!"

Half-way up the stairs it stands,
And points and beckons with its hands
From its case of massive oak,
Like a monk, who, under his cloak,
Crosses himself, and sighs, alas!
With sorrowful voice to all who pass,—
"Forever—never!
Never—forever!"

By day its voice is low and light;
But in the silent dead of night,
Distinct as a passing footstep's fall,
It echoes along the vacant hall,
Along the ceiling, along the floor,
And seems to say, at each chamber-door—
"Forever—never!
Never—forever!"

Through days of sorrow and of mirth,
Through days of death and days of birth,
Through every swift vicissitude
Of changeful time, unchanged it has stood,
And as if, like God, it all things saw,
It calmly repeats those words of awe,—
"Forever—never!
Never—forever!"

In that mansion used to be
Free-hearted Hospitality;
His great fires up the chimney roared;
The stranger feasted at his board;
But, like the skeleton at the feast,
That warning timepiece never ceased,—
"Forever—never!
Never—forever!"

There groups of merry children played,
There youths and maidens dreaming strayed;
O precious hours! O golden prime,
And affluence of love and time!
Even as a miser counts his gold,
Those hours the ancient timepiece told,—
"Forever—never!
Never—forever!"

From that chamber, clothed in white,
The bride came forth on her wedding night;
There, in that silent room below,
The dead lay in his shroud of snow;
And in the hush that followed the prayer,
Was heard the old clock on the stair,—
"Forever—never!
Never—forever!"

All are scattered now and fled,
Some are married, some are dead;
And when I ask, with throbs of pain,
"Ah! when shall they all meet again?"
As in the days long since gone by,
The ancient timepiece makes reply,
"Forever—never!
Never—forever!"

Never here, forever there,
Where all parting, pain, and care,
And death and time shall disappear,—
Forever there, but never here!
The horologe of Eternity
Sayeth this incessantly,—
"Forever—never!
Never—forever!"

IMPROVING RHYTHM

Rhythm has been held as the final consideration because the subject includes most of the factors discussed earlier. Pitch, intensity, and rate, as well as articulation and pronunciation, influence and are influenced by speech rhythm.

Clement Wood[1] has carefully defined rhythm in English speech, as " . . . the movement of words marked by the recurrence of, or alternation in, accented and unaccented syllables and pauses." This definition is essentially correct, but the reader must remember that many underlying factors, not mentioned in the definition, are involved in rhythm. For example, accent is achieved through changes in pitch, intensity, and rate. "Movement of words" implies changes in cadence or rate and duration. A rise or fall in pitch, an increase or decrease in intensity, an increase or a decrease in the duration of a pause, or a change in the cadence of the words may result in the emphasis of a word or phrase. The recurrence of these accent factors combined with the flow or movement of the words serves to make pronunciation and all the factors of vocalization—with the possible exception of vocal quality—components of rhythm.

The word *rhythm* is usually thought of in connection with poetry. Some people do not think of this factor as part of speech at the dinner table or on the public-speaking platform. Actually, it is as important in the one medium of expression as in the other; it is as important a part of prose as it is of verse.

CAUSES FOR FAULTY SPEECH RHYTHM

Jerkiness in the flow of words and poor accenting and emphasis result from bad speech habits, emotional upset, a lack of understanding or

[1] Wood, C., *Poets' Handbook*, Garden City Publishing Company, Inc., New York, 1942, p. 105.

knowledge of the subject, and disorganized thinking. In some instances the child imitates one of his parents or an older person in the family who has a faulty rhythm pattern. This may occur even though the irregularity in the other person is only slight. Poor rhythm habits may develop from these early imitations and become a permanent part of the child's speech patterns. Such temporary conditions as a disturbed emotional state, excitement, temporary hypertensions, and lack of familiarity with the material being discussed may result in irregular speech rhythms.

The speech of most of us contains vocalized pauses, hesitations, poor timing, and improper accenting in varying degrees of severity. Slight falterings may serve to give spontaneity and freshness to vocal utterance, and some will say, "I prefer it that way. I don't like a speaker to be too fluent." Of course, the steady flow of words on a single tone (frequently referred to as *tonal perseveration*) is not acceptable because the speech tends to become "ministerial," indirect, and lacking in conversational quality.

However, rhythm irregularities do little or nothing to improve the communication of ideas. Well-timed pauses of proper duration, varied accent and cadence, and a pleasing voice without tonal perseveration will accomplish this purpose without detracting from the ideas, and as a result communication will be more efficient.

RHYTHM OF POETRY AND SPEECH

Normal speech is much like poetry. Listen to the person who is mentally and physically alive, and you discover that his speech has a marked rhythm. If you are adept at scansion, you will be able to mark off the metric feet while he speaks as readily as you scan lines from Shakespeare or Sarett. Of course, the rhythm varies considerably more in speech than in poetry because rhythm in poetry results from the regular repetition of the accent pattern. However, poetry varies from simple iambic feet to highly varied rhythm patterns, and usually, in prose the variation is even more irregular.

Poetry and prose are very useful to the student who wishes to improve the rhythm of his speech. They can be used to bring together all the factors of pitch, intensity, and rate which were considered individually earlier in the text. It must be remembered, however, that this material is directed toward voice training only and not designed for the purpose of teaching the oral interpretation of literature.

EXERCISES TO DISCOVER RHYTHM

Prose, as well as poetry, has rhythm which is easily discovered when the material is read aloud. By stressing the words that express the important ideas and by giving more value to words that contain emotional content, the natural rhythm of the sentence is brought to light almost immediately.

EXERCISE 166. As a practice exercise, underscore the words in the following passage that you believe have important meaning and emotional content, and then read the material aloud stressing those words. Note what happens to the rhythm.

Crabbed age and youth cannot live together:
Youth is full of pleasure, age is full of care;
Youth like summer morn, age like winter weather;
Youth like summer brave, age like winter bare.
Youth is full of sport, age's breath is short;
Youth is nimble, age is lame;
Youth is hot and bold, age is weak and cold;
Youth is wild, and age is tame.
Age, I do abhor thee, youth, I do adore thee;
O, my love, my love is young!
Age, I do defy thee; O, sweet shepherd, hie thee,
For methinks thou stay'st too long!
—SHAKESPEARE, from "The Passionate Pilgrim"

Joy! shipmate—joy!
(Pleas'd to my Soul at death I cry;)
Our life is closed—our life begins;
The long, long anchorage we leave,
The ship is clear at last—she leaps!
She swiftly courses from the shore;
Joy! shipmate—joy!
—WALT WHITMAN

'Twas on the day, when Thorold rich and grave,
Like Cimon, triumph'd both on land and wave:
(Pomps without guilt, of bloodless swords and maces,
Glad chains, warm furs, broad banners, and broad faces)
Now night descending, the proud scene was o'er,
But lived, in Settle's numbers, one day more.
Now mayors and shrieves all hush'd and satiate lay,
Yet eat, in dreams, the custard of the day;
While pensive poets painful vigils keep,
Sleepless themselves to give their readers sleep.
—ALEXANDER POPE, from "The Dunciad"

EXERCISE 167. You may find it helpful to mark off the content of your material into smaller partials which may be designated as thought groupings. At the end of each group, use the — symbol, but remember that these markings do not indicate pauses. Read with a smooth flow of speech, placing emphasis upon those words which are most important in carrying the thoughts and feelings to the audience. Be careful that the markings do not cause the reading to become jerky and irregular.

Deep—in the shady sadness—of a vale—
Far—sunken—from the healthy breath—of morn,—
Far—from the fiery noon,—and eve's one star,—
Sat—gray-hair'd—Saturn,—quiet—as a stone,—
Still—as the silence—round about—his lair;—
Forest—on forest—hung—about his head—
Like cloud—on cloud.—No stir—of air—was there,—
Not—so much life—as on a summer's day—
Robs—not one light seed—from—the feather'd grass,—
But—where the dead leaf fell,—there—did it rest.—
A stream—went voiceless—by,—still—deadened—more—
By reason—of his fallen—divinity—
Spreading—a shade:—the Naiad—'mid—her reeds—
Press'd—her cold—finger—closer—to her lips.
—JOHN KEATS, from "Hyperion" Book I

The curfew—tolls—the knell—of parting—day,—
The lowing—herd—winds—slowly—o'er the lea,—
The ploughman—homeward—plods—his weary—way,—
And leaves—the world—to darkness—and to me.—

Now—fades—the glimmering—landscape—on the sight,—
And—all—the air—a solemn—stillness—holds,—
Save—where—the beetle—wheels—his droning—flight,—
And drowsy—tinklings—lull—the distant—folds.
—THOMAS GRAY, "Elegy Written in a Country Churchyard"

SCANSION AS A MEANS OF DEVELOPING RHYTHM

When the practice medium is verse, it may be helpful to scan the material. This will show where the principal emphasis should fall. Division of the material into feet may be found helpful because such division ". . . follows the normal division that the voice uses in speaking the words."[1]

[1] *Ibid.*, p. 106.

EXERCISE 168. Using principally the rhythm of iambic verse (ta TUM), we can practice the following selections in developing improved rhythm. The / symbol indicates short pauses, and / / indicates the longer pauses.

Forget not yet / the tried intent
Of such a truth / as I have meant; / /
My great travail so gladly spent, /
Forget not yet!
—SIR THOMAS WYATT, "Forget Not Yet"

God of our fathers, / known of old, / /
Lord of our far-flung battle-line, / /
Beneath whose awful Hand / we hold
Dominion / over palm and pine, / /
Lord God of Hosts, / be with us yet, / /
Lest we forget, / / lest we forget.
—RUDYARD KIPLING, "Recessional"

All in a moment through the gloom were seen
Ten thousand banners rise into the air
With orient colors waving: / / with them rose
A forest huge of spears: / / and thronging helms
Appear'd, / and serried shields in thick array.
I—JOHN MILTON, "Paradise Lost"

EXERCISE 169. Using trochaic lines (TUM ta), practice the following selections to improve the rhythm.

Round about the caldron go; / /
In / the poison'd entrails / throw; / /
Toad, / that under co-old stone /
Days / and nights hath thirty-one /
Swelter'd venom sleeping got, /
Boil them first / i' the charmed / pot. /

Double, / double, / toil and trouble, /
Fire, / burn; / and caldron, bubble.
—SHAKESPEARE. *Macbeth*

EXERCISE 170. A desirable effect is produced when varied metric feet are used in the practice of poetry and prose.

By the flow of the inland river, / /
Whence / the fleets of iron have fled, / /
Where the blades of the grave-grass quiver, / /
Asleep are the ranks of the dead: / /
Under the sod and the dew, /
Waiting the Judgement Day, /
Under the one, / the Blue; / /
Under the other, / the Gray.
—FRANCIS MILES FINCH, "The Blue and the Gray"

Proceed, / Solinus, / to procure my fall, / /
And, by the doom of death, / end woes and all.
—SHAKESPEARE, *The Comedy of Errors*, Act I, Scene i.

Not so much life / as on a sum- mer's day
Robs not one light seed from the feath- ered grass.
—JOHN KEATS, "Hyperion"

EXERCISE 171. Scan the following prose selections, and read them over. If you are not satisfied with the rhythm as you have marked it off, change your markings and read it again.

Sir, I love the acquaintance of young people; because, in the first place, I don't like to think myself growing old. In the next place, young acquaintances must last longest, if they do last; and then, Sir, young men have more virtue than old men: they have more generous sentiments in every respect. I love the young dogs of this age: they have more wit and humor and knowledge of life than we had; but then the dogs are not so good scholars. Sir, in my early years I read very hard. It is a sad reflection, but a true one, that I knew almost as much at eighteen as I do now. My judgment, to be sure, was not so good; but I had all the facts. I remember very well, when I was at Oxford, an old gentleman said to me, "Young man, ply your books diligently now, and acquire a stock of knowledge; for when years come upon you, you will find that poring upon books will be but an irksome task."
—JAMES BOSWELL, *Young People*

When I was about four years old my father found himself able to buy the lease of a house on Herne Hill, a rustic eminence four miles south of the "Standard in Cornhill"; of which the leafy seclusion remains, in all essential points of character, unchanged to this day; certain Gothic splendors, lately indulged in by our wealthier neighbors, being the only serious innovations; and these are so graciously concealed by the fine trees of their grounds, that the passing viator remains unappalled by them; and I can still walk up and down the piece of road between the Fox tavern and the Herne Hill station, imagining myself four years old.

—JOHN RUSKIN, *Daily Life at Herne Hill.*

PRACTICE SELECTIONS

AN ESSAY ON CRITICISM, *Alexander Pope* [From *The Collected Poems of Alexander Pope,* edited by Ernest Rhys, J. M. Dent & Sons, Ltd., London, 1924. Reprinted 1931.]

Of all the causes which conspire to blind
Man's erring judgment, and misguide the mind,
What the weak head with strongest bias rules,
Is PRIDE, the never-failing vice of fools.
Whatever Nature has in worth denied,
She gives in large recruits of needless pride;
For as in bodies, thus in souls we find
What wants in blood and spirits, swell'd with wind:
Pride, where wit fails, steps in to our defence,
And fills up all the mighty void of sense.
If once right reason drives that cloud away,
Truth breaks upon us with resistless day.
Trust not yourself; but your defects to know,
Make use of every friend—and every foe.
A little learning is a dangerous thing;
Drink deep, or taste not the Pierian spring:
There shallow draughts intoxicate the brain,
And drinking largely sobers us again.

HAMLET, PRINCE OF DENMARK, *William Shakespeare* [From *Hamlet, Prince of Denmark* by William Shakespeare, edited by Joseph Quincy Adams, Houghton Mifflin Company. Copyright, 1929, Joseph Quincy Adams.]

HAMLET. To be, or not to be: that is the question:
Whether 'tis nobler in the mind to suffer
The slings and arrows of outrageous fortune,
Or to take arms against a sea of troubles,
And, by opposing, end them.—To die, to sleep:
No more: and, by a sleep, to say we end

The heart-ache and the thousand natural shocks
That flesh is heir to—'tis a consummation
Devoutly to be wish'd!—To die, to sleep.
To sleep? perchance to dream! Ay, there's the rub!
For in that sleep of death what dreams may come,
When we have shuffled off this mortal coil,
Must give us pause. There's the respect
That makes calamity of so long life!
For who would bear the whips and scorns of time,
The oppressor's wrong, the proud man's contumely,
The pangs of dispriz'd love, the law's delay,
The insolence of office, and the spurns
That patient merit of the unworthy takes,
When he himself might his quietus make
With a bare bodkin? Who would fardels bear,
To grunt and sweat under a weary life,
But that the dread of something after death,
The undiscover'd country, from whose bourn
No traveller returns, puzzles the will,
And makes us rather bear those ills we have
Than fly to others that we know not of?
Thus conscience does make cowards of us all.
And thus the native hue of resolution
Is sicklied o'er with the pale cast of thought,
And enterprises of great pith and moment,
With this regard, their current turn awry,
And lose the name of action.—Soft you now!
The fair Ophelia? Nymph, in thy orisons
Be all my sins remember'd.

THE RIME OF THE ANCIENT MARINER, *Samuel Taylor Coleridge*
[From *The Rime of the Ancient Mariner* by Samuel Taylor Coleridge, edited by Pelham Edgar, Appleton-Century-Crofts, Inc., New York, 1900.]

Part I

It is an ancient Mariner,
And he stoppeth one of three.
"By thy long gray beard and glittering eye,
Now wherefore stopp'st thou me?

The Bridegroom's doors are opened wide,
And I am next of kin;
The guests are met, the feast is set:
May'st hear the merry din."

He holds him with his skinny hand,
"There was a ship," quoth he.
"Hold off! unhand me, graybeard loon!"
Eftsoons his hand dropt he.

He holds him with his glittering eye—
The Wedding-Guest stood still,
And listens like a three years' child:
The Mariner hath his will.

The Wedding-Guest sat on a stone:
He cannot choose but hear;
And thus spake on that ancient man,
The bright-eyed Mariner.

THE LISTENERS, *Walter de la Mare* [From *Selected Poems* by Walter de la Mare. Copyright, 1927, Henry Holt and Company, Inc., New York.]

"Is there anybody there," said the Traveller,
  Knocking on the moonlit door;
And his horse in the silence champed the grasses
  Of the forest's ferny floor;
And a bird flew up out of the turret,
  Above the Traveller's head;
And he smote upon the door again a second time:
  "Is there anybody there?" he said.
But no one descended to the Traveller;
  No head from the leaf-fringed sill
Leaned over and looked into his grey eyes,
  Where he stood perplexed and still.
But only a host of phantom listeners
  That dwelt in the lone house then
Stood listening in the quiet of the moonlight
  To that voice from the world of men;
Stood thronging the faint moonbeams on the dark stair,
  That goes down to the empty hall,
Hearkening in an air stirred and shaken
  By the lonely Traveller's call.
And he felt in his heart their strangeness,
  Their stillness answering his cry,
While his horse moved, cropping the dark turf,
  'Neath the starred and leafy sky;
For he suddenly smote on the door, even
  Louder, and lifted his head:
"Tell them I came, and no one answered,
  That I kept my word," he said.

Never the least stir made the listeners,
  Though every word he spake
Fell echoing through the shadowiness of the still house
  From the one man left awake:
Ay, they heard his foot upon the stirrup,
  And the sound of iron on stone,
And how the silence surged softly backward,
  When the plunging hoofs were gone.

PART EIGHT

SUMMARY AND APPLICATION FOR THE STUDENT

20

WORKING FOR IMPROVED VOICE

This text was designed as your "guide to action" with the essentials of the speech-improvement program presented in a logical training sequence. If you hope to accomplish the objectives set forth in this text, you must have a sincere desire to bring about general improvement and to correct faults. Unless you are motivated to do this and are willing to "dig in," you will fail to change your manner of speaking. The process of altering habits requires work.

You must follow a regular program of exercises and be willing to apply the new principles every time you speak. Briefly, the steps suggested for improving your voice and articulation are:

1. Hearing your voice as it actually sounds to others and recognizing your faults as such.
2. Discovering techniques that help to replace old habits with new ones.
3. Learning to do these correctly.
4. Practicing each of them many times.
5. Making a constant effort to utilize new principles in actual practice.
6. Making applications consciously at first. Later, having them so well fixed that they occur spontaneously, without conscious effort.

CULTIVATING A GUIDE

At the outset, you need to train the ear, because the hearing mechanism serves as a guide during vocalization, regulating pitch, loudness, and quality. As a first step in this part of the program, you must improve the attention factor so that you are able to focus the attention on sounds in the environment. Next, you need to improve auditory alertness to develop full hearing potentialities. Finally, you should improve your ability to discriminate pitch, loudness, and quality. This will help you to develop your ability to isolate the basic elements of voice readily.

This step includes the analysis of your own voice as well as the voices of others. You should not only add to your own general voice-improvement possibilities but correct slight vocal and articulation defects as a result of ear training. Furthermore, with this foundation firmly established, you will be better prepared to avoid slipping back into old speaking habits and you will have an indispensable guide during practice periods.

MECHANICS OF VOCALIZATION

Since frequent reference is made to anatomical structures and physiological functions, you need to make a brief introductory study of the mechanics of vocalization and articulation. Such knowledge on your part makes discussion of the subject understandable to all concerned. It puts you and the teacher on common ground and thereby accelerates the program.

In addition to gaining this necessary understanding, you learn about many factors that have tangible application in the voice training program. For example, you learn that the tone produced as a result of the vibration of the vocal folds is amplified in the resonators and, furthermore, that the size, shape, and texture of the resonators determine vocal quality. This information gives you a clue regarding the importance of the resonators during speech. By using them properly, you are able to increase loudness and improve vocal quality.

MAKING PHYSICAL PREPARATION FOR VOCALIZATION

Your first step in physical preparation is relaxation. You must learn to sense the difference between tension and relaxation and then to develop ability to relax throughout the body. You do this by practicing conscious control of the muscles at first and then by doing exercises to relax the trunk and extremities. When you can relax the large muscles of the body, you should practice exercises to relax the throat, jaw, and tongue and try to carry the principle over into vocalization. Your entire effort should be directed toward having the proper amount of tonicity in the muscles involved in producing speech.

An easy, erect posture which prepares your body for the speech act and avoids hindering the movement of the muscles involved is part of the physical preparation you make for vocalization.

This, in combination with quiet, coordinated breathing of the combined thoracic and abdominal type, is recommended as most satisfactory for voice production. First, you may need to learn abdominal breathing and, later, the combined thoracic and abdominal type of breathing.

DEVELOPING BASIC ELEMENTS

The three basic elements discussed are quality, pitch, and loudness. First consideration is given to developing a clear, vibrant tone which is produced without effort and free from such defective qualities as *breathiness*, *nasality*, *denasality*, *throatiness*, and others. Exercises to open the pharynx, develop nasal and oral resonance, and utilize all the resonators are given, and suggestions made for correcting faulty tonal quality. The defects of quality fall into three categories: the *throaty*, *thin*, and *nasal and denasal*.

Steps in improving pitch include:

1. Finding the structural pitch for which the vocal equipment is best suited and adjusting accordingly. Two methods are recommended: the use of spoken sounds and Fairbanks's 25-percentile test.
2. Achieving variety in the pitch of the voice.

Causes for the weak voice are considered, and the following principles suggested for achieving adequate loudness:

1. Forceful air column.
2. Open resonators.
3. Clear, resonant tones.

Exercises for increasing loudness, tempering a loud voice, and varying loudness are given.

IMPROVING ARTICULATION

Movement of the articulatory mechanisms is a prerequisite for clear, distinct speech. By moving these parts with precision action, understandability is improved, and thus the speaker develops ability to project his voice to the ears of the listener. Students can learn to activate the lips, jaw, and tongue through the practice of the exercises which are included for this purpose. Their aim should be the establishment of the proper degree of muscle tonicity for improved articulation and projection. Overpreciseness should be avoided.

Articulation of consonants and vowels is considered next in the program. Consonant and vowel sounds are defined, and exercises are given for improving the articulation of the nasal sounds, plosives, fricatives, semivowels, vowels, and vowel blends. Problems of pronunciation are discussed. Some of these are inconsistency of vowels, unstressing the vowels, silent and variant consonants, accent, regional differences, and levels of usage. Errors and rules of pronunciation are listed.

IMPROVING SPEECH RHYTHM

The program is rounded out with a chapter on improving rhythm. Causes for poor speech rhythm are found to be bad speaking habits, emotional upset, a lack of understanding or knowledge of the subject, and disorganized thinking. Prose, like poetry, possesses natural rhythm, and unless it is present, the speech or reading pattern is not pleasant to the listener's ear. Exercises to discover the rhythm of a sentence are given, and means are presented for developing rhythm when poetry is used as the speech medium.

CONCLUSION

Having learned all the basic elements and gradually improved his abilities, the student should have eliminated individual problems and by now have a fairly well-established set of new habits of vocalization and articulation. He needs to continue to integrate all the factors he has learned so that these habits will become firmly fixed. If, at any time, he finds himself slipping back into old habits, he should moreover, practice the related exercises he learned previously. Moreover, an occasional review of all the principles is recommended for maintaining high standards of voice and articulation.

21

CAREFUL USE OF THE VOICE

Most of us quietly wait for our favorite sport season to come around, and when it does, we get out our megaphone and start yelling at the umpires and players with all the gusto we can muster. We have made no preparation for such vocal activity, and we break all the common-sense rules of vocalization. As a result, we suffer some vocal Charley horses. The vocal cords become irritated, and the voice sounds husky and thin. Sometimes we put so much strain on the mechanism that we are required to whisper for a spell before we can speak in a normal voice again. We usually recover, however, and it is not long until we are ready to repeat the mistake.

Our voices can stand this punishment for a while, but if we are vocally overindulgent too often, we may suffer some drastic consequences. A high-school teacher of the author made the mistake of abusing his vocal mechanism when he was a boy, and at sixty, he was speaking with a thin, high-pitched squeak. He had ruined his voice while he was in the grades. The school he had attended held oratorical contests, and at regular intervals he was required to speak. He suffered from severe stage fright in the first two performances and was about to face the dreaded third when he ran into what appeared at the time to be a streak of good luck. On the day preceding the festival, he was playing with several friends and yelling so strenuously that his voice "gave out." Because of his huskiness, he was excused from speaking. His problem of facing the audience solved itself so easily on this occasion that, when the time came for his next appearance, he decided to use the husky-voice excuse again. He sneaked into the neighboring hills, where no one would hear him, and shouted until he was hoarse. The trick worked, so he repeated it every time his turn came to speak. Later, he learned that he had been very unwise in his use of this escape; it had robbed him for life of a pleasant speaking and singing voice.

The author is constantly faced with the problem of improving a voice that has "broken down" late in life. Most of the persons who come to the clinic with this type of vocal problem are in their fifties. The voice is throaty in quality; it sounds forced and tired. In some instances, there is a pathological involvement of the tissues; in others, there is no sign of any organic disturbance whatever, but there are factors in the history which are common to all these cases. One of the most prominent is vocal overindulgence. Usually, the individual admits that he has spoken frequently under adverse conditions, has placed an undue amount of strain on the vocal instrument, and has often forced the voice when he did not feel like speaking.

Recently, a woman called for an appointment. Over the telephone, she sounded like a woman of seventy, but in her first conference it was discovered that she was only thirty-five. Her voice betrayed her age because of its tonal qualities—it sounded like a flat tire on a gravel road. I asked her how much she had used her voice and under what circumstances. "Oh, I've been in a lot of plays and spoken before large audiences. I always had a forceful voice until this happened," she bragged. She should have learned early that you must "take it easy" on precision machinery. You just do not dare to kick it around.

She was referred to a physician. Then later, with his approval, suggestions were given as to how she might improve her voice. I have not seen her since, but I fear that my efforts bore no fruit. She became interested in vocal care too late. She had worn the vocal cords "to a frazzle" and was destined to have an aged voice the rest of her life.

The muscles involved in vocalization move with rapid precision. They can stand some abuse, but their owner must use good judgment. Too much wear and tear over a long period result in throat irritation and chronic hoarseness.

Use the same good judgment in vocalizing that you use in breaking in a new car. You would not drive at a speed of 90 miles per hour the first day out. You would ruin the motor, because the parts are tight. Similarly, during speech you would ruin the voice if the muscles involved were tense. Speech sounds result from the movement of muscles. The vocal cords open and close as many as 500 times a second. Lips, tongue, jaw, and vocal cords should move together in easy precision. Unless the mechanism is relaxed, vocalization will be forced and you will get the same effect as "gunning" a new car.

The rules of vocal hygiene are simple. If you learn what they are and put them to use every time you speak, you should have a good voice for a lifetime.

SOME RULES OF VOCAL HYGIENE

The experiences of the high-school teacher and the lady thespian demonstrate that you should *never abuse the voice.* The muscles that are involved in vocalization are delicate, and they can be ruined through improper use.

The following suggestions regarding vocal hygiene should be observed if you hope to retain a pleasant, resonant voice:

1. Relax the muscles of the throat and larynx during speech.
2. Stay within an easy pitch range.
3. Prepare for unusually loud speech by learning to relax the vocal mechanism and by applying the principles of breathing.
4. Be careful to avoid straining the vocal folds if it is necessary to affect unusual quality variations.
5. Speak softly or whisper when the voice is husky.
6. If the voice is persistently husky, see a physician.

You will always be vocally safe if you relax the muscles of the throat and larynx and avoid hypertension in all parts of the vocal mechanism every time you speak.

If you find that you must make your voice perform in an unusual manner, for example, speaking loudly or in an exceedingly high or low pitch, you should train yourself to accomplish the end in view without placing stress on the mechanism.

Some time ago the author watched one of the sopranos in the choir of the local church as she tried to reach the high notes. The cords of her neck stood out like posts designed to prop her head in place. Either her vocal mechanism was not suited to singing in the upper registers, or she was using the vocal mechanism improperly. Since she was unable to sing her part with ease, she should have joined the audience.

You need to discover your optimum pitch—the one that is best suited to your vocal mechanism. The voice should be varied around this.

You must be careful to keep within an easy range, going neither too high nor too low.

USING THE VOICE WITH CARE

Likewise, you must be careful about speaking loudly. Usually, when you want to make your voice carry for a hundred feet or so, you tense the throat and yell. You would get much better results if you would inhale, open and relax the mouth and throat, apply abdominal pressure, and speak clearly and distinctly. Less strain then would be placed on the larynx, and the quality of the sound produced would be far more pleasant to listen to.

CARE WHEN STRUCTURES ARE AFFECTED

When the voice becomes husky as a result of a cold or because you have been careless in its use, you should give it a rest by speaking softly or by remaining silent, the latter precaution being preferable.

If the period of silence or soft utterance does not remove the huskiness, you should see a physician and have him study the vocal folds to determine whether or not there is a pathological condition that should receive treatment. Frequently, in these cases, a singer's node (a small corn) appears on one or both of the cords. This causes a deviation in the glottis (the opening between the cords), and as a result the vocal quality becomes distorted. The condition is a serious one and should be treated immediately. However, an operation for removing the corn should never be necessary if the rules of vocal hygiene suggested earlier in this chapter are conscientiously adhered to. By following these rules, you avoid the possibility of developing structural deviations and tend to retain for a longer time the youthful tonal qualities.

PART NINE

SUGGESTIONS TO TEACHERS

22

SUGGESTIONS TO TEACHERS

The author's experience in teaching courses in voice training and articulation over a period of several years prompts the following suggestions to teachers. Some of these may be found helpful in planning and conducting group work in this subject; others may not be feasible in a particular academic situation or not suited to the procedures used by certain teachers. In any event, they are offered for what they are worth to those who are planning to introduce such a course or alter one that already exists.

THE TEACHER'S QUALIFICATIONS

The teacher should have a pleasant, well-modulated, and expressive voice and distinct articulation free from provincialisms and substandardisms. He needs a knowledge of the vocal mechanisms and the ability to teach students how to use their vocal and articulatory equipment effectively in speech. It is most helpful to students if the instructor can give vocal demonstrations of principles which are under consideration at the time. Such matters as variation of pitch and intensity, the development of resonance, and projection are best understood when students are given firsthand demonstrations.

ROOMS AND EQUIPMENT

The text was designed mainly for group work with people with average to poor speech. For most effective teaching, the number of pupils in any group should not exceed twenty-four.

THE CLASSROOM. The classroom should be approximately 24 by 33 feet. Acoustics should be good, with no echo, and walls should be constructed so that sound will not be conducted to adjoining rooms. Chairs should be movable in order to allow sufficient space for exercises devoted to physical preparation for vocalization.

Plans should be made to use a large auditorium or ampitheater after the class is prepared for work in vocalization. In many instances, the author's classes adjourn to nearby open spaces for work with increased resonance, loudness, and projection.

RECORDING EQUIPMENT. A recorder with playback is considered an essential for this course. Recording may be made on tape, disc, or wire. The disc recorder has the following advantages: (1) the disc can be played on standard phonographs in the home of the student as he studies and analyzes his voice, and (2) the playback, which is a regular part of the equipment, is useful for playing selected samples of speech. If the tape or wire equipment is used, then it is necessary to purchase an extra piece of equipment for the latter purpose. With tape- and wire-recording equipment it is sometimes necessary to play the recordings of several members of the class in order to find an individual recording.

The uninitiated are prone to accept a convenient piece of equipment at face value without placing sufficiently stringent requirements upon faithful reproduction. Budgets sometimes require the purchase of low-price recording equipment. In many cases these devices—whether they be wire, disc, or tape—fail to achieve faithful reproduction, and both the student and the teacher attempt to evaluate a distorted reproduction. In a course where results are determined in large part by ear training, faithful reproduction is vital because the student must hear his voice as others hear it, or as close to this as is possible.

The most important factors to be considered as one contemplates the purchase of recording equipment are wide frequency range, low distortion, low noise output, uniform quality, and high- and low-frequency response. Other factors are recording time, special requirements, ease of manipulation, life of the recording, compactness of the recording, its usability on student-owned playbacks, attention to equipment during its use, ease in reproduction of the recorded selection, and portability of the equipment.

If at all possible, the equipment should be stationary and its use limited to only a few qualified persons. Too often inexperienced people are allowed to use the expensive equipment without proper instruction, and it soon falls out of adjustment. The recording equipment should be checked by an expert at frequent intervals to assure that all parts are functioning properly. Like the choice of a hearing aid or an audiometer, recording equipment should be purchased only after an extended trial period.

If the budget will allow, equipment with a range of 15,000 cycles should be used in voice recording. Equipment with a low distortion source and an 8,000-cycle upper limit should be the minimum requirement for speech purposes. Generally, the microphone and loudspeaker which come as part of inexpensive equipment are inadequate, and the buyer would be wise to purchase the best in these.

C. J. LeBel[1] gives an excellent discussion of the advantages and disadvantages of wire, disc, and tape recording which every teacher would be wise to read. Regarding quality bottlenecks, he points out that

> . . . a great deal of the quality impairment in a portable machine results from the accessories used. The microphone and loudspeaker are particularly at fault. Occasionally the means of measuring recording level is inadequate—a flashing neon lamp is much too crude, for example, and an excessively sluggish meter is almost as bad.
>
> Almost anyone can change these accessories easily. The cost of such a step may be unpleasantly high—half the cost of the original machine—since the market for high quality microphones and loudspeakers is as limited as that for high quality recorders. It is believed that a number of low-cost tape machines, which will hit the market in the next three months, will be of high enough quality to warrant the cost of such improved accessories.
>
> High quality equipment has been available if the buyer knew where to look. In the professional field, wide range tape recorders have been on the market for about a year. At the start nine thousand cycle range costs about $300, and 15,000 cycles cost at least $3000; but within the last four months 15,000 cycle equipment has become available at about $800. Within the next three months several tape machines will reach the market, priced in the $125 to $150 range. At least one of these will offer usable response up to seven thousand cycles (excluding microphone and loudspeaker).

OTHER ITEMS OF EQUIPMENT. Other important items are records suitable for use during training in relaxation, recordings of superior voices, consonant charts, vowel charts, metronome, charts and models illustrating the vocal mechanisms, tuning forks, and the Seashore Tests of Musical Talent (Manual and Records).

Although regular classroom chairs will probably be used in most instances, cots, mats, or adjustable chairs would be most desirable for work in general relaxation.

[1] LeBel, C. J., "An Engineer Looks at the Problems of Speech Recording," *The Quarterly Journal of Speech*, vol. 35, pp. 210–213, 1949.

The audiometer is highly desirable but is not included as a minimum essential. Often this is available in the speech clinic or another department of the school. Some instructors find the piano most helpful in training the ear and the speaking voice.

RECORDING THE CLASS

Before any work is started, a recording should be made of the voice of each student. This will serve as a strong motivating as well as ear-training device and can be used immediately in an analysis of students' voices. Additional recordings should be made periodically during the course. If this is not possible, at least a second recording should be made at the close of the course.

The value of repeated hearing by the student of his own record cannot be overstressed. Just one quick replaying either in class or outside hardly justifies the expense of making the records. Every effort should be made to provide time, space, and equipment for students to do this work. A voice and articulation laboratory with a well-qualified attendant instructor to assist in operating the equipment and analyzing voice and articulation problems would be ideal in accomplishing this purpose. The tape-recorder type of equipment would be most suitable in such a setup because of the desirability of recording the voice and playing it back immediately. For such purposes, the tape recording is less expensive than the disc because the tape can be used over and over.

It is interesting to compare the first recording made of the student's voice with the last recording made to determine whether there has been satisfactory progress. The author has the student record the same material at the beginning as at the end of the semester. Both recordings are played for each student, and the entire class makes judgments as to whether the first record played was the first or the last record made. For one student, the second record played may be the first record made; for another, the first record played may be the first record made. All the first and last records for the entire class are played as the students make their notations. A key sheet is kept, and the students' notations are compared with the actual order of playing the records. The blank used for the students' notations is shown in Fig. 15. The results of these studies are always most enlightening when carefully evaluated. They tend to indicate individual as well as class achievement. If sufficiently standardized, the approach might serve as a basis for an experimental study in the field of voice training.

Date ______________________ Your Name ______________________

Group ______________________

You will judge the voices of students who have been enrolled in a course in voice training. The students worked on general relaxation, voice placement, prcjection and vocal variety. The purpose of this work was to develop a clear, resonant, weil-projected voice which varied in pitch, intensity and rate and was suited to the age and sex of the individual.

Write the stuaent's name before the record is played. Listen to both recordings. Then place a Roman numeral I in the "1st Record Played" column, if you believe the first record played was the first record made. Write "II" if you believe the first record played was the second record made. If you place a "I" in the first column, place a "II" in the second and vice versa.

Name	1st Record Played	2nd Record Played

FIGURE 15

THE SILENT CRITIQUE. A new procedure developed by the author to save time and give the student an evaluation of his voice while he is listening to his record has been found to be most useful in classwork. Two large charts, one listing vocal flaws and another listing what the student must do to correct his faults, are hung at the front of the room. As the records are played, the instructor uses a pointer to indicate each student's vocal problems and what he must do to correct them. This timesaving procedure serves as a motivating device as well as an excellent means of training the ears of all students in the class simultaneously.

EAR TRAINING

The author has found it most desirable to proceed with the course in voice training and articulation in the order in which the material is organized in the text.

EAR-TRAINING PROGRAM. The ear training should be started early and continued throughout the course. It is advisable to start training the student to be analytical about his own and other voices at the very first meeting of the class. After that, a portion of each class meeting should be devoted to the furtherance of ear training. During the class periods devoted to study of the vocal and articulatory mechanisms and exercises in physical preparation for vocalization, much can be accomplished toward the development of auditory attentiveness and discrimination which will be helpful as students attempt to produce pleasant vocal tones.

The teaching of the phonetic alphabet is a useful device for training the ear to recognize slight differences in speech sounds as well as to develop the student's ability to reproduce the sound correctly. The ear-training aspects of this work are as vital as the visual aspects and should be emphasized.

Teacher's record library. As part of this program, the teacher should have the student listen to samples of good and poor vocalization and articulation. A library of records can be built up over a period of time which will be most helpful in this phase of the work.

Students with outstandingly thin, metallic, hollow, monotonous, and other types of deficient voices will register in the teacher's classes from year to year. A few students with superior voices may enroll also. He will be wise to make recordings of both of these for use with future classes. The records will serve the purpose of supplying the student with auditory impressions of poor and good voices and can be used for comparative purposes. In like manner, he should secure samples of inferior as well as superior articulation among his students. After several periods devoted to ear training, the teacher can use these records as a means of testing the students' ability to identify defective speech sounds and vocal characteristics correctly.

He would be wise to add to his library examples of speech as recorded by outstanding speakers of the day. Some recommended selections appear in Appendix D. The Linguaphone records, although developed as a guide to standard American pronunciation, are useful in studying vocal elements as well as articulation and pronunciation.

KNOWLEDGE OF STRUCTURES

Frequent reference will be made to the anatomical and physiological aspects of vocalization; therefore an understanding of the vocal mechanisms becomes a requirement. Some teachers believe that the voice training program should be preceded by a course in voice science. The author believes that this is not necessary if sufficient time is devoted to a study of the anatomical and physiological mechanisms involved in voice and speech production as contained in Chaps. 3 and 4. It is incumbent upon the teacher to assist the students with the material presented in these two chapters, and because the space is limited here, he may find it necessary to make additional assignments in texts included in the bibliography. Furthermore, it seems desirable to offer voice and articulation training early in the college program—possibly in the freshman year—so that the student will not be handicapped by poor voice and articulation in future college courses. It would seldom be possible for him to take voice science prior to voice training inasmuch as the course in voice science is usually offered at the junior and senior levels.

GROUP EXERCISES

The author strongly believes that little or nothing can be accomplished with voice and articulation retraining unless the teacher leads the way toward the development of new habits in his students. One of his best means of doing this is through having the entire class participate in ear-training activities and in exercises in relaxation, posture, breathing, and voice production. To attempt to get voice improvement through a series of lectures would be about as effective as trying to teach the follow-through in golf by having the student read a book on the subject.

The course should resemble physical education courses in many respects, especially while the student is making physical preparation for vocalization. The instructor must know how to execute each exercise so that he can lead the group during the early stages of training. Later, as a check on the students' practice, he may want to ask members of the class to serve as leader.

Relaxation exercises. The instructor can help the student discover the value to be derived from the relaxation exercises if he will emphasize the passive phase of each exercise. During the relaxation periods, he should lift the students' arms and legs and move their heads to ascertain whether or not a relatively complete state of relaxation exists. He can test jaw relaxation by moving the jaw of each student down and up several times. By placing the fingers on the throat, he will be able to discover excess tension in the larynx and neck muscles during vocalization.

Posture and breathing. Blackboard pictures, teacher demonstrations, and individual instruction will be helpful in teaching the principles of correct posture and breathing.

Some instructors will prefer to teach only the combined thoracic and abdominal breathing without first devoting time to abdominal breathing. This is a choice that the individual teacher will have to make. Some hold the view that manner of breathing should receive no attention at all in a voice training program. The validity of this concept will not be discussed here, but in those cases where a shallow, clavicular type of breathing is being used, new habits should certainly be developed.

The author approaches breathing in the manner suggested in the text because he has achieved best results from such procedures. By starting first with abdominal breathing and then going to the combined type, the student exerts voluntary control over the expiratory phase with greater ease. He tends to avoid creating hypertensions in those muscles directly or indirectly effecting vocalization (muscles of the neck, larynx, and pharynx) when he seems to exert pressure beneath the air stream. Whether the concept of abdominal breathing is scientifically correct is not an important point as long as the voice is improved as a result of such practice. Those teachers who can achieve their purposes without developing a controlled type of breathing are strongly urged to continue their procedures.

PRACTICE SELECTIONS

Although some well-known practice selections are included, the author has purposely chosen an adequate sample of poetry and prose selections which are not familiar to most students. He has done this to avoid having students read the selections using melody and rhythm patterns that are already established. In instances where a student is already familiar with a passage, the teacher may want to require the use of another selection, especially when the object of the lesson is to develop variety of pitch, rate, and intensity.

PRACTICE AND APPLICATION

Considerable emphasis must be placed upon practice and application of the principles learned in the course. It has been found that students tend to allow their work in voice and articulation to suffer toward the end of the semester when other lessons begin to take their time. The teacher must guard against this tendency and make a constant effort to motivate regular practice.

Students should be encouraged to practice their assignments at least three times each day, devoting a minimum of 10 minutes to each practice period.

They should find a place where they can practice aloud without disturbing others or being embarrassed by their utterances. If possible, the school should provide such a place for practice activities.

There are many times during the day when the student can contribute to his progress in voice and articulation improvement without taking time out from routine activities; for example, each time the student steps in front of a mirror, he can check his jaw relaxation. While brushing his teeth, he can stand with the back to the wall to check posture.

PRACTICE SCHEDULE

NAME ______________________ SEMESTER ______________________

CLASS ______________________ INSTRUCTOR ______________________

WEEK	NUMBER OF MINUTES SPENT IN EAR TRAINING AND PRACTICE							
	MON.	TUES.	WED.	THURS.	FRI.	SAT.	SUN.	TOTAL
1ST								
2ND								
3RD								
4TH								
5TH								
6TH								
7TH								
8TH*								

* SPACES SHOULD BE ADDED TO PROVIDE FOR THE TOTAL NUMBER OF WEEKS IN THE TERM OR SEMESTER.

FIGURE 16

A practice schedule similar to the one shown in Fig. 16, which is mimeographed and handed out to each student at the first class meeting, may be found helpful in motivating practice.

The teacher should stress the importance of application of principles at every meeting, for it is only through constant repetition that new habits are established.

SOME PRECAUTIONS

Teachers in courses involving the vigorous use of the vocal mechanism should not allow students to participate in activities if there are active pathologies. In like manner, persons with enlarged thyroid (goiter) should not practice any of the exercises involving the neck.

Even though it is possible to learn to effect changes in vocal quality, the text does not include a discussion of this subject. It is well known that the quality of most persons' voices changes automatically with changes in the emotional state. If an individual has a normal voice and personality, the qualities of his voice will be many, depending upon the state of his mind and emotions. The instructor in dramatics and oral interpretation may want to deal with affected qualities. This problem is not considered in this text. However, it should be emphasized that, in working to effect unusual voices, overstrain should be avoided and the affected voice should not be employed for a prolonged period.

The teaching of courses in voice training and articulation can be most satisfying because results are tangible. However, improvement cannot be obtained without earnest desire and effort on the part of the student. Therefore, if the student lacks self-motivation, then it is the teacher's problem to create in him the desire for better speech. Sometimes, the reproduction of a poor voice will cause the student to become alarmed. Improved auditory discrimination may prove to the person with the average voice that he needs further improvement. These evidences of need plus effective guidance, the use of a variety of exercises, and provision for adequate equipment and practice space will be helpful in assuring student interest and effort.

APPENDIX A

ADDITIONAL PRACTICE SELECTIONS

The exercises presented in this text have been suggested as means of establishing new habits which would carry over into an improved manner of speaking. They were by no means ends in themselves. It has been the purpose of the volume to roll the snowball slowly until all the elements of the program have been integrated into a new pattern of speaking habits. Assuming that this has been accomplished, such items as the proper amount of muscular tonicity in the throat and jaw; easy, erect posture; quiet, coordinated breathing; suitable pitch level, and other new habits of vocalization should be working together to produce improved voice and articulation. Practice the following additional selections to fix these new habits further. If you find that you are failing in one or the other principle, go back and review the exercises suggested for that purpose.

TELLING THE BEES, *John Greenleaf Whittier* [From *Complete Poetical Works of John Greenleaf Whittier*. Edited by Horace E. Scudder, Cambridge ed., Houghton Mifflin Company, Boston, Copyright, 1894, New York.]

Here is the place; right over the hill
  Runs the path I took;
You can see the gap in the old wall still,
  And the stepping-stones in the shallow brook.

There is the house, with the gate red-barred,
  And the poplars tall;
And the barn's brown length, and the cattle-yard,
  And the white horns tossing above the wall.

There are the beehives ranged in the sun;
  And down by the brink
Of the brook are her poor flowers, weed-o'errun,
  Pansy and daffodil, rose and pink.

A year has gone, as the tortoise goes,
  Heavy and slow;
And the same rose blows, and the same sun glows,
  And the same brook sings of a year ago.

There's the same sweet clover-smell in the breeze;
  And the June sun warm
Tangles his wings of fire in the trees,
  Setting, as then, over Fernside farm.

I mind me how with a lover's care
  From my Sunday coat
I brushed off the burrs, and smoothed my hair,
  And cooled at the brookside my brow and throat.

Since we parted, a month had passed—
  To love, a year;
Down through the beeches I looked at last
  On the little red gate and the well-sweep near.

I can see it all now,—the slantwise rain
  Of light through the leaves,
The sundown's blaze on her window-pane,
  The bloom of her roses under the eaves.

Just the same as a month before,—
  The house and the trees,
The barn's brown gable, the vine by the door,—
  Nothing changed but the hives of bees.

Before them, under the garden wall
  Forward and back,
Went drearily singing the chore-girl small,
  Draping each hive with a shred of black.

Trembling, I listened: the summer sun
  Had the chill of snow;
For I knew she was telling the bees of one
  Gone on a journey we all must go!

Then I said to myself, "My Mary weeps
  For the dead to-day:
Haply her old blind grandsire sleeps
  The fret and the pain of his age away."

But her dog whined low; on the doorway sill,
  With his cane to his chin,
The old man sat; and the chore-girl still
  Sung to the bees stealing out and in.

And the song she was singing ever since
  In my ear sounds on:—
"Stay at home, pretty bees, fly not hence!
  Mistress Mary is dead and gone!"

MUSIC, *Edward Rowland Sill* [From *The Poetical Works of Edward Rowland Sill*, Houghton Mifflin Company, Boston, authorized publishers.]

  The little rim of moon hangs low—the room
Is saintly with the presence of Night,
And Silence broods with knitted brows around.
The woven lilies of the velvet floor
Blend with the roses in the dusky light,
Which shows twin pictures glimmering from the walls:
Here, a mailed group kneels by the rocky sea—
There, a gray desert, and a well, and palms;
While the faint perfume of a violet,
Vague as a dream of Spring, pervades the air.
Where the moon gleams along the organ-front,
The crooked shadow of a dead branch stirs
Like ghostly fingers gliding through a tune.
  Now rises one with faintly rustling robes,
And white hands search among the glistening keys.
Out of the silence sounds are forming—tones
That seem to come from infinite distances,—
Soft trebles fluttering down like snowy doves
Just dipping their swift wings in the deep bass
That crumbles downward like a crumbling wave;
And out of those low-gathering harmonies
A voice arises, tangled in their maze,
Then soaring up exultantly alone,
While the accompaniment wails and complains.
—I am upon the seashore. 'Tis the sound
Of ocean, surging on against the land.
That throbbing thunder is the roar of surf
Beaten and broken on the frothy rocks.

Those whispering trebles are the plashing waves
That ripple up the smooth sand's slope, and kiss
The tinkling shells with coy lips, quick withdrawn;
And over all, the solitary voice
Is the wind wandering on its endless quest.
—A change comes, in a crash of minor chords.
I am a dreamer, waking from his dream
Into the life to which our life is sleep.
My soul is floating—floating, till afar
The round Earth rolls, with fleece of moonlit cloud,
A globe of amber, gleaming as it goes.
Deep in some hollow cavern of the sky
All human life is pleading to its God.
Still the accompaniment wails and complains;—
A wild confusion of entangled chords,
Revenge, and fear, and strong men's agony,
The shrill cry of despair, the slow, deep swell
Of Time's long effort, sinking but to swell,
While woman's lonely love, and childhood's faith
Go wandering with soft whispers hand in hand.
Suddenly from the ages one pure soul
Is singled out to plead before the Throne;
And then again the solitary voice
Peals up among the stars from the great throng,
Catching from out the storm all love, all hope,
All loveliness of life, and utters it.
  Then the hushed music sobs itself to sleep,
And all is still,—save the reluctant sigh
That tells the wakening from immortal dreams.

BLEAK COUNTRY, *Gilbert Maxwell* [From *Look to the Lightning* by Gilbert Maxwell, used by permission of the publishers, Dodd, Mead & Company, Inc.]

Here is the season when a man alone
Is like a tree stripped naked to the cold;
This is a wind to chill the staunchest bone
And send the white sheep shivering to the fold.
Even the hare along the broom-sedge track,
Leaps to his hidden burrow underground,
Knowing the hunted scent the wind throws back;
Fearing the distant baying of the hound. . . .
By the uneven hoof-prints in the snow
Along this wide-deep rutted wagon road,
A man may walk this way alone and know
That mules have stumbled here beneath a load;
A man may walk this way at dusk and weep
For driven mules and frightened hares, and sheep.

OPPORTUNITY, *Edwin Markham* [From *Gates of Paradise* by Edwin Markham, Doubleday & Company, Inc., New York, 1924. Copyright, 1920, Edwin Markham, reprinted by permission.]

In an old city by the storied shores
Where the bright summit of Olympus soars,
A cryptic statue mounted toward the light—
Heel-winged, tip-toed, and poised for instant flight.

"O statue, tell your name," a traveller cried,
And solemnly the marble lips replied:
"Men call me Opportunity: I lift
My winged feet from earth to show how swift
My flight, how short my stay—
How Fate is ever waiting on the way."

"But why that tossing ringlet on your brow?"
"That men may seize me any moment: *Now*,
NOW is my other name: to-day my date:
O traveller, to-morrow is too late.'"

DOG DAYS, *Jay S. Sigmund* [From *Drowsy Ones* by Jay S. Sigmund, Prairie Publishing Company, Cedar Rapids, Iowa, 1925. Copyright, 1925. Prairie Publishing Company, reprinted by permission.]

Hear how the killdeer by the pasture stream,
Harassed by mad suns, vents a high-piped scream!

The water-snake—this morning filmed of eye—
Now leaves his dead and curling robe to dry.

Over the yellow field where oat-shocks stand
A black crow flutters with his pirate band.

Crickets that droned like viols all night long
Are silenced by the sickle's metal song.

Welcome is night, lit up by pale ghost moons,
After a span of days with scalding noons.

I shall be grateful when the witch of dusk
Cools the hot venom of this heat-hag's tusk!

HER SONG, *Alfred, Lord Tennyson* [From "Maud" by Alfred, Lord Tennyson, in *Poems of Alfred, Lord Tennyson, 1830–1865*, Oxford University Press, New York, 1910.]

A voice by the cedar tree
In the meadow under the Hall!
She is singing an air that is known to me,
A passionate ballad gallant and gay,

A martial song like a trumpet's call!
Singing alone in the morning of life,
In the happy morning of life and of May,
Singing of men that in battle array,
Ready in heart and ready in hand,
March with banner and bugle and fife
To the death, for their native land.

Maud with her exquisite face,
And wild voice pealing up to the sunny sky,
And feet like sunny gems on an English green,
Maud in the light of her youth and her grace,
Singing of Death, and of Honor that cannot die,
Till I well could weep for a time so sordid and mean,
And myself so languid and base.

Silence, beautiful voice!
Be still, for you only trouble the mind
With a joy in which I cannot rejoice,
A glory I shall not find.
Still! I will hear you no more,
For your sweetness hardly leaves me a choice
But to move to the meadow and fall before
Her feet on the meadow grass, and adore,
Not her, who is neither courtly nor kind,
Not her, not her, but a voice.

THE WOOING OF KATHERINE, *William Shakespeare* [From *The Taming of the Shrew* by William Shakespeare, Yale University Press, New Haven, 1921.]

PETRUCHIO: Good morrow, Kate; for that's your name, I hear.
KATHERINE: Well have you heard, but something hard of hearing:
They call me Katherine, that do talk of me.
PETRUCHIO: You lie, in faith; for you are call'd plain Kate,
And bonny Kate, and sometimes Kate the curst;
But Kate, the prettiest Kate in Christendom;
Kate of Kate-Hall; my super-dainty Kate,
For dainties are all Kates; and therefore, Kate
Take this of me, Kate of my consolation;
Hearing thy mildness praised in every town,
Thy virtues spoke of, and thy beauty sounded,—
Yet not so deeply as to thee belongs,—
Myself am moved to woo thee for my wife.
KATHERINE: Moved! in good time: let him that moved you hither
Remove you hence: I knew you at the first,
You were a moveable.
PETRUCHIO: Why, what's a moveable?

KATHERINE: A join'd-stool.
PETRUCHIO: Alas, good Kate, I will not burden thee!
For, knowing thee to be but young and light,—
KATHERINE: Too light for such a swain as you to catch:
And yet as heavy as my weight should be.
PETRUCHIO: Should be! should—buzz!
KATHERINE: Well ta'en and like a buzzard.
PETRUCHIO: O slow-wing'd turtle! shall a buzzard take thee?
KATHERINE: Ay, for a turtle, as he takes a buzzard.
PETRUCHIO: Come, come, you wasp: i' faith, you are too angry.
KATHERINE: If I be waspish, best beware my sting.
PETRUCHIO: My remedy is, then, to pluck it out.
KATHERINE: Ay, if the fool could find it where it lies.
PETRUCHIO: Who knows not where a wasp does wear his sting? In his tail.
KATHERINE: In his tongue.
PETRUCHIO: Whose tongue?
KATHERINE: Yours, and so farewell.
PETRUCHIO: What, nay, come again,
Good Kate: I am a gentleman.
KATHERINE: Then I'll try. (She strikes him.)
PETRUCHIO: I swear I'll cuff you, if you strike again.
KATHERINE: So may you lose your arms:
If you strike me, you are no gentlemen;
And if no gentleman, why then no arms.
PETRUCHIO: A herald, Kate? O, put me in thy books!
KATHERINE: What is your crest? a coxcomb?
PETRUCHIO: A combless cock, so Kate will be my hen.
KATHERINE: No cock of mine: you crow too like a craven.
PETRUCHIO: Nay, come, Kate, come: you must not look so sour.
KATHERINE: It is my fashion, when I see a crab.
PETRUCHIO: Why, here's no crab; and therefore look not sour.
KATHERINE: There is, there is.
PETRUCHIO: Then show it me.
KATHERINE: Had I a glass, I would.
PETRUCHIO: What, you mean my face?
KATHERINE: Well aim'd of such a young one.
PETRUCHIO: Now, by Saint George, I am too young for you.
KATHERINE: Yet you are wither'd.
PETRUCHIO: 'Tis with cares.
KATHERINE: —I care not.
PETRUCHIO: Nay, hear you, Kate: in sooth you 'scape not so.
KATHERINE: I chafe you, if I tarry: let me go.
PETRUCHIO: No, not a whit: I find you passing gentle.
'Twas told me you were rough and coy and sullen,
And now I find report a very liar;
For thou art pleasant, gamesome, passing courteous.

But slow in speech, yet sweet as spring-time flowers:
Thou canst not frown, thou canst not look askance,
Nor bite the lip, as angry wenches will;
Nor hast thou pleasure to be cross in talk;
But thou with mildness entertain'st thy wooers,
With gentle conference, soft and affable.
Why does the world report that Kate doth limp?
O slanderous world! Kate, like the hazel-twig,
Is straight and slender, and as brown in hue
As hazel-nut and sweeter than the kernels.
O let me see thee walk: thou dost not halt.

KATHERINE: Go, fool, and whom thou keep'st command.

PETRUCHIO: Did ever Dian so become a grove
As Kate this chamber with her princely gait?
O! be thou Dian, and let her be Kate:
And then let Kate be chaste and Dian sportful!

KATHERINE: Where did you study all this goodly speech?

PETRUCHIO: It is extempore, from my mother-wit.

KATHERINE: A witty mother! witless else her son.

PETRUCHIO: Am I not wise?

KATHERINE: Yes: keep you warm.

PETRUCHIO: Marry, so I mean to, sweet Katherine.
And therefore, setting all this chat aside,
Thus in plain terms: your father hath consented
That you shall be my wife; your dowry 'greed on;
And, will you, nill you, I will marry you.
Now, Kate, I am a husband for your turn;
For, by this light, whereby I see thy beauty,—
Thy beauty, that doth make me like thee well,—
Thou must be married to no man but me;
For I am he am born to tame you, Kate,
And bring you from a wild Kate to a Kate
Conformable as other household Kates.
Here comes your father: never make denial;
I must and will have Katherine to my wife.

AFTER BLENHEIM, *Robert Southey* [From *Prose, Poetry and Drama for Oral Interpretation* selected and arranged by William J. Farma, Harper & Brothers, New York, 1930. Copyright, 1930, William J. Farma.]

It was a summer evening;
Old Kaspar's work was done,
And he before his cottage-door
Was sitting in the sun;
And by him sported on the green
His little grandchild, Wilhelmine.

She saw her brother Peterkin
  Roll something large and round,
That he beside the rivulet,
  In playing there, had found:
She ran to ask what he had found,
  That was so large and smooth and round.

Old Kaspar took it from the boy,
  Who stood expectant by;
And then the old man shook his head,
  And with a natural sigh,
"'Tis some poor fellow's skull," said he,
Who fell in the great victory."

"I find them in my garden,
  For there's many here about;
  And often, when I go to plough,
  The ploughshare turns them out;
For many thousand men," said he,
  "Were slain in that great victory."

"Now tell us what 'twas all about,"
Young Peterkin, he cries;
And little Wilhelmine looks up
  With wonder-waiting eyes;
"Now tell us all about the war,
  And what they fought each other for."

"It was the English," Kaspar cried,
  "Who put the French to rout;
But what they fought each other for
  I could not well make out;
But everybody said," quoth he,
  "That 'twas a famous victory."

"My father lived at Blenheim then,
  Yon little stream hard by;
They burned his dwelling to the ground,
  And he was forced to fly;
So with his wife and child he fled,
  Nor had he where to rest his head.

"With fire and sword the country round
  Was wasted far and wide,
And many a childing mother then,
  And new-born baby, died;

But things like that, you know, must be
  At every famous victory.

"They say it was a choking sight
  After the field was won;
For many thousand bodies here
  Lay rotting in the sun:
But things like that, you know, must be
  After a famous victory.

"Great praise the Duke of Marlborough won
  And our good Prince Eugene."
"Why, 'twas a very wicked thing!"
  Said little Wilhelmine.
"Nay, nay, my little girl," quoth he,
  "It was a famous victory.

"And everybody praised the Duke,
  Who this great fight did win,"
"But what good came of it at last?"
  Quoth little Peterkin.
"Why, that I cannot tell," said he;
  "But 'twas a famous victory."

ABOU BEN ADHEM, *Leigh Hunt* [From *Prose, Poetry and Drama for Oral Interpretation* selected and arranged by William J. Farma, Harper & Brothers, New York, 1930. Copyright, 1930, William J. Farma.]

Abou Ben Adhem (may his tribe increase!)
Awoke one night from a deep dream of peace,
And saw within the moonlight in his room,
Making it rich, like a lily in bloom,
An angel, writing in a book of gold;
Exceeding peace had made Ben Adhem bold,
And to the presence in the room he said,
"What writest thou?" The vision raised its head,
And with a look made of all sweet accord,
Answered, "The names of those who loved the Lord."
"And is mine one?" said Abou. "Nay, not so,"
Replied the angel. Abou spoke more low,
But cheerily still; and said, "I pray thee, then,
Write me as one that loves his fellow-men."
The angel wrote and vanished. The next night
It came again, with a great awakening light,
And showed the names whom love of God had blessed,
And, lo! Ben Adhem's name led all the rest.

WHAT'S O'CLOCK, *George Borrow* [From *The Romany Rye* by George Borrow, E. P. Dutton & Co., New York, 1906.]

The next morning, having breakfasted with my old friend, I went into the stable to make the necessary preparations for my departure; there, with the assistance of a stable lad, I cleaned and caparisoned my horse, and then, returning into the house, I made the old female attendant such a present as I deemed would be some compensation for the trouble I had caused. Hearing that the old gentleman was in his study, I repaired to him. "I am come to take leave of you," said I, "and to thank you for all the hospitality which I have received at your hands." The eyes of the old man were fixed steadfastly on the inscription which I had found him studying on a former occasion. "At length," he murmured to himself, "I have it—I think I have it"; and then, looking at me, he said, "So you are about to depart?"

"Yes," said I, "my horse will be at the front door in a few minutes; I am glad, however, before I go, to find that you have mastered the inscription."

"Yes," said the old man, "I believe I have mastered it; it seems to consist of some verses relating to the worship of the Spirit of the Hearth."

"What is the Spirit of the Hearth?" said I.

"One of the many demons which the Chinese worship," said the old man; "they do not worship one God, but many." And then the old man told me a great many highly-interesting particulars respecting the demon worship of the Chinese.

After the lapse of at least half an hour I said, "I must not linger here any longer, however willing. Horncastle is distant, and I wish to be there to-night. Pray can you inform me what's o'clock?"

The old man, rising, looked towards the clock which hung on the side of the room at his left hand, on the farther side of the table at which he was seated.

"I am rather shortsighted," said I, "and cannot distinguish the numbers at that distance."

"It is ten o'clock," said the old man; "I believe somewhat past."

"A quarter, perhaps."

"Yes," said the old man, "a quarter, or—"

"Or?"

"Seven minutes, or ten minutes past ten."

"I do not understand you."

"Why, to tell you the truth," said the old man, with a smile, "there is one thing to the knowledge of which I could never exactly attain."

"Do you mean to say," said I, "that you do not know what's o'clock?"

"I can give a guess," said the old man, "to within a few minutes."

"But you cannot tell the exact moment?"

"No," said the old man.

"In the name of wonder," said I, "with that thing there on the wall ticking continually in your ear, how comes it that you do not know what's o'clock?"

"Why," said the old man, "I have contented myself with giving a tolerably good guess; to do more would have been too great trouble."

"But you have learnt Chinese," said I.

"Yes," said the old man, "I have learnt Chinese."

"Well," said I, "I really would counsel you to learn to know what's o'clock as soon as possible. Consider what a sad thing it would be to go out the world not knowing what's o'clock. A millionth part of the trouble required to learn Chinese would, if employed, infallibly teach you to know what's o'clock."

"I had a motive for learning Chinese," said the old man, "the hope of appeasing the misery in my head. With respect to not knowing what's o'clock, I cannot see anything particularly sad in the matter. A man may get through the world very creditably without knowing what's o'clock. Yet, upon the whole, it is no bad thing to know what's o'clock—you, of course, do? It would be too good a joke if two people were to be together, one knowing Armenian and the other Chinese, and neither knowing what's o'clock. I'll now see you off."

APPENDIX B

DESCRIPTIVE PASSAGES FOR USE IN RELAXATION PERIOD

SHANGRI-LA

Lie on your cot or sit in a comfortable chair, and quiet your busy nerves and muscles. Take away from them the strains which come with struggling and achieving in our busy world. Let go the tensions; forget all those worries which cloud your life, and allow yourself to slip quietly into the serene, peaceful land of the imagination.

Recall the Valley of the Blue Moon in Frank Capra's phantasmagoria, *The Lost Horizon.* Call to mind those illusive views of rocky, snow-capped mountains—the valley entrapped by towering, dew-laden cliffs, the golden sun from the azure sky bathing the scene with morning light and causing the picturesque view to shimmer with gemlike splendor.

Dividing the valley is a sparkling stream descending from its snowy source to ripple laughingly over its pebbly bed. Fields of grain quilt the valley in an irregular pattern. The blanket seems held together by rows of trees, with here and there a knot of shrubbery.

The villagers go about their tasks without hurry. There is the joyful chatter of children; the soft murmur of Mother Nature, the birds, the soft clarion breezes; the scent of wild flowers; the lowing of cattle; and the chiming of the distant silver bells. Overlooking it all is the home of Father Pieron, a white marble structure surrounded by gardens and crystal fountains. In this land of peace and quiet, people live in moderation. There is not the hurry and rush that fills the lives of us in this world. It is a utopia called *Shangri-La.*

As you think of this scene, feel that the arms and hands, the legs, the trunk, the shoulders, the neck, face, and jaw are free from excess tension. When all the strains of your daily living are gone you will come closer to entering your own Shangri-La.

NIAGARA

Free your muscles from their tensions, and travel in imagination to the Empire State. Visualize tons of water as they pour over mammoth rocks at Niagara Falls. You are standing far from these powerful waters, but you can see them clearly and hear them faintly.

The sun has gone, and, from the Canadian side, lamps are shining across the river. They light the white foam and mist which you see in the distance. Great shafts of colored light cast beams upon the white water. Under rainbow hues, the pleated overlappings move slowly and forcefully.

Below you, you hear the waters of a rumbling, tumbling river. There is the pleasant scent of rich warm earth, of grass and flowers. The stars and the moon are bright tonight and there is a soft, warm breeze.

Visualize these works of God and man as you rest from your little journey.

MOUNT RAINIER

Forget about all those "cares that infest the day" and take a "mental trip" with the author to a far western state where stands a proud mountain called *Rainier*. As you view it from afar, it seems to rise out of Puget Sound like an enormous tree stump capped with white cotton—a volcanic cone, towering above its great base. You see the crowning snow mound which bears the proud name of Columbia Crest, a huge snow dune heaped up by westerly winds. From this distance the arms of ice extending down from the snowy summit; the gardens of wild flowers which carpet Paradise Valley; trails winding through enchanted woods—all enter into a great Gestalt. The vastness of this glacial mantle and the striking sculpture of its cliffs are so overwhelmingly impressive that you are magically drawn to examine it at closer range.

You move across the arm of the sea on a quiet, peaceful summer's day and up an open road through dense evergreen forests to wide alpine meadows carpeted with vividly colored flowers which extend upward to the very edge of snowfields and ice packs. You see columbine, daisies, larkspur in this rich, subalpine garden, mirror lakes, grassy meadows, a forest of all ages, and a trail of shadows.

There is a soft, warm, washed breeze stirring these natural gems, and you are permeated with the peace, the quiet, and the strength that comes from walking beneath Liberty Cap and Point Success. Review with me this scene, feel that there are no longer the tensions which crowd into your everyday life, feel the freedom which comes from forgetting all else but this picture of nature's wonderland.

CAMPUS SCENE

Take a comfortable sitting position. Place the hands in the lap, and allow the head to fall slightly forward. Think of the arms and hands, the legs, the trunk, the neck and face, and free them from tension. Forget all your worries and cares while I describe a peaceful scene. It is a springtime picture of—I have heard it called—the most beautiful of all college campuses, that of Michigan State College.

The verdant grass is pastelled with tulips, forsythia, spiraea, and the lacy shadows of trees. Gray ribbons divide the green plots so that from above we see a silken crazy quilt. Winding Cedar River is high on its banks; it glitters gaily as it wanders along beneath a warm sun.

The foliage on each tree takes its own comfortable time as it protrudes from closed buds. The rugged evergreens stand firm in robes which have cheered the eyes of college men and coeds the winter through. They are bold as they stand there so proudly; you can almost hear them say, in the vernacular of their compatriots, "We can take it." The oaks are timidly poking out tiny leaves; wise trees these, they know the wiles of the climate in which they have stood for many years and do not want it to rob them of their precious ornament.

The red brick buildings, in their varied shades, have been washed clean by spring rains. Above the peaceful scene is a soft delphinium blue sky and white clouds tinted with golden sunlight.

Life stirs—the ladies and gentlemen of M.S.C. walk proudly beneath a conservative clarion tower. They have laid aside winter garments and now, like the landscape, are bedecked in brighter hues. Tennis courts, the hockey field, the baseball diamond are centers of activity again after a long winter season.

The bells of Beaumont continue to chime their merry tunes and strike out the quarter hours while the Michigan State students quietly pursue the right of every American youth, the right "to be educated."

APPENDIX C

RECORDINGS FOR USE DURING THE RELAXATION PERIOD

Some records in the following sets will be more satisfactory than others. The student will soon discover which selections serve best during the relaxation period.

Beethoven, Symphony No. 3 in E Flat, "Eroica," The Austrian Symphony Orchestra, Fritz Busch, Conductor, Remington Record Album, RLP-199-21.

Beethoven, Symphony No. 5 in C Minor, Op. 67, Hans Wolf, Conductor, Remington Record Album, RLP-149-9.

Brahms, Symphony No. 1 in C Minor, Op. 68, The Symphony Orchestra of the Viennese Symphonic Society, H. Arthur Brown, Conductor, Remington Record Album (recorded in Europe), RLP-199-5.

Brahms, Symphony No. 2 in D Major, Op. 73, The Austrian Symphony Orchestra, Hans Wolf, Conductor, Remington Record Album (recorded in Europe), RLP-199-19.

Mozart, Symphony No. 40 in G Minor (K 550), The Salzburg Festival Orchestra, Paul Walter, Conductor, Remington Record Album, RLP-149-23.

Tschaikovsky, Symphony No. 6 in B Minor, "Pathétique," H. Arthur Brown, Conductor, Remington Record Album, RLP-199-13.

APPENDIX D

RECORDINGS TO USE IN EAR TRAINING PROGRAM

The following recordings are recommended for use in the ear-training program. They are not models to be imitated but represent voice and articulation in certain professional situations. You would never ask for a cup of coffee or recite in history class as Archibald McLeish presents *America Was Promises*. Rather, you should listen to these records, attempting to improve your ability to analyze voices. After some concentration on these records, they can serve worth-while purposes in studying articulation.

Title and reader*	Record number	Number of records
American English—Vowels and Diphthongs, George Bernard Shaw *American English—Vowels in Groups*, W. Cabell Greet	Part I, AMPH-1CC; II, AMPH-1D	1
The Joy of Teaching, William Lyon Phelps	Part I, CS-048562-1; II; CS-048563-1	1
Interlude on Cats, William Lyon Phelps	Part I, CS-048564-1; II, CS-048565-1	1
Spoken English and Broken English, George Bernard Shaw	Part I, SH-1-E; II, SH-2-E; III, SH-3-E; IV, SH-4-E	2
For Us The Swing, Alexander Woollcott	Part I, PT-1-1A; II, PT-2-2A; III, PT-3-3B; IV, PT-4-4A	2
Pronunciphone—A Course in Standard American Pronunciation	Part I, Pron 4917-A1850; II, Pron 4918-A1851; III, Pron 4919-A1852; IV, Pron 4920-A1853; V, Pron 4921-A1854; VI, Pron 4922-A1855; VII, Pron 4924-A1856; VIII, Pron 4923-A1857; IX, Pron 4925-A1858; X, Pron 4926-A1859; XI, Pron 4927-A1860; XII, Pron 4928-A1861; XIII, Pron 4929-A1862; XIV, Pron 4930-A1863	7
America Was Promises, Archibald MacLeish	Part I, D8CC-768-1; II, D8CC-769-1; III, D8CC-767-1; IV, D8CC-770-1	2
Lincoln's Gettysburg Address, Raymond Massey	Part I, 76744B; II, 76743A	1

* Recorded by Linguaphone Institute, RCA Building, New York.

APPENDIX E

REFERENCES

Voice

ANDERSON, V. A., *Training the Speaking Voice*, Oxford University Press, New York, 1942.

BRYANT, D. C., and K. R. WALLACE, *Oral Communication*, Appleton-Century-Crofts, Inc., New York, 1948.

CROCKER, L., *Public Speaking for College Students*, 2d. ed., American Book Company, New York, 1950.

FIELDS, V. A., and J. F. BENDER, *Voice and Diction*, The Macmillan Company, New York, 1949.

HOLMES, F. L. D., *A Handbook of Voice and Diction*, F. S. Crofts & Co., New York, 1940.

HUSTON, A. D., and R. A. Sandberg, *Everyday Business Speech*, Prentice-Hall, Inc., New York, 1943.

NORVELLE, L., and R. G. SMITH, *Speaking Effectively*, Longmans, Green & Co., Inc., New York, 1948.

SARETT, L., and W. T. FOSTER, *Basic Principles of Speech*, rev. ed., Houghton Mifflin Company, Boston, 1946.

THONSSEN, L., and H. GILKINSON, *Basic Training in Speech*, D. C. Heath and Company, Boston, 1947.

WILLIAMSON, A. B., C. A. FRITZ, and H. R. ROSS, *Speaking in Public*, rev. ed., Prentice-Hall, Inc., New York, 1948.

Articulation

BAIRD, A. C., and F. H. KNOWER, *General Speech*, McGraw-Hill Book Company, Inc., New York, 1949.

DOLMAN, J., JR., *A. Handbook of Public Speaking*, Harcourt, Brace and Company, Inc., New York, 1945.

FAIRBANKS, G., *Voice and Articulation Drillbook*, Harper & Brothers, New York, 1940.

KENYON, J. S., and T. A. KNOTT, *A Pronouncing Dictionary of American English*, G. & C. Merriam Company, Springfield, Mass., 1944.

McCALL, R. C., *Fundamentals of Speech*, rev. ed., The Macmillan Company, New York, 1949.

OLIVER, R. T., D. C. DICKEY, and H. P. ZELKO, *Essentials of Communicative Speech*, The Dryden Press, Inc., New York, 1949.

POWERS, DAVID GUY, *Fundamentals of Speech*, McGraw-Hill Book Company, Inc., New York, 1951.

THOMAS, C. K., *An Introduction to the Phonetics of American English*, The Ronald Press Company, New York, 1947.

WISE, C. M., *et al.*, *Foundations of Speech*, Prentice-Hall, Inc., New York, 1941.

Voice and Articulation Disorders

JOHNSON, W., *et al.*, *Speech Handicapped School Children*, Harper & Brothers, New York, 1948.

VAN RIPER, C., *Speech Correction, Principles and Methods*, rev. ed., Prentice-Hall, Inc., 1947.

WEST, R., L. KENNEDY, and A. CARR, *The Rehabilitation of Speech*, rev. ed., Harper & Brothers, New York, 1947.

Related Sciences

EDWARDS, L. F., *Synopsis of General Anatomy*, The Blakiston Company, Philadelphia, 1948.

FOWLER, E. P. (ed.), *Medicine of the Ear*. Thomas Nelson & Sons, New York, 1947.

GRAY, G. W., and C. M. WISE, *The Bases of Speech*, rev. ed., Harper & Brothers, New York, 1946.

GREISHEIMER, E. M., *Physiology and Anatomy*, J. B. Lippincott Company, Philadelphia, 1945.

JUDSON, L. S., and A. T. WEAVER, *Voice Science*, F. S. Crofts & Co., New York, 1942.

KUNTZ, A., *A Text-book of Neuro-Anatomy*, Lea & Febiger, Philadelphia, 1945.

MARSHALL, C., and E. L. LAZIER, *An Introduction to Human Anatomy*, W. B. Saunders Company, Philadelphia, 1947.

POLYAK, S. L., G. McHUGH, and D. K. JUDD, *The Human Ear in Anatomical Transparencies*, published by Sonotone Corporation, distributed by T. H. McKenna, Inc., New York, 1946.

Trans-vision Anatomy of Head Structures Involved in Oral Prosthesis, Published by Wernet Dental Manufacturing Company, Jersey City, N. J.

WILLIAMS, J. F., *A Textbook of Anatomy and Physiology*, W. B. Saunders Company, Philadelphia, 1943.

INDEX

O

P